BURN RATE

BURN RATE

LAUNCHING
A STARTUP
AND LOSING
MY MIND

ANDY DUNN

CURRENCY
NEW YORK

Copyright © 2022 by Andy Dunn

Published in the United States by Currency, an imprint of Random
House, a division of Penguin Random House LLC, New York.

CURRENCY and its colophon are trademarks of
Penguin Random House LLC.

Hardback ISBN 978-0-593-23826-4
Ebook ISBN 978-0-593-23827-1

crownpublishing.com

1st Printing

First Edition

For Usha, Monica, and Charley.
Without you, I have no past.

For Manuela. Without you, I have no present.

For Isaiah, and for Bella. Without you, I have no future.

CONTENTS

AUTHOR'S NOTE

THIS BOOK ISN'T WHAT YOU THINK IT IS.

It is not a self-aggrandizing tale of entrepreneurial success. It is not an insider's guide to launching a startup, brimming with insights packaged for tech bros or corporate leaders looking for an edge.

This book is a ghost story.

My Ghost first arrived in the year 2000 and would haunt me for the next sixteen years. It was a secret, known only to a handful of my closest loved ones.

My Ghost is an illness—one that can amplify human potential and seek to destroy it at the same time. For some, a ghost like mine might even seem life-expanding—jet fuel for the entrepreneurial drive—before the liabilities rip it all apart.

Here is the tabloid-ready summary of my book: In 2016, on the precipice of selling Bonobos, the startup I'd been building for the previous nine years, I flew into a manic spiral and was hospitalized for a week in the psych ward at Bellevue in New York. When I was discharged, I was met by NYPD officers, who took me to jail, where I was charged with felony and misdemeanor assault.

Thanks to my Ghost, I came within an inch of losing the

woman who is now my wife, the company, and everything I cared for in the world.

Here's the thing: I still live with it—but the Ghost, my diagnosis of bipolar disorder, isn't a secret anymore.

It has taken five years of therapy to be able to write those words.

NORMALLY WHEN YOUR most shameful life events have been hidden behind a veil of secrecy, you keep them under the rug, or in the closet, unexcavated. But what if there is nothing to be ashamed of? Then why would they need to be secrets at all?

If there was not a profound stigma around mental illness, this book would not be necessary. Perhaps it could make a good startup yarn—about the time a couple of guys hit the e-commerce moment right, despite a lot of bad ideas along the way.

The truth, though, is that the stigma is here, and it *is* profound. Mental illness is one of the final taboos. The business community values stability. When it comes to leading teams, shepherding capital, and governing enterprises, a steady hand is what is sought. So even as we have entered a new era, one where assumptions surrounding race, gender, and power are being interrogated more deeply, issues of mental illness in the workplace go largely unmentioned. For most of my professional life, my mental illness has felt unspeakable: a fast track to an awkward silence, a closed door, or a lost opportunity.

The thing is, a lot of us have it. A *lot*. The illness I deal with—bipolar disorder—affects 3 percent of the population and, by one estimate, is seven times more prevalent in entrepreneurs. That might mean 20 percent of entrepreneurs have bipolar disorder. It is an illness where suicide attempt rates approach 60 percent, and suicide "success" rates approach 20 percent. One study by the National Institutes of Health indicated that almost half of entrepreneurs deal with mental health issues. The figure was 32 percent for non-entrepreneurs, staggering in its own right.

In the world of sports, the mental health conversation is beginning, thanks to Naomi Osaka, Simone Biles, Mardy Fish, and many others. In entertainment, it's understood and accepted that artists face mental health challenges: witness Kanye West, Demi Lovato, and Britney Spears.

In the business world, though, no one talks.

I'm lucky to be in a position where I have a voice—my "exited startup" good fortune insulates me from the fear of financial loss, if not social stigma or personal embarrassment. So why go there? By not discussing what transpired, I would be letting the delusion continue to masquerade as fantasy: It never happened. It won't happen again.

To see this Ghost clearly, I needed to bring him out of the closet, to acknowledge the impact he has had on my life as a matter of public record. To deny this Ghost is to deny myself. I write this memoir to surface the darker story behind the airbrushed "living the dream" bullshit. This is a book about mental illness told by an entrepreneur lucky to have made it to the other side, even if the other side is an impermanent place full of surprises.

This book is my own story. My account is based on my own recollections, triangulated as much as possible with those of others: family members and friends and loved ones who were there for the ride. It's impossible that I got everything right. In chapters in which I depict an episode of full-blown mania, I switch the narration to the present tense, to emphasize both the impulsive chaos of these experiences and the blurred nature of my memories of them. In some cases, I've chosen to alter names or identifying details, or only provide a first name, where I felt it wasn't important for readers to know a person's real identity, and where the imperfections of my memory would be a disservice to them.

I WRITE THIS for the families out there coping with the maddening, challenging people they desperately want to help. Let this be a reminder that there will be thanks later, that on the other side is unending gratitude for your sacrifices and for your love.

Most of all, I write this for all of you struggling with a secret you feel you can't talk about. I hope this book serves as a reminder that there can be a path to health, integration, and healing. For me, it came in the form of a complex daily regimen of medication; therapy sessions multiple times a week with my psychiatrist, Dr. Z; a lawyer when I needed one; a sleep tracker and daily sleep report; the privilege to be able to afford it all; and the unbending, redemptive love and eventual clear-eyed determination and acceptance of a small band of family members and friends who rallied around me and who helped keep me sane. And who still do.

Let me tell you a ghost story.

PART I
ORIGIN OF THE SPECIES

The Chinese believe that before you can conquer a beast you must first make it beautiful. In some strange way, I have tried to do that with manic-depressive illness. It has been a fascinating, albeit deadly, enemy and companion; I have found it to be seductively complicated, a distillation both of what is finest in our natures, and of what is most dangerous.

—Kay Redfield Jamison, *An Unquiet Mind*

First the fall, and then the recovery from the fall, and both are the mercy of God.

—Julian of Norwich

CHAPTER 1

WINDU

IN HINDI, THERE ARE AT LEAST TEN WORDS FOR "AUNT" OR "uncle." Your mother's sister, mother's brother, father's sister, father's brother, mother's sister-in-law, mother's brother-in-law, and on and on: they all have different names. The most affectionate term of all is *masi*, reserved for your mother's sister. For my sister and me, our mom's family was the strongest force in our childhood. Our mom has four sisters, so I have four *masis*; it was a profoundly and proudly matriarchal upbringing. What I didn't know at the time was that I would one day spend thirteen years building a company named for a species of matriarchal chimpanzee.

Mom's parents, Prakash and Dhian, were born in Rawalpindi, a city in Punjab State. In 1947, the British split Punjab in two, creating a Pakistani side and an Indian side: Muslims over here, Hindus over there. My grandparents, a Hindu and a Sikh, had to leave in the middle of the night with their two daughters. The region was thrown into chaos, with an estimated fifteen million people displaced, and at least one million killed.

Usha Ahuja, my mother, was born in this context, in a refugee town called Kurukshetra, during her family's multiyear journey from Rawalpindi to New Delhi, where they eventually settled. My mom's mom, our Badi Mummy (Prakash), was a child bride, not educated beyond the sixth grade. She lost two children in infancy before she turned eighteen. Then she had seven kids: five girls and two boys.

My mom and her sisters adored their father, and they feared him, too. The level of his expectations for their success was daunting. He was an enterprising building contractor, a chain-smoker, and an alcoholic. He instilled in his daughters a progressive message, ahead of its time in 1950s and '60s India: "You don't want to be dependent on a man like me." His vision for his children was for them to get educated and make it to the United States. By the time he fell ill with emphysema, my mom had graduated college and been shipped first to Canada and then to the United States, to live with my Ashi Masi, by then an obstetrician-gynecologist. My aunt would go on to deliver both my sister and me.

My mom's mandate was to get trained as an X-ray tech and send money home, living with her sister so that she could pass on 100 percent of her income. With her father ill, they desperately needed the money, and my mom—a most dutiful human—answered the call to the sublimation of her own possibilities. Any dreams she had of becoming a doctor, like two of her older sisters, were subsumed by that short-term need in the late 1960s. She never complained about it. She never complains. Money was so tight that when my grandfather died, in January 1969, my mom couldn't afford to go home to New Delhi for his cremation. It haunts her still. She has never gotten closure.

Mom's sisters built the clichéd Indian American immigrant family, filled with doctors and married to them, too. Ashi Masi's husband is a radiation oncologist; Shano Masi, an internal medicine physician, married a surgeon; and Dolly Masi, my mom's younger sister, is a physical therapist. My dad's side of the family is smaller, but also filled with medical professionals.

As I was growing up, doctors were everywhere. My older sister, Monica, and I felt invincible—there was always medical help ready for any issue we faced.

Except, of course, for the one that came.

For Monica and me, Mom was a hands-on cultivator of empathy, a self-awareness developer, and, like her own father, a setter of high hopes and expectations. She was a rare mixture of caring—tough, compassionate, and candid. She was the same at work: in her twenty years of leading a team of a dozen women in a hospital ultrasound department, no one ever quit.

"You have to love the person behind the person that works for you," she'd say.

IN MY CHILDHOOD home we had paintings from Mackinac Island, in northern Michigan: gulls, pine trees, windy skies, rocks, and bluffs. There is a gray-blue hue where the horizon meets the lake. My dad's eyes are that color. At six feet two inches, Charles Dunn, my father, seemed to me a gentle giant. "I love you" rolled off his tongue easily; unique, perhaps, for midwestern dads of his vintage. As a parent, he was a watchful protector, a role model for how to treat your wife, the answerer of all questions, and an ascetic who abstained from all forms of hedonistic consumption, save for ice cream. He was a walking encyclopedia. On a trip to Madrid, in 2003, I was three years out of college. Dad and I headed into the

Museo Nacional del Prado. I asked if he wanted to get the tour-by-audio headset. "I'll provide the audio," he quipped. And then he did.

Dad's family is multigenerational Irish, Danish, English, Norwegian, and Swedish American. One of three children, he was raised as an evangelical Christian, a Swedish Baptist. His father was adopted, so tracing the lineage becomes hazy: picture some Danish immigrants on a farm in Wisconsin, a Swedish bartender and his Irish bride, and you start to get the idea. His family moved nine times in twelve years before landing on Chicago's West Side.

Before all that moving, and before her mood swings began, my paternal grandmother, Alva Georgina North (Nana), was a World War II hero. Nana was born in Chicago. She was a surgical army trauma nurse who arrived on the beaches of Normandy on day ten, treating frontline soldiers' wounds on the march to Berlin and Victory in Europe, or V-E, Day. She was present for the liberation of the Buchenwald concentration camp. Back in the States, she had treated an airman named Charles Willard Dunn II, my grandfather (Dada), who would win the Distinguished Flying Cross as a path-finding navigator on a B-17 Flying Fortress, leading bombing raids over Europe. They exchanged nine hundred love letters on the European front, which Dad discovered in a trunk in the basement after his parents were gone. He spent ten years writing the story of their wartime romance, titling it *The Nurse and the Navigator*.

Dada dropped out of Harvard, but after the war eventually made it to medical school and became a psychiatrist. Nana became, informally, one of his patients, and he started medicating her. In an unpublished appendix to my father's memoir, he writes of my grandfather: "Dad's decision to become a psychiatrist was made with the expectation that his resulting expertise would mitigate the effects of Mom's disorder. But it also gave him dark powers that could be wielded against her."

The treatment plan included barbiturates, tranquilizers, at least two institutionalizations, and frequent moves to avoid the "embarrassment" of Nana's difficulties. One of Nana's commitments was a few weeks long, another a few months. When my grandmother returned home, in true Scandinavian spirit, it was swept under the rug. My dad writes of his siblings and himself: "During the good times, Jane, Bob and I— taking our cue from Dad [my dad's father]—always pretended that everything was okay. Indeed, during the good phase, Dad himself always proceeded as if there was no reason to be concerned that the bad times were going to recur, although they always did." In a theoretical world, my grandmother's psychiatric issues and my grandfather's career as a psychiatrist might have prepared us for what was to come. Instead, the family tradition did the opposite: it prepared us to bury it all.

From my vantage point, they seemed like normal grandparents, sending us money on our birthdays and taking us on trips to Marshall Field's, where Nana, doused in perfume, would buy us Frango mint chocolates. According to Dad, by the time Monica and I met them, they had transcended the turmoil, though they bore little resemblance to the war heroes he later encountered in those letters.

Even a decade after my own issues emerged, it never occurred to me to wonder if, or how, mental illness runs in a family, let alone how shame and stigma compound generationally. A house filled with ghosts.

Growing up in the suburbs of Chicago, I grasped very little of my family's history, and even less of the impact it would ultimately have on me. What I did know was that I was the son of an ultrasound tech and a teacher, living in a fairly modest, twenty-two-hundred-square-foot house in suburban Downers Grove, an upbringing that, looking back, was solidly middle-class.

Our parents were expert savers, lived within their means, and invested everything above our cost of living in us. They did everything for Monica and me, and had no discernible social lives beyond their kids and our extended family. When I begged for a saxophone, they saved for months to buy me one. Monica was seven and I was five one Christmas when they woke us up in the middle of the night to head to the airport. They ushered us out the door for a surprise trip to San Diego, where the main attraction for a boy obsessed with animals was a visit to the zoo.

We wanted for nothing, it seemed, but we were by no means wealthy. I wasn't introduced to the concept of a millionaire until the seventh grade. If class differences mostly eluded me as a child, some part of me did recognize that I looked different: brown skin in a sea of white classmates. My sense of "other" translated as a form of uniqueness. Instead of burgers and hot dogs, we'd have Italian beef on the grill, with corn coated in garam masala and lime.

WHEN I WAS in second grade, my parents pulled me aside. I thought I had done something wrong. They let me know that they'd been speaking with the teacher about my skipping third grade. They wanted to know what I thought.

"How long have you been talking to Ms. Bostedo about this?" I asked, incredulous that they'd kept this from me.

"About a month," my mom replied. I squinted at her, disbelieving.

The truth was, I couldn't wait to skip a grade. Even at that age, I processed this as a sign that I was some kind of outlier (well before I knew the term), capable of things other kids weren't.

Despite my mom's attempts to keep me grounded, this sense of being special, or "gifted," became bedrock for my psyche. The root mixture of self-importance and hubris, prerequisite for many entrepreneurs, is in some ways traceable to that year. While it wasn't necessarily a precursor to delusion, it incepted something in me that my biochemistry would later exploit.

Andy is the most gifted student we've seen around here in a long time.

While the leap from "being gifted" to "being a gift" is a dizzying stretch, the possibility became a twinkle in my eye when I was eight years old.

MY TIME AT Herrick Junior High was dominated by fantasy novels, computer games, and math. While I was reading books by David Eddings and J.R.R. Tolkien, and cultivating my inner superhero complex, my friend Gavin, the school's only Jewish student, was reading Tolstoy and Zola. We'd shoot baskets in his driveway, play chess in his living room, and eat Peppermint Patties from a jar near his front door.

One day, in seventh grade, Gavin came to class with a new jacket, saturated with brilliant colors: purple and yellow and red. I asked him what it was for, and he said skiing. That winter break, his family went on a ski trip to Aspen. I'd never heard of such a thing. No one else I knew went skiing. It was expensive, and it seemed dangerous.

His family lived in Oak Brook, where homes regularly

sold for over a million dollars. The sum was inconceivable to me.

From what I could tell, there were two kinds of people in Oak Brook: doctors and entrepreneurs. Gavin's dad, Rick, owned an auto parts retailer. One day Gavin told me his father had an office filled with security cameras. I used to picture him there, in a command center of sorts. Rick would play basketball with us in the driveway, and we'd watch movies together in the family's home cinema. He didn't believe in credit cards and carried around a wallet brimming with cash at all times. Most impressively, Gavin's family had season tickets to the Chicago Bulls. To twelve-year-old me, in my corner of the world, this was the Holy Grail of professional triumph.

Looking back, I admired Gavin's family, and I envied them, too. I didn't know any other entrepreneurs growing up. My preteen brain sensed that there was something different about Gavin's dad—that in running his business and employing working-class people, he knew how to relate up and down the class spectrum, and profit from his acumen. Connective tissue was forming in my head around entrepreneurship and the notion of being my own boss—and, perhaps, the ability to go to Bulls games with a wad of hundos in my pocket.

WINDU.

White Hindu.

It stuck.

Two years later, I was a sophomore in high school, and a new nickname for me was making the rounds. We were exiting CAT, college algebra trigonometry, a class of mostly juniors and a small cabal of precocious sophomores. As the only one of those sophomores who had skipped a grade, I was fourteen years old in a class full of sixteen- and seventeen-year-olds. Late to puberty, I was a baby-faced boy in a classroom of young men. An easy target.

The nickname was invented by Joe, a junior. He was a year older than me and a star on the varsity soccer team. I was a mediocre member of the sophomore team, two rungs down. What made it worse was that we were friends, at least in the way a striving younger teenager thinks about friends: someone you hang out with, look up to, and want to be around because they travel in cooler circles. It was a confusing and pernicious mixture of sharing affinity in private and taking the piss in public.

It got to me. I was the kid who'd run upstairs after losing a game of Monopoly and cry behind a lounge chair to hide my hurt. My skin was thin. As the boy prince in a matriarchal family, with no brothers, a doting older sister, an adoring mom, and a gentle father, I had none of the armor most boys have by the time they get to high school. Though I was wounded, I made little of it when I told my parents, almost in passing, about the nickname.

They started laughing. It was a rare moment of my parents not being empathetic—but since I hid my hurt from them, too, they couldn't help but react with amusement. After all, it was kind of funny. Nicknames that stick, particularly derogatory ones, stick for a reason.

What was that reason? It was a clever play on words. Sure. But beyond that, it was kids weaponizing difference, and I didn't have the tools to process that. Our culture was a long way from caring about or even recognizing the feelings of "otherness" for a brown-skinned half-Indian kid, and so I started developing skills to pretend those feelings weren't there. Hiding vulnerability became a survival skill for me, and like other young men, I learned to stash it behind a veil of indifference fabricated by feelings of rejection.

That's where anger begins: sublimated hurt. If the anger and hurt are not surfaced, acknowledged, and dealt with, the combination of emotions can metastasize into depression. It would be years before I understood that possibility, and that it all begins with hiding things from yourself.

My sister knew, though. She intuited that I was bruised. A senior at the time, Monica gathered a bunch of her friends, the you-don't-want-to-mess-with-me variety, and word got to Joe that if he kept making fun of me, he was going to get his ass kicked by a bunch of seniors. The harassment died down.

In Hindi, we reserve a special term of respect for our older sisters.

Didi.

And a good *didi* will always protect her little windu.

BY SENIOR YEAR, my status had solidified: king of the nerds. I captained the quiz bowl team and was in the top five on the math team. I kept at it with soccer and tennis for a few years but was never good enough to make varsity. Mentally, I blamed it on being a year younger than everyone, owing to the skipped grade, but the truth is, my competitive drive was not matched by my athleticism. In senior year, I didn't bother coming out for either team. It was a quiet defeat.

Although I was not much of a heartthrob, one girl eventually came around. When senior prom arrived, I was dating Melanie. On the way up to the summer house where a bunch of us were staying, we made a stupid decision. We went off-road. Not with pickups or a Wrangler, but with a minivan and my little Dodge Neon, a compact sedan that looked like a hyperactive frog. We got stuck in the wet dirt. As the tires spun, mud flew, clogging the small tire wells, spitting grit all over the car.

Walton was the prom date of one of Melanie's friends. He was driving the other car, a maroon minivan, which did not get stuck. His leer irritated me, as did the way he leaned out of the driver's window of the minivan, laughing. Angry at being made fun of, I bottled up my resentment and focused on extricating the car.

After arriving at the house, we filled the bathtub with cans of beer, partied late, and did what teenagers do when they get to spend a rare night away, unsupervised.

Early that morning, still awake and foggy from the depleted bathtub beer stash, I snuck out and transferred as much mud as I could, by hand, from my car to Walton's. He had humiliated me. Now it was my turn. The deed complete, I went to sleep. What I didn't consider was that my actions would only deepen my own humiliation come daylight.

In the morning, everyone saw what I had done. The mood grew somber on the drive home. We went full midwestern: nobody talked about it. My girlfriend was especially quiet. I felt ashamed. Mine was the injured pride of a frail ego, laid bare for all to see. I didn't address it, I didn't apologize, and nobody called me out. The only referendum was the group's silence.

Dr. Z and I talk frequently about my desire to out-alpha any male I feel challenged by. We're still searching for the headwaters. I revered my dad for his devotion to all of us, for how funny he was, for how he seemed to know everything. We loved watching competition together—the Cubs, Bulls, and Bears—but he was never competitive with me at all. I begged him to play chess. He didn't enjoy beating me, and seemed pleased only once I beat him. Then we gave it up. Somehow this absence of expressed dominance, a subtle form of dominance in its own way, turned into a mixture of me sanctifying him and wanting to show every other male I met that they weren't as good as either of us. Deifying him would turn out to be a problem.

Meanwhile, although I wanted to be No. 1, I had to settle for less. I graduated third in my class at Downers Grove North. For the high school yearbook, I was named "most likely to be a millionaire." I was both flattered and surprised. I had no interest in business, I didn't read books about entrepreneurs, and I wasn't particularly coin-operated. While I tried my hand at mowing lawns, I was more candy striper than side hustler. My dream was to be a doctor, not an entrepreneur.

Maybe my high school classmates saw something I didn't.

Do goal-driven future doctors treat quiz bowl like the Super Bowl, obsess over status, or coat their friends' cars with mud because of a small slight?

I don't know. But emotionally fragile, hypercompetitive, mercurial teenagers do, and those qualities, for better and worse, line up nicely with the central-casting traits of the male entrepreneur.

CHAPTER 2

INSANE INGREDIENTS

AT NORTHWESTERN, I LIVED IN A FRESHMAN PARTY DORM called Bobb Hall, where alcohol was the defining fixture of extracurricular life. In high school I had been a late bloomer when it came to partying and dating; those activities had been on the back burner relative to academic work. Now I began to wing it in the classroom while my focus turned entirely to my social life.

I knew that joining a fraternity would mean a built-in schedule of one party after another, and I pledged at Sigma Chi. If Gavin's dad was my original entrepreneurial role model, Sigma Chi was a new jolt of inspiration, as well as status recalibration. While a handful of our friends would go on to medical school, most guys in the house were all about business. Some came from money, but even those born with a silver spoon were ambitious. One such trust funder had a black BMW M3, a vehicle I envied (it was standard issue for a bunch of brothers), with the license plate MLTS. Rumor was that it had been a high school graduation gift from his dad. The letters stood for:

Most Likely To Succeed

He was mocked for it behind his back, and deservedly so.

What he was putting out there, though, was something most guys in the house were already thinking.

Today, I'd call my experience in Sigma Chi at Northwestern a playground in white male privilege. My first internship and my first job out of college both came directly from brothers in the house getting me interviews at their firms. But the bonds were genuine. Guys cared about each other. They were mentors, sounding boards, and role models.

Beyond the schoolwork and the academic pathways into the world of enterprise, the swagger of the brothers was magnetic to me as a seventeen-year-old. There was a relentless "study hard and play hard" mentality. The outward posture was all chivalry and class. The conversations on the inside were different. I didn't have the good stories. Compared to other guys, I wasn't someone who got noticed a lot. When a sophomore started dating a woman who'd dumped me, it sank my narrative that "nice guys" finish first, and it opened a new frontier for my alpha pathologies to metastasize.

Though alcohol was the fraternity's currency, one friend in the house, Reuben, was doing some harder drugs and having what were termed "episodes." He went to Europe for a study-abroad semester, and rumor had it that he came home in a straitjacket. My Northwestern buddies talked about him in hushed tones, and only in passing. The less we talked about his situation, the less real it seemed. As I flew out to New York City in 1999, in between my sophomore and junior years, for a summer internship, Reuben's predicament was far from being at the forefront of my mind. I'd never had any mental health issues, and I didn't do any hard drugs. I drew a hard, if arbitrary, line after booze and pot. What I forgot, or never knew, is that a sound mind is a gift that the good Lord can rip away whenever He fucking feels like it.

My internship—landed with the help of a fraternity connection—was at Deloitte, a management consulting firm where smart senior people give clients advice and junior people, who have no idea what they're trying to do, make PowerPoint presentations, run Excel models, and pretend they're not frauds. It was my first real job in the business world, and I loved it.

I met my boss, Debbie, in the shadow of the Twin Towers, at the marina right outside the World Financial Center. As Manhattan buzzed with the energy of enterprise, we sat at one of the tables that doubles as a chessboard. I had no foundation in business whatsoever. Studying economics was a great way to pretend I did, but marginal cost curves and ivory tower equations have little application in the real world. Nevertheless, I would pontificate to Debbie about vendor management during her cigarette breaks. I was twenty years old, arguing that rather than beating on your suppliers, Lee Iacocca–style, you have to treat them the same way you treat your customers: as partners in the ecosystem. Debbie looked at me quizzically.

The idea of mentioning Iacocca had come from my dad, a left-wing Advanced Placement U.S. History teacher who took a historian's view of American business. Why attack the people who make your product possible? Sure, you want to buy stuff at the lowest cost. But do you? Doesn't making sure your suppliers are winning, too, ensure the long-term success of your business? I must have seemed like such a naïve kid to Debbie, but the gist of the idea was one I'd still be discussing twenty-one years later with the CEO of the largest company in the world.

One day that August, while I was sitting in an ocean of cubicles in Deloitte's office at 2 World Financial Center, my phone rang. It was my dad. I wondered if my neighbor would hear, from her cubicle, the calamity about to unfold in mine. I was being charged with a crime by the state of Illinois.

In our sophomore year, one of the fraternity brothers helped a number of us secure fake IDs. They were Indiana driver's licenses and looked so good that we put our real names on them. It was a foolproof way to get in anywhere, because we could show backup, usually a credit card, if there was ever any doubt. Now we could party in Chicago. This worked beautifully for two years. Until it didn't.

Crobar was a busy night spot in Chicago at the time. Think: industrial beats, Dennis Rodman doing shots at the bar, bare midriffs, and expensive tattoos. Thanks to that Indiana fake ID, I'd been to Crobar many times. Then one night, as my friends streamed in, I was stopped. The bouncer said that I wasn't getting in, and that he wasn't giving me my ID back. It was freezing outside, with the kind of Chicago winter wind that doubles as a buzz saw. I had lost my golden ticket into bars, and by summertime in New York City I had entirely forgotten about it.

Until the call from my dad.

As it turns out, that ID had ended up with law enforcement. The state of Illinois authorities sent a letter to my house in Downers Grove, and on the phone with my dad, I struggled to catch up to what he was telling me. I ducked into a small conference room, and my brain finally comprehended. I was being formally charged with a misdemeanor: possession of false identification.

Throughout my childhood, I'd been in trouble with my dad fewer than five times. The first time was as a four-year-old, when I said I didn't want to give my grandmother a kiss on the cheek because her skin was too wrinkly. Badi Mummy couldn't hear me, but I can still remember the expression on Dad's face: briefly withering, then shifting to disappointment. Though crumbling inside, I stood my ground, and refused to kiss her goodbye. But this time was different. I was twenty. This was anger and disappointment, simultaneously. I'd never felt both of those together before, let alone regarding something with real legal repercussions. It terrified me.

Toward the end of the conversation my dad said that the whole ordeal was *a dagger in the heart*.

Those words haunted me for a long time. They laced a cocktail of emotions. Fear of the legal system. Shame. Sadness. Guilt. Self-pity for being singled out for something "everyone" did. And another feeling I wasn't in touch with, one that grew as I reflected in the weeks and months ahead: anger. Anger at Dad for what I perceived to be an uncalibrated reaction, a puritanical worldview, and an unwillingness to forgive.

For my entire life he'd been the perfect dad. And I thought that in many ways, I'd been a perfect son.

Dr. Z would one day explain the father-son relationship to me this way: For the son, his father begins as a deity on a pedestal. The father can do no wrong. As the son ages, he discovers that his father is flawed, mortal, and full of frailty: an oedipal fall from grace. The son is filled with disappointment, hurt, and anger over his dad's imperfections. The father starts to sink in the son's eyes, slowly sometimes, and other times all at once. What follows is conflict and resentment. As the son's psyche grinds against his father's, men are forged. Boys become men. Or they don't.

Only some dads survive the son's journey intact.

Before they do, they all fall down.

.   .   .

SIX MONTHS LATER, and it was winter again. I was in Steamboat Springs, Colorado; summer in New York was a distant memory, as was the ID scandal. My license had been suspended for one year, but the charges against me had been dropped. A group of us were there for Northwestern's annual ski trip. I had never skied. It was a sport, and a lifestyle, I was trying on for the first time, the once-mysterious pastime of my affluent childhood friend. I fell in love with all of it—the views, the snow, the mountains, the skiing itself, and another, unspoken feeling as well: being among those who could afford it.

The front door of our rental house was wide open. We were splayed out on the porch, without jackets, but not cold. We were of this world, but we were not in it.

Jack, one of my best friends, was drinking from a jug of water. He gave me a sip. The water tasted like it flowed from the faucet of a glacier. The Rocky Mountains looked impossibly beautiful, surrounding us like snow blankets, flecked with proud and brave pines.

In the bathroom, the tiles were transmogrifying, shape-shifting spirits. They were alive. We had eaten the mushrooms on an omelet. Not porcini, not shiitake, definitely not enoki.

These mushrooms were magic. It was the first time in my life I'd shroomed.

At some point that afternoon we decided to go to Wendy's. The fries were hot, salty, and terrific. What I remember most is the yellow of the cup and the scorching red of Wendy's hair.

The jacket I'd bought with my mom before I'd left was not as shiny or as expensive as my childhood friend's, but I was slopeside nevertheless. I was also in a serious adult relation-

ship for the first time in my life, with a woman named Camila. She had luminous green eyes, a dry sense of humor,
and an industrious work ethic. She was an exceptional skier,
having been raised in a Chilean ski town, and waited for me
patiently as I skidded and fell, again and again, on my way
down the hill.

WHAT MY FRIENDS couldn't be expected to notice about me, a
twenty-year-old kid in a state of psychedelic rapture, mesmerized by the mountains and falling in love with a woman,
doing mushrooms, laughing, drinking beer and smoking pot,
and talking fast and thinking faster, was that I was beginning
to climb a volcano.

This is how a manic episode starts. It's incremental at first.
I didn't know it was happening. Nobody did.

A week or so later, back at the apartment I shared with my
three housemates at the corner of Ridge and Noyes in Evanston, we decided to have a New Year's Eve party to usher in the
new millennium. My housemates were Paymon, whom I'd
known since junior high; Brent, a premed student who was
my sophomore year roommate; and Eric, a sparring partner
on Middle Eastern politics. We all lived on the same hall
freshman year, and by senior year we were all still close. As
one of the hosts at the party, I was hyper-focused on making
sure I asked everyone for their coat when they came in. Getting those jackets onto the bed, neatly stacked, was of para-
mount importance. Something was starting to shift inside me.

Obsessive, goal-directed behavior, Dr. Z would tell me
twenty years later, is one of the indicators of ascending hypomania. According to Google, the hallmarks of hypomania
also include an upbeat, jumpy, or wired mood; increased en-

ergy or agitation; an exaggerated sense of self-confidence; mild euphoria; a decreased need for sleep; racing thoughts; and some distractibility. But at a college party, who could decipher between a spirited and talkative guy drinking Canadian Club with Dr Pepper and someone becoming hypomanic?

My sister, a recent grad of the University of Illinois, drove up from our parents' house, where she was living, to the party that night. From a balcony, Monica and I looked down on the street. We both feared heights, we learned, for different reasons.

"What if I fall?" Monica said.

"What if I jump?" I said.

Dr. Z says that inside all of us is a death wish.

A TV was on in the house. A news report showed a group of South Koreans. They were waiting for the Messiah to arrive, praying on their knees.

The next day my friend Daniel and I went to the mall to see *The Cider House Rules*. As I rocketed up, I became convinced that the movie was a revelatory event in my life. The film is based on the John Irving novel and stars Michael Caine and a young Tobey Maguire. It is a story about a man who breaks with his father figure, only to become just like him later in life. After I saw it I told anyone who would listen that it was the best movie I had ever seen. It's a good book and a decent movie—but it's not *The Godfather*.

The next day, I got a ride from school to our fraternity house from a friend. She was struggling with a relationship that was ending with a mutual friend. I felt terrible for her. Now, in my increasingly perilous state, I decided to make something up to help her feel better.

He's gay.

How do you know?

He told me.

Who is he with?

His brother.

I meant his actual brother. My underlying intent was to make her feel better. To do so, I invented a story that wasn't true. As I got out and closed the car door, I felt a clear sense of having helped her, a good deed complete.

To say that I was lying would be inaccurate. Lying is what we do when we intend to mislead someone. In my decompensating state, I had no intentions, just unfiltered dream-state experiences. Imagine waking up one day and being like, "That was a crazy dream," except it was a dream for you and real for everyone else.

FROM THERE, my memories race and blur.

I'm no longer hypomanic at this point. I've crossed the line to mania. Hypomania is talking excitedly about the guy you just met who you are going to marry. Mania is talking excitedly about the watermelon you just ate that is the reincarnation of your grandfather. Hypomania is a vibrant experience of reality. Mania is inventing your own reality, living out your unconscious in Technicolor.

In a room in the fraternity house, I talk to my parents on the phone. First Mom, then Dad. I go back and forth between crying and not crying. This rapid cycling of moods is textbook for someone who is losing it. I bring up what my dad had said to me that summer, in the wake of the fake ID incident, and I let him know that drinking *is* wrong—he'd been right all along. All substance use is wrong.

At this point I am (1) making up reality for myself and others; (2) experiencing a gurgling grandiosity; and (3) cycling between mood states.

I am also on a college campus where the norm, for me, is staying out late, pulling all-nighters, having weird conversations, and abusing substances. Dr. Z says that everything is overdetermined. While we search for clean-line narratives, there is no one clear singular input that catalyzes a breakdown. There are usually multiple vectors, working together.

Now the ingredients are all percolating.

Gothic conflict with Dad, weathering his disappointment. The first earthshaking love of my life, and the rising biochemical joy produced by intimacy. Ecstasy the previous summer, mushrooms two weeks prior, marijuana and alcohol as daily staples. Some powerful acne medication to treat the volcanic archipelagos on my back. Throw in the arrival of the year 2000, to which I, in my mood-altered state, attach great significance. Then the fatal decision to stop sleeping, eating, and drinking water—and with it, a flash of divine insight.

I am on foot, striding across campus, walking wherever my feet take me. The whirlwind of thoughts and feelings brings tears to my eyes as I pass the Charles Deering library. President Bill Clinton suddenly comes to my mind. Choking up with joy and gratitude, I know that one day I will be the president, too.

It is the year A.D. 2000. Wait. Those initials are the same as my initials.

The Messiah *is* coming back.

And I know who He is.

It's Me.

CHAPTER 3

GOD IS A WOMAN

LEAVING CAMPUS FILLED WITH MESSIANIC ZEAL, I HEAD TO THE only twenty-four-hour spot in town: Burger King. It is two A.M., and there are only a handful of customers. I strike up a conversation. Society isn't right, I declare. It isn't fair that some people have more opportunities than others. The inequality of the world, the country's history of racism: It is criminal. And I will fix it.

The non-manic person processes day-to-day interactions alongside private thoughts, selectively sharing what they think. For the manic me, there is no gauge. I say whatever comes to mind to whomever I want, whenever I want. There is no such thing as a stranger. Every thought and interaction is seismically important. It is my own personal *Truman Show*. Dr. Z tells me there is even now something called the Truman Show delusion, where everyone is an actor in your personal life movie.

In this state, uncomfortable truths are confronted, sometimes surprisingly coherently, other times entirely unintelligibly. Feelings I have about society that I had bottled up, including anger or anguish about the state of the world, surge like a geyser. Homelessness, a horrible fixture of daily life, becomes a cruelty that requires immediate, personal action.

The people who tolerate it, who don't welcome the homeless into their homes: they are the ones who are insane. As I empirically depart from sanity, in my own mind I become the only sane person there is. I am the seer. Everyone else is my flock, a people in need of enlightenment, conversion, and transcendence.

The truth: that night, as I moonlight as a remedy to the world's ills, I transform into the liability in chief. Here I am, a walking stereotype, a Northwestern undergrad in jeans and an Abercrombie & Fitch sweater, standing before three random Burger King customers, and not shutting up. They regard me with indifference, perhaps a hint of amusement at my cosmic ranting. I make a declaration that I will be giving a speech later in the week. They say they'll come. I believe them.

At some point I leave BK. I haven't eaten a thing. There is simply no time to eat or drink. There is too much to do to save the world. Sleep is the farthest thing from my mind. It is, I realize, something that I will never need to do again.

It is nearing five A.M., after hours of roaming, when I ring the doorbell of a random Evanston house. I pick a residence by instinct, knowing that no matter which one I choose, I will be well received.

The man who answers the door has disheveled brown hair. I ask if I can come in and talk to him. My fundamental knowledge is that he will say yes. Who wouldn't want to talk to a prophet? Manic me experiences life as destiny, an inevitable future with absolute truth, where wishes and ideas are manifest, without question. The world unfurls from my imagination like a solipsistic version of that self-help book *The Secret*. Solipsism: the belief that there is only one mind in the

universe, and you yourself are that one mind. I am now conjuring reality.

The guy at the door looks at me like I'm . . . insane. The
door slams.

I am undeterred.

There is no fear and no filter.

AS MY CONDITION deteriorates, on the streets of Evanston, I
run into Nick Ehrmann, one of my best friends at school. It
wasn't an accident. My friends are increasingly attuned to
something amiss. They are looking for me.

Nick had been with me on the ski trip. He knows me as
well as anyone, and how big of a deal it is for me to be in a
healthy, serious relationship for the first time, with Camila.
His mom, Lisa, is a trained psychologist. When he finds me,
he gets me on the phone with her. I explain to her that Camila and I are to have a baby, who will be the Second Coming.

Offline, Nick's mom tells him to get me to the hospital.
What she doesn't tell him is that my delusional state is likely
an indicator of drug use, mania, or schizophrenia. After we
hang up, she prays it's not schizophrenia. I am noncompliant
on going to any hospital, and escape from the clutches of my
conversation with Nick by telling him I am going home to
sleep.

BY DAWN, I have wandered back to my shared apartment. I
run into my housemate and friend Eric later that morning. I
tell him about the speech I'll be giving later in the week, and

the folks from Burger King who are coming. He is concerned, but chalks it up to a friend who has been going out too much. I have no memory of the next twenty-four hours. Eric sees me again the following morning; I am looking harrowingly tired, bags under my eyes. I tell him I rode Chicago's elevated train, the "L," all night. Then I slip in that I am speaking to birds.

He looks at me quizzically.

"You're talking to birds, Andy?" he says. "Like, they speak English to you?"

"No," I say, growing irritable. "Of course not. I talk to them in my head." I loved Dr. Dolittle books as a kid. Now I am part Dr. Dolittle.

Eric and our other housemates, Brent and Paymon, are gravely concerned. After another unaccounted-for twenty-four hours, they surmise that I've been up for three nights in a row. Dr. Z says that a manic person can stay up for four or five nights before crashing. That is how much the runaway brain disconnects from the body.

When I next see Eric, I inform him that Camila is God.

"Camila is God?" he asks me.

"Yes," I confirm.

"So who does that make you?" he asks me.

"I'm going to be her Moses. I'm going to spread the word. God is not a man. The Bible has been wrong the whole way. God is a woman, Eric. Just think: Who gives us life? Mother. Mother Nature. Our own mothers. And yet we venerate our fathers."

So who at this point is the Messiah? My answer keeps changing. It's me. It's Camila. It's our unborn child. We would have needed an ecumenical council to sort this all out.

I show my housemates a manifesto I've written that lays out my thinking. It is a hybrid of delusions and babble.

As they read it, I'm pacing in the room. The group huddles, then they call my parents. Mom and Dad are already concerned by my dead cellphone and my strange call earlier in the week. Dad is dispatched to see what's going on. When I notice that my flip cellphone is dead, I begin to wonder if I'm dead, too. Some delusional people, Dr. Z says, actually think they are dead, like in *The Sixth Sense*. That's me. Now the walking dead, I know that I will live forever. A Holy Ghost.

Manic me sees symbols in everything: everything means something, and everything is a sign. Dad finds me outside the apartment building when he pulls up in his green Pontiac. I get into the car willingly. The sign is this: the first man I am to convert is my own father.

At this point, I have been awake for three nights, but I am not mentally tired at all. Physically, I'm falling apart. Wired and loquacious, I proceed to confront Dad, on the drive home, about three things: white men, forgiveness, and drugs.

On white men: Can't he see that so many of the so-called heroes of history were white men, like him? Washington, FDR, Lincoln, Jerry Sloan—what did they all have in common? I have recently read *Guns, Germs, and Steel*, and I am grappling with its theories about why white Europeans ascended, why Pizarro sailed to conquer the Incas, and not the other way around. I am also ready to apply these ideas to my own family. In my manic mind, Dad colonized Mom. As the son of a Scandinavian Irish American white man and a Punjabi immigrant mother, I find myself deep in some Freudian clichés. I explain to my father that he is failing to grasp his own unconscious preferences for white culture, and how this lack of awareness embodies the worst of white men everywhere. In this way, it is my closest loved ones who become avatars of my manic firestorm of emotions.

On forgiveness: Why can't he forgive his family for their unspoken grievances? On drugs: Why be so puritanical? Toggling between angry diatribes and sanctimonious lecturing, I channel all my being into leading Dad to a new truth. Trying to avoid any escalation, Dad just drives.

When Dad and I arrive at home, I strip down to my underwear and begin roving through the house. I sit in a chair upstairs and continue to teach Dad, asking him questions, issues that were previously subconscious now bursting forth, freeform, from the unconscious. He nods, not engaging, stone-faced. It is a remarkable performance.

My family is stalling.

My Ashi Masi, her husband, Uncle Yash, and their son Neil come over. All three are doctors. Ashi Masi had delivered me into this world. Now I am on the verge of slipping back out of it. The group of us pile into their car. I am guided to the middle of the back seat, surrounded on all sides by family. They spare me the ambulance and the struggle. And because I trust them on an innate level, to the hospital we go.

AS TEENAGERS, Paymon and I volunteered as candy stripers at Good Samaritan Hospital, where my mom was the head of the ultrasound department. We sat up front in our red-and-white-striped uniforms, which made us look like we were wearing tablecloths from Pizza Hut. We had two relatively simple jobs: answer the phone and greet visitors. We'd been tasked with one set of special instructions, however. When someone came in looking for someone in the North Pavilion, the psychiatric ward, we were instructed to say:

I don't see anyone here by that name.

The anonymity of those patients had to be protected. Enterprising family members would sometimes ask where the mental ward was. We could point them in that direction, and then from there, somehow it got figured out. We were never sure how. "Up North" may as well have been the North Pole in terms of our understanding of how things worked.

He's headed up North became our joke, inside and outside of the hospital, for anyone who was acting strangely.

One day someone walked in and said they were looking for Mrs. Ellen.

Paymon checked the computer. There she was. Elizabeth Ellen.

"Elizabeth Ellen?"

"Yes," the young woman replied. I imagined she might have been Elizabeth's daughter.

Paymon looked back at the screen. There was a zero before the phone number, which meant she was a North Pavilion patient.

"She's not here," he replied.

"What do you mean? You just gave me her first name."

Paymon gulped. He was trapped. He looked over at me, but I wouldn't make eye contact. I was focused ahead, giving nothing away.

At that point, Paymon had no choice. He sent the visitor up to the North Pavilion.

My first associations with mental illness came from this time volunteering at the hospital: mockery and secrecy.

. . .

THE CAR, filled with family, pulls up, and my parents bring me into the emergency room at Good Sam. We stand before a desk I had manned as an emergency room EMT greeter a couple years earlier. In a role reversal, now I'm the one getting checked in.

Once inside, I explain to the medical staff that my girlfriend, Camila, is the Messiah. My housemates drive down from school to meet me there, and bring my favorite food: Taco Bell. Brent asks me what kind of car I will drive as a prophet. I reply, "A Porsche convertible."

Paymon, who has known me the longest of any of my friends, looks at me pointedly: "Andy! Camila is not the Messiah," he says. "You know that, right?" Reason isn't the most winning strategy when dealing with people experiencing mania. Anger, also, not so much.

I insist that Camila is. The medical staff takes note that I am extremely dehydrated, perhaps have not had water in days, and certainly not food. They hook up an IV. I go in and out of bouts of crying uncontrollably, in anguish at the state of the world. Nick arrives to join my housemates, to survey the damage. My mom interrogates all of them: she thinks my state must be due to drugs, and wants to know what they know as my partners in substance use. Dr. Z will later tell me that she wasn't entirely wrong to question the role of the drugs involved: for many, even a "chill" drug like marijuana can stimulate a manic episode.

"Paymon," I exclaim proudly, chugging a bottle of water. "Look, I can drink as much water as I want, and I don't need to pee!" My dad's in the room, arms crossed: confused, upset, overwhelmed.

"Okay, Andy," Dad says. "Okay. Okay."

. . .

WHEN THEY ASK if I want to commit myself to the psych ward, I happily sign. I'm on a manic carpet ride. At times it feels like an adventure. I can still remember the calm, resolute walk of my sister in her long green coat as I am wheeled by a crew of healthcare professionals and security personnel to the North Pavilion. I am headed up North.

As I settle into my room in the mental ward, I see my parents in the doorway—the look of fear and concern on their faces. I've flipped to wanting to impress upon them the idea that drugs are not that bad for you, that they're maybe even good for you—the irony being the role ecstasy and mushrooms might have played in altering the chemistry of my brain. My puritanical dad is the target of my incoherence.

Love or drugs, I remember saying to Dad, *love or drugs.* Over and over.

The first priority for an admitted manic patient is sleep. The hospital staff loads me up to knock me out. An antipsychotic plus sleep medication plus mood stabilizers. And that first night I sleep for sixteen hours—like Rip Van Winkle. That hibernation allows my brain to relax at last, my synapses to begin to be restored, my body to reset, catch up, and begin a multiday journey back to sanity.

My next memory of the North Pavilion is from the following day—filling out a questionnaire. It starts with job and compensation. I proudly write down $58,000: the starting salary of my upcoming job at Bain & Company, the consulting firm, which I am slated to begin in August 2000. But I also note in the margins how backward it is that the first question concerns my job and income. I am fixated on teaching the healthcare professionals that the capitalist cancer of our society begins with asking mentally unwell people how much money they make.

The first will be last, and the last will be first. Material things are an illusion. Conspicuous consumption is evil. Manic me saw inequality in the world as untenable.

The manic state is a real-time processing of the unconscious. It's a rushing to the surface of everything gurgling beneath it. There is a jumble of truth, hyperbole, and nonsense alike in what I am thinking. But it adds up to profound realization, a new spirit of concern. The idea is that the world is profoundly unequal, and that it is time to grant the justice largely conferred to white men to all people, that after tens of thousands of years of being the subjugated gender, it is time for women to become the equals of men. The turn of the millennium, too, is involved—a marker of significance, urgency. It all condenses and crystallizes into a single concept:

God is a woman.

And then a second thought:

And she wants to have a child.

Male priests. Male gods. Men segregated from women by religion. The men who wrote all the books.

He.

His story.

Women, who make humans, who give birth, who give life, Mother Earth, they were the sideshow.

Camila will give birth to our child, the Second Coming. My matriarchal upbringing, the oppression of my maternal grandmother as a child bride, the echoes of colonialism in the racial differences between my parents, my deification of my own mother, my admiration for and resentment of the purity—and pure whiteness—of my own father, and the bio-chemical halo of falling in love with a woman for the first time converge into a narcissistic and megalomaniacal delu-sion: I am to be the savior of men.

It is obvious to me that God is a woman. My life's mission, once I get out, is to bring that message to the world, set the record straight, and, in so doing, save us all.

I LOVE MY fellow inpatients on the mental ward. They are, like me, from the other world, so there is no need to teach them anything: they already *know*, and they *know me*. We play ping-pong. We watch *Jeopardy!* together. I don't have my contact lenses, but for a period of time, I am convinced that I can read the answers perfectly from afar. As I return to sanity, am fed more and more medication, my eyesight reverts to nearsighted, and I can no longer read the clues. The patients, all in their own worlds, are a happy bunch. The staff mem-bers are our guardian angels.

After a few days, a lot more medication, and a lot more sleep, I was beginning to come back. I was becoming the me everyone knew, again. It was a volcanic explosion on the way up; on the way down, it was a slow descent. The lava dried, and I moved toward base camp and reality.

About a week in, the doctors decided I was ready to go. At that point, I thought, *Thank God*. With my psychosis reced-ing, being in a mental ward became less fun. I started to think, *Get me the hell out*.

I sat down for a discharge briefing with the psychiatrist, a woman from India. Coming from a family of Indian doctors, she cut a familiar figure. What she said was unfamiliar.

Her diagnosis: bipolar disorder type I, which is the most severe kind.

The words fell like a sledgehammer in slow motion. I was not yet sane enough to be in shock, or to cling to the belief that everything happened for a reason. In a separate discussion with the same doctor, my parents and sister sparred with her. Was the Accutane I'd been taking for severe acne to blame? Or the psychedelic mushrooms? The doctor said that if I didn't have another episode for five years, that might mean it was a one-off psychotic event, that bipolar disorder was a differential diagnosis, whatever that means.

One-off. That term became a life raft our family clung to for years.

I was already entering the emerging depressive state that frequently follows mania. What goes up that high doesn't just come down. It stays down.

I had heard the term "bipolar" used in hushed tones to describe others—it always seemed to refer to people who were constantly up and down. When we got back to my parents' home, I couldn't even look it up. It became a forbidden word. If I had bothered to learn more, I would have known that it's a forever diagnosis. If I had, I would have known that five years isn't the right timeline—that mania can return twenty years later, out of nowhere. If I had looked it up, I might have learned that there is no cure, that it's like a bomb in the brain, one that might go off at any point and that, on the flip side, can lead to prolonged periods of depression and stunningly high rates of suicide.

Meanwhile, the simplicity of the diagnosis's terminology, the suggestion of simply two states, *manic* and *depressive*, the notion that I was "disordered," simply didn't square with how I felt. I felt like someone who had been on a dream journey, someone who had seen the world more clearly—for all its inequalities—and who was now on a mission in the real world to do something about it.

A few days after my release, my Punjabi grandmother, our Badi Mummy, came to visit. I was blinking my eyes unnaturally, I don't know why, while attempting to sleep in my high school bed. "*So jaen mera beta*," she said as she rubbed my head, meaning "Go to sleep, my boy." That primal feeling of being in my grandmother's care, the acceptance, the love, the belonging, felt like a warm blanket for the soul as I descended, slept, and progressed on the road to recovery. I returned to a childlike state. With that recovery, with each passing day, the delusions of grandiosity diminished, and kernels of shame, of shock, emerged. I began to accept that what had been an ethereal dream for me had been a nightmare for everyone else. That nightmare was now becoming my reality, too.

I was twenty years old. I had bipolar disorder type I. For the rest of my life, *disordered*? This didn't seem like something that could be happening to me. The possibility that this new, unknowable thing was a forever diagnosis? A future filled with wild upward swings; periodic hospitalizations; long, catatonic depressive phases; and maybe time in an institution? No sir. No thank you. Too much. Oh, and suicide rates? Okay, let me look that up: "Researchers estimate," noted a National Center for Biotechnology Information (NCBI) abstract, "that between 25% and 60% of individuals with bipolar disorder will attempt suicide at least once in their lives and between 4% and 19% will complete suicide."

I cracked in half. If somebody told you that this is what your future might look like, would you want to believe it? Would you be willing to? A few days after I got out of the hospital, my mom drove me, against my will, to see an out-patient psychiatrist for follow-up, a step recommended on my exit from the North Pavilion.

"Mom," I protested, "there's no need. I am not bipolar." When we say someone "is bipolar" rather than "has bipolar disorder," that's like saying that someone "is cancer" rather than "has cancer." The hardest part is that that's what we hear when we are diagnosed. *I am bipolar.* Or when others whisper: *He is bipolar.* Which is why it's easier to not say it at all, and deny the whole thing.

The doctor I visited took notes and listened calmly as I rejected dozens of years of accumulated psychiatric science. I lectured him on how devastating the name of the diagnosis is and informed him that it didn't apply to me.

When I returned to the car, where my mom had been waiting patiently, I told her I wasn't going back.

Whenever the word "bipolar" came up in my stream of consciousness, I put it back in the bottle. The shame became hidden, the memories of what had transpired frozen in amber. I didn't talk with my family about what had happened. I tried to erase it from my mind. I tried to delete a part of myself. My only way to cope with the diagnosis was to categorically reject it.

Despite my efforts, flickers of things I had said and done were refiring and coming back to me. The Ghost had arrived.

I knew I had to get back to school to show everyone I was okay. I had missed a week of classes, and my goal was to pretend nothing had happened. Within ten days, stunningly, I was back at Northwestern—studying and socializing among a group of friends, many of whom knew that I had lost my mind, from my girlfriend to my fraternity brothers who had visited me in the hospital. I didn't know what to say about it.

I couldn't possibly talk about it. So we did something simultaneously gothic and midwestern: we never did. It was like it never happened.

The medication I was prescribed was called Depakote. In the heavy dosage I took, 500 milligrams, it's a big pink pill. For some months, I took it, on and off. It dulled me. It removed my joie de vivre, my creative spark. As I would learn, it's common for the recently diagnosed to go off their meds. It's not because we're idiots. It's because we'd rather roll the dice and be ourselves than be someone we don't know. And it's easier to do this if everyone is trying to pretend that what happened didn't happen. It's easier to do this if the diagnosis itself is being questioned or denied. The stigma around mental illness makes it logical to skip meds, too. If something is so shameful that it's unspeakable, why take medication and internalize that shame?

The number of intersecting forces—conscious and subliminal, societal and cultural, biochemical and otherwise—conspiring to cause a patient to stop taking their medication is enormous.

If I'd had an ongoing relationship with a therapist or a psychiatrist, maybe it would have been a different conversation. Maybe we could have tinkered with different medications and dosages to find an equation that worked. But I didn't. My mom took me to see someone, once. I gave him a speech about how I didn't have bipolar disorder, and I refused to go back.

TWO YEARS AFTER graduation and two years into my tenure at Bain, the consulting firm, I brought up the episode with one of my college friends. He and I were sitting at Ghost Bar in

Chicago. Was I unconsciously drawn there because of the name? With liquid courage, I revisited the episode. I knew he knew, because he'd been there at the hospital when I was admitted. It felt terrifying to finally broach the topic. My heart was exploding.

He did his best to engage, but the conversation stalled out. That in and of itself would have been awful, but not long after, he proactively said he didn't want to discuss what we had talked about at Ghost Bar ever again. As if it were his burden to hear about more than it was mine to bear. As if he was more ashamed by the memory than I was by my reality. By banishing the subject as taboo, after I had finally found some sliver of fortitude to talk about it, he solidified my desire to not bring it up with anyone ever again. A small bid for help can be, privately, a gigantic effort, imperceptible to its recipient, and crushing to the bidder if rejected.

I lived by pretending that what had happened had never happened. I took each passing day of sanity as evidence that the events of early 2000 had been an aberration, a glitch in the matrix. No blue pill, no red pill, and no pink pills, either. The problem had probably been the mushrooms, or the ecstasy the previous summer, or both, mixed in with my state of romantic rapture. Or maybe it was that I hadn't been sleeping, or had been drinking too much, or taking Accutane, or all five things combined. It couldn't be what I had been medically diagnosed with.

I hid what had transpired from the real world because the real world had no desire to talk about it or process it. Everyone was happier if it seemed like the episode hadn't happened. Including me.

My diagnosis became a ghost. Not visible to the living, but

always there. Like a half-dead person, I was no longer fully seen, by myself or others.

I chose not to engage with the diagnosis, not because I didn't want to, but because I just couldn't. I didn't know how. I was dancing on the knife's edge, mistaking it for a springboard.

CHAPTER 4

WANTREPRENEUR

SOME DAYS I FELT THAT BRIAN SPALY WAS JUST LIKE ME, ONLY better in every way.

Spaly was my new roommate on campus at Stanford Graduate School of Business, or simply "the GSB," as insiders call it. A three-letter acronym to rival the school's rival: HBS, or Harvard Business School. If business schools were houses at Hogwarts, HBS would be Slytherin, all cunning and ambition, and the GSB would be Gryffindor, all courage and compassion, and with a slightly self-righteous undercurrent of moral and entrepreneurial superiority. In other words: perfect for me.

Stanford was notoriously the hardest business school to get into, but the least competitive, and the most collaborative, once you were in. The grade nondisclosure policy, the focus on the touchy-feely side of leadership, and the unabashed embrace of all things entrepreneurial created an atmosphere of grandeur and possibility. The question wasn't how you could beat your classmates and get the best job; it was which of your classmates was going to become your cofounder. This was the milieu I had been dreaming of.

Between the consulting job at Bain and Stanford, I spent two years as a private equity associate. The best way I can describe what that job entails is acting like you're super important when you're not. Your bosses buy and sell companies, mostly with other people's money, and earn outsize returns by leveraging those investments with debt. As a junior number cruncher, I got to go along for the ride: board meetings in Connecticut, ski trips to Park City, closing parties with bankers in Vegas, and investor meetings in South Beach and New Orleans.

It was a prestigious and lucrative profession, a true Masters of the Universe club. It was also an advanced course in alpha male overcompensation, literally and figuratively. The partners in consulting were worth millions of dollars. The partners in private equity were worth tens of millions, and more. They treated me well. I learned a lot about owning companies, but not much about building them. Directionally, I was bad at the job. My entire second year was dedicated to buying a company that made bathrooms smell better. I wanted to be the person building something inspired from the beginning, not the one who buys it later. I didn't want to be known just for covering up the smell of other people's farts.

Spaly and I arrived at the GSB with virtually the same post-college experiences: we'd both spent time in consulting, at the same firm no less, then worked in private equity. We'd been introduced by a mutual friend, first meeting up in Austin the summer before the program. We were both from the Midwest: Spaly grew up in Ann Arbor, Michigan.

We became fast friends and decided to room together at Schwab, the dorm where most first-year Stanford business school students lived. I admired Spaly. He was better at sports. He was funnier. He had more money. He was self-reliant, disciplined, and frugal. I was none of those things.

What I was most jealous of: while I was barely an athlete, he was an exceptional one. We'd both played soccer in high school—I'd been a JV grunt; he'd been a star. He'd played hockey, too, and had picked up squash as an undergrad at Princeton, then made the team. He was good, and he knew it. After he beat the son of one of our Stanford professors, Spaly sent the kid an email outlining all the ways his dispatched opponent could tighten up his game. He was an outstanding skier, floating over moguls and bombing down hills, always in control.

What defined our future, though, was this difference: he was fashionable and I was not. His style was tailored, colorful, even flamboyant. He'd wear a psychedelic pink bow tie and a seersucker suit one day, white jeans and a faded Lakers T-shirt the next. He knew where in San Francisco you could buy used $500 Italian leather shoes at 80 percent off, and how to pair them with a subtly pin-striped pair of wool pants. In sartorial matters, he was not a hockey player from Ann Arbor at all.

After I drove down from Stanford to run the San Diego marathon, I reported back to Spaly, an Ironman triathlete, with my time.

"Holy shit," he replied, "that's fast! Amazing. You worked for that."

It was like reporting to a coach, and in many ways that's what Spaly was. He was a workout freak and a nutritionist with an ironclad Trader Joe's regimen. He would remind me to steer clear of what he called the five white devils: mayonnaise, sour cream, sugar, cocaine, and Dick Cheney. He even gave me pointers on how to clean the counter of our shared first-year kitchen, including the right way to use a sponge.

At the GSB, talking about startups is core to the culture. In Chicago, people thought my startup ideas were cute, but no one took my overtures to raise capital seriously. I built a business plan for a nationwide falafel-and-hummus chain and shopped it around to my mentors, people who could have afforded to write a check. Not one taker. Upon returning from a consulting engagement in El Salvador when I worked at Bain, I devised a scheme to import premium Guatemalan rum. Lots of cheerleaders, but no dollars.

Angel investors are the people who will invest in your company at the very beginning—before there is any traction. A typical check might be anywhere from $25,000 to $100,000 for a modest stake in the enterprise, generally maxing out at 1 or 2 percent of the company. Typically, angel investors back a founding team and an idea. At the time, I couldn't find any angels in Chicago. It was an old-school business town: commodities, industrials, airplanes, and cheeseburgers. I headed to California not just to find money for new ventures but to brush up against people who wanted to make the future.

At Stanford, in the heart of Silicon Valley, the atmosphere from 2005 to 2007 was exactly as advertised. The sense among my new classmates was that anything was possible. Google, launched by two Stanford engineering students, had gone public in 2004, was mapping the globe, and had just acquired a fledgling mobile operating system called Android. In downtown Palo Alto, right across El Camino Real from campus, a company known as Facebook had recently incorporated, after its founder dropped out of Harvard. Skype was enabling people from all over the world to talk face-to-face. Jobs was working on the iPhone. YouTube was acquired by Google for more than $1 billion, just one year after launch. In class, we debated whether the acquisition was justified. It seemed like a ridiculous price at the time, though several classmates argued with prescience that it was a brilliant move.

We were swimming in the bathwater of Silicon Valley at the peak of its powers: the rise of social media and the launch of smartphones. When Mark Zuckerberg came to visit one of our classes, fresh out of college, the oxygen got sucked out of the room and replaced with awe.

With such startups-turned-juggernauts serving as ever-present inspiration, students came up with ideas constantly and tested them out on each other. Here, without jobs, and with all the time in the world to dream, this Silicon Valley mindset was taken to the next level. If Sigma Chi at North-western was an airport for my entry into privilege, Stanford business school was a space station.

OVER WINTER BREAK that first year at the GSB, I took a trip with Spaly and Bryan Wolff to Bogotá, Colombia. Spaly and Wolff were two of a kind: two dusty blonds with blue eyes. If Spaly was the charismatic and brash front man, a little more like *Top Gun*'s Maverick, then Wolff was the wingman and color commentator, a little more Goose.

It was in Bogotá that I first took stock of Spaly's love of men's fashion. While in Colombia we received an email in-vite to a friend's wedding in Lima, where we'd soon be travel-ing. We didn't have anything to wear, so a local classmate of ours took us to his family tailor. Inside the atelier, Spaly lit up. He used terminology I'd never heard of, picking a Super 140s Italian wool and a contrasting pale blue silk for the liner, ask-ing for heavier construction in the shoulder. It was the best suit I'd ever worn, and with an improbably mundane but pleasing feature: pants that actually fit.

Bogotá is hilly. As we wound down a quiet road from the tailor's shop, I felt energized and impressed by a talent of Spaly's I'd never fully appreciated: he really knew his stuff when it came to the make of men's clothing. I should have known. From the moment we'd arrived at school, Spaly had been talking only about one entrepreneurial idea:

Pants.

He believed that most men's pants didn't fit. During our first year, he launched an independent research project to see if it was just his hunch or a widely shared view. He devised a survey and sent it to our classmates. What he found was that guys didn't like the way their pants fit, they didn't like shopping for pants, and so whenever they could, they resorted to the default: jeans.

I never took Spaly's business idea seriously. It seemed a hobby, a passing interest, something fun to talk about. In my narrative, I was the one who was going to do something entrepreneurial, and his pants thing was just a curious little idea, a toy project. What I didn't know at the time was that a lot of great companies start out as toys.

WHILE SPALY WAS talking pants, I was fixated, that first year at Stanford, on the concept of cultural arbitrage, the business equivalent of bridging different cultures. This was a natural idea for a windu with a developing travel addiction. How do you take something one group of people love, fanatically, and bring it to a broader audience? In addition to importing Guatemalan rum and rolling out a national falafel chain, I developed a third obsession: commercializing a market in the United States for South African biltong.

A remarkable form of cured meat, biltong is to beef jerky what filet mignon is to ground round. It's raw beef, originally cured by sunlight, infused with salt, pepper, oil, and coriander. During the spring term of our first year at Stanford, I recruited a team of five classmates to evaluate the opportunity to make biltong in the United States. I couldn't believe that carnivorous Americans hadn't already stumbled upon it.

The biltong team sat down for the final presentation with our professor, Joel Peterson, who was overseeing the project. Joel was beloved among the students. He'd been a CEO of a large real estate concern, he'd invested hundreds of millions of dollars during his career, and he had served on dozens of boards. Joel was unusual in that he was an experienced investor in companies up and down the life cycle, from backing start-ups with venture capital, to scaling later-stage enterprises with private equity, to governing and growing public companies.

Although his students showed up in flip-flops, Joel wore a navy suit and silk tie to class. He had a Wheaties box in his office that read, FEEDBACK: BREAKFAST OF CHAMPIONS, a gift from students, in acknowledgment of a previous teaching award. A Mormon from Michigan and a Detroit Tigers fan, Joel had a Socratic style in class that often manifested in role-playing management scenarios. He pushed us to treat difficult conversations with care, but to never shy away from the heart of the matter. He would pepper in a wealth of insights from his time in the trenches, along with more than a little life wisdom gained as a father of seven and a grandfather of twenty, his stories always infused with self-deprecation and humility.

We sat down in a conference room adjacent to Joel's modest office for the presentation. We laid out the case for how Americans, who by and large love red meat, might gravitate toward a much-better-tasting version of it in dried form.

Aside from my mom, Joel is the best listener I know. He'd stare at me with lucid blue eyes and a calm nod, inviting me to go on. Meanwhile, he never broke my gaze, never interrupted. When he did speak, it was almost always to ask a thoughtful question, never sharply posed but always incisive, or to offer a prompt that would drive the conversation further. His typical construction was this:

"Well, I'm the last guy who'd know anything about this, so take this for what little it's worth." Then he'd drop a perspicacious insight no one else had ever raised. After meeting Joel, I realized that the most self-confident leaders are not the ones who need to talk, but the ones who ask the best questions.

As we sat down that day to present the plan, the team was excited. We'd been slogging for the entire term, and our audience with Joel was the moment we'd been working toward.

Somewhere in mid-conversation he offered one of his pointed questions:

"Andy, is this a company or a product?"

Turning the question over in my head, I wondered what the difference was. I don't remember what I said. A little bit of the oxygen left the room.

As we talked through the risks to the business, we explained that biltong was a cured meat, not cooked in a traditional way, and that it currently hadn't reached the U.S. market because, since it was an uncooked meat sold in ready-to-consume form, it might not be legal.

Joel made a joke: "It's illegal. Well. That could be a minor challenge."

Everyone laughed. Such an experience might have put

me in a funk. But my Ghost was nowhere to be found. While I was in Northern California, I was running forty miles some weeks. I got a lot of sunshine. Grandiose dreaming was encouraged. No depression, no mania. I had never felt more distant from the diagnosis.

ANDY RACHLEFF WAS another Stanford legend. Whereas Joel's experience was across stages, Andy's was in Series A investing: the first meaningful round of venture capital a company takes, usually after friends and family and angel investors have come in, but before there is much proof of concept. The firm he had co-founded, Benchmark Capital, quickly became one of the three biggest names in Silicon Valley at the time, along with Sequoia and Kleiner Perkins.

What made Andy remarkable was that he, at the apex of his career in venture capital, had left it behind to share his learnings with all of us at the GSB. His insider knowledge of how great technology companies got funded, and the art and science of backing the best entrepreneurs, made his classes as popular as Joel's. Andy coined the term "product-market fit," the moment in startup iteration when you know you have something that the people want. When I heard about Andy during my first year, knowing that I couldn't take his class until the second year, I pestered him for a call to get his advice on my concept of taking my cultural arbitrage ideas and turning them into a venture capital firm. The thought was that while any one of the ideas might fail, by investing in an entire range of like-minded startups, I could earn a return for investors.

Like Joel, Andy had an uncanny way of leaving silence for

his conversational partner to step into—and sometimes, as in my case, stumble all over.

After I hurriedly described the idea to him, the first full sentence he ever spoke to me was this:

"It's a terrible idea."

I'd never experienced a relative stranger being so brutally honest with me at first blush. He had no qualms about offering an unequivocal opinion the first time we spoke. Whereas Joel would lay out his assessment artfully, Andy would just drop his opinion right on you. His candor left me speechless. It was a paradox: while so much of Silicon Valley culture involved being supportive of other people's ideas, Andy's form of support was telling the truth, especially when it hurt.

Andy's rationale was that a venture capital firm focused on consumer products and retail, with businesses that relied on brick-and-mortar stores, couldn't work. "The size of your wins isn't big enough to cover all your ones and zeros," he explained. It was my introduction to venture capital math. Andy, as a technology investor, knew something I didn't yet: information technology, software, and the developing internet made possible asymmetric returns that you couldn't access in businesses where you had physical inventory and real estate.

AS I WORKED through my entrepreneurial ideas, I landed a summer internship at a venture capital firm in Seattle called Maveron, which focused on consumer investments. At the end of the summer, I was lucky to receive an offer. Over lunch on Lake Washington, I shared the news with a mentor and a departing partner at the firm.

"You're not taking that offer," he told me.

"What are you talking about? I've been working toward this for years."

What he said next is one of those things you never forget, a spur-of-the-moment zap of advice that ended up altering the trajectory of my life.

"You're not a venture capitalist, Andy," he said. "You're an entrepreneur."

As someone who had never started a company, wasn't particularly focused on money, and couldn't figure out how to sell hummus, rum, or biltong, I didn't know where his confidence came from. He had been both a VC and an entrepreneur in his own right, though, so I tucked away his advice.

I didn't take the job.

Before I returned to Stanford, something unusual started happening in Seattle. After a full night's sleep, I would rise from bed, eat breakfast, and get ready for the day. Before leaving, though, the orange futon in the corner of my sublet would whisper to me to lie down again for just a moment. Fully clothed, I would comply. Just a quick nap? I would sleep the entire day. An unrecognizable feeling appeared: I didn't care about anything. I lacked the energy to do anything. Returning for my second year at Stanford pulled me out of this slump, and I put it out of my head that it even happened. Since it hadn't happened, there was no reason to give it a name.

CHAPTER 5

BIRTH OF BONOBOS

IN OUR SECOND YEAR AT STANFORD, SPALY AND I WERE housemates with three others on El Camino Real in Atherton. The house was decorated like a movie set for *Scarface*. Crystal vases, glass tables, white sofas—the only thing missing was cocaine on the kitchen table. Spring break was approaching, and Spaly faced a dilemma.

"What should I do?" he asked me.

We were upstairs in his lofted bedroom. It looked like an attic with a gray carpet. He sat at a small desk set flush against the wall. I was standing near the doorway when he refined the question:

"Should I go to the wedding, or should I drive down to L.A. and buy fabric and start making pants?"

Friends of ours were getting married in Brazil. Dozens of our classmates were going. Spaly was feeling the momentum on his pants project. His research from the independent study exploration he'd undertaken the previous year had produced two clear takeaways. First, while the denim world had evolved—fabric with stretch, multiple fits—the world of men's chinos and wool pants had seen no such innovation. Second, our male classmates had confirmed that they didn't like the traditional way of shopping for pants: going to stores and trying them on. Guided by this feedback, and his own intuition, Spaly felt ready to start making prototypes.

I hadn't yet grasped how serious he was about his idea.

"You have to go to Brazil."

AFTER SPRING BREAK, Spaly and I got together to talk. I was just back from Nairobi. A prior commitment to join some classmates on a service trip to East Africa had kept me from the wedding in Brazil.

"How was the wedding?" I was excited to hear the stories.

"I didn't go to Brazil. I went to L.A. and bought fabric."

What? I was the one who wanted to be the startup guy. He was the one doing it.

In his room were several huge rolls of fabric. They were soft pinwale corduroy, fine to the hand and with a bit of stretch, in a few colors, including a velvety chocolate and an incandescent turquoise blue. For each, Spaly had bought contrasting fabric to line the inside of the pants and create the signature peek-through, or "wink," of the back pockets. He'd purchased the fabrics with his personal savings, paired them with the contrasting linings, and before long would be importing buttons and zippers from Italy.

Spaly also found what might have been one of the last remaining clothing manufacturers in San Francisco. The company had a little cut-and-sew shop on Townsend Street, a couple blocks from the Giants' baseball stadium. "Cut and sew," I would learn, is jargon for the core activities in an apparel factory: reams of fabric are cut, then sewn together into garments. There were two partners in the little factory: Hong

Ning, a female Chinese immigrant, and Seymour Jaron, an older Jewish man from Brooklyn.

"I don't know, Brian," I can hear Seymour saying in his thick Brooklyn accent, drawing out the vowels in the middle of the name. "Pants, that's a tough business."

Spaly paid them in cash, up front. We would sit down with Hong Ning and Seymour at a Chinese restaurant in San Francisco. Spaly always picked up the tab. Years later, before Seymour's passing, I returned to the factory to find the walls plastered end-to-end with press clippings on the rise of Bonobos.

The factory had dozens of sewing machines. Only four were up and running—and that enabled the garment workers to make a few dozen pairs of pants a week. Every cut ticket had four samples taped to it: the main fabric, the contrasting liner fabric, the contrasting thread, and a carefully considered button. Spaly began selling the pants. He'd carry them around in appropriately floral-patterned red Trader Joe's grocery bags and sell them to our friends for around $100.

The main collection of inventory, maybe a hundred pairs or so, was stacked in his attic room. Spaly also kept a stash of mobile inventory, in a few different sizes and styles, in the trunk of his car. Guys would try on pants behind parked cars or trees, and with a little bit of word-of-mouth momentum, Spaly went from selling a couple pairs a week to a few pairs a day. It was energizing to watch the sales trickle in. I had a front row seat to seeing Bonobos go live.

But I wanted to play.

ONE DAY AS we sat in class, Spaly passed me a note on a yellow Post-it pad; it contained a list of names. Everyone had been calling the pants Spaly Pants, and it was time to give the brand a name. One possible candidate caught my eye, but it was a word I didn't recognize:

Bonobos.

Like everyone does, I mispronounced it at first. It'd be a while before I got it right: buh-NOH-boze.

"What are bonobos?" I asked Spaly.

"They're peace-loving monkeys that like to have sex," he replied. It turns out they're apes. I should have rolled my eyes. Instead, I bought in. I wanted to be a bonobo, too.

As the venture picked up steam, I started helping out: taking pictures of Spaly as our pants model, selling product, working on a rudimentary version of the website, writing copy, joining Spaly on trips to San Francisco to put in orders and pick up inventory. We scheduled a pants party at our house one day, and during the run-up, we hustled to build our inventory to maybe two hundred pairs. We sold more than $10,000 worth of pants that day.

What we were learning wasn't just that people loved the fit of the pants. They also loved being freed from the hassle of buying them the traditional way: in stores. While at Bain, I'd spent a year in Dodgeville, Wisconsin—working as a consultant on the acquisition of Lands' End by Sears. It indoctrinated me in the advantages of a direct-to-consumer catalog retailer. At the time, Lands' End was rated one of the top companies in America for its service. I did some research. So was L.L. Bean. It occurred to me that this was not widely understood but intuitive upon examination: they both delivered better service as apparel brands precisely because they were catalog retailers rather than store-driven. It's hard to deliver good service in stores. The catalog folks could "outservice" the competition with their rapid response call and email centers, and they could "out-assort" their competition, too. The assortment advantage came from being able to offer more options: more colors, more sizes, and more fits. They could do this because they were aggregating demand at the national level, rather than limiting the assortment to the local demand of a brick-and-mortar store.

It was a subtle point, but with massive implications for the power of building a brand centered on fit. An internet-based company could be like a catalog retailer, but more dynamic, and—with the power of technology—more personalized. Given our early reputation for good fit and bold styles, we thought we could do something that hadn't, to our knowledge, been done before: build the brand digitally from the ground up. The momentum of Zappos, a hot e-commerce company selling shoes, inspired us. They were also out-assorting people, offering sizes that were hard to find, and being recognized for great customer service and fast response times. Tony Hsieh had proved that you could sell soft goods from existing brands online, if you offered a great customer experience. Why couldn't the same be true for a new brand?

The better things went at the company, now officially called Bonobos, the more involved I got. At some point as we approached graduation, something funny happened. Spaly and I body-swapped. I had introduced him to the private equity fund I'd worked for before Stanford. They made him an offer and he accepted the job. To this day, I'm not entirely sure why he wasn't willing to go all in on his new venture. Was it fear of failure? A sense of duty to the offer he'd signed? Or a free option to see what I could do and then rejoin the company if it was "working"? In any case, it opened up a window for me. He became who I might have been, and I became who he might have been.

We struck a deal: I would become the co-founder and CEO of the company, and Spaly would stick with the private equity gig, while working nights and weekends for Bonobos on the side. We agreed that if we gathered enough momentum, and were able to raise more money, he'd rejoin the company full-time when we could afford him.

Why was he willing to entrust his idea to me? He had conceived of the whole thing. He had identified the opportunity through careful research. He had built the initial supply chain. He had designed the pants. He had put $50,000 of his savings to work buying inventory. All I had done to date was be a sounding board, a pants photographer, and a part-time blogger.

Spaly, I think, saw me as having the hustle, grit, and cunning to take his kernel of an enterprise and turn it into a company. My belief in the developing idea was perhaps reciprocally contagious. Beyond that, from our time together as classmates, he'd seen me galvanize others, including by starting a TED Talk–style series at Stanford called Talk 07, in which a classmate would share a deeply personal story each week. (I never took the proverbial stage. Deep down I knew I had a good story to tell, but I was far from ready to tell it. The Ghost went unmentioned.)

Spaly didn't know that I had bipolar disorder. None of my classmates did. My diagnosis wasn't even a thought I could hold in my own mind for more than a few seconds without experiencing a sinking feeling. The concept would perform evasive maneuvers, and then vanish, like a fast-darting octopus, back into the algae.

.   .   .

SPALY AND I were on a run. He made a comment that should have served as a bit of a warning.

"My only problem with you running this company is you're just not that fashionable." It was cutting and true.

My willingness to run the new enterprise day to day put me in the driver's seat, causing the power dynamics of the decision-making to shift. Spaly, the originator of the concept and the inventor of the product, slid to the passenger side. Laced into that was the dynamic of risk-taking: Spaly, who'd put up the initial money to start the company, was now going the safer route. With a truckload of school debt and nothing in the bank, I cashed in a 401(k) to fund a few months of living expenses and took the plunge. Initially, we cut a fifty-fifty deal. At a taqueria on Woodside Road, I offered a counterproposal: if he didn't return to the company full-time, the equity split would flip from fifty-fifty to two-thirds me, one-third him. Our startup lawyers would soon make it official.

With our deal struck, and the inventory bills piling up, it was time to raise some money.

THERE ARE TWO kinds of professors at the GSB: the academics, who do research and teach, and the practitioners, high-achieving people from the world of business who lead coursework from their experiences. The latter type, in select cases, will invest in a graduating student's startup. It is rare but not unheard of.

Joel Peterson was one of the practitioners. He was an early riser, I met him at his office at the break of dawn. I took him through a simple ten-page pitch deck on how we were going to turn Spaly's pants into an internet movement. As the presentation unfolded, Joel was virtually silent. While one track of my mind was sharing the idea with him, a second track was running in parallel—imagining all the reasons he'd think this was an awful concept. I dreaded missing the mark with him again.

He asked how much money we were raising.

"Three hundred thousand dollars," I replied. "Enough to fund inventory, the website, marketing expenses, and a couple of employees for the first year."

"And how much of the company are you looking to sell?"

"Ten percent."

"Okay," said Joel, "that implies roughly a three-million-dollar valuation. At two million, I'd be inclined to take the whole thing—but at three, I'm in for one hundred thousand."

Joel said something about this being reminiscent of his first meeting with the founder of JetBlue, and how we were going to go into a stagnant industry and shake things up with a more customer-centric approach. I'll never forget that moment—where I was sitting, the steadiness of his gaze, the gleam of belief. He was the same age as my dad, staring out from a strikingly similar set of blue eyes. Professionally he'd play the same role: a father figure whose respect I coveted, and whose disappointment, I'd find, could be a dagger. Years later, he'd tell me that my readiness to walk away from the biltong idea was the reason he had invested in the pants concept: I'd shown myself willing to listen, to change my mind, and to come up with something new. It occurred to me then that the best way to build influence with someone is to accept their influence to begin with.

Early the next week, I drove to Andy Rachleff's office at his old VC firm. Andy was no longer an active partner at the firm, but he did take meetings there. I drove down on the hallowed grounds of Sand Hill Road. At the end of our conversation, he also offered to invest $100,000. My mind was blown. Andy didn't like consumer investments, let alone ones with inventory or retail dynamics. I'd known that ever since he'd swatted down my cultural arbitrage venture capital idea. With Bonobos, though, he bought into the story that we'd do things differently by building the brand on the internet. He liked the distribution model. And I think he liked us.

"Where are you going to build the company?" Andy asked.

"New York," I replied, without hesitation. I'd recently taken a trip there to sell pants, and I'd felt a crackle of energy from a symphony of diverse industries, the vibe different from that in one-note Silicon Valley. The tech scene was on the West Coast, undoubtedly, but the fashion and creative capital of the country was New York. My instinct was that if the technology and fashion worlds were going to meld, New York City was more likely to be the epicenter. I also sensed that it would be a lot more fun there.

"Why New York?" Andy asked.

I ran through a list of reasons, from a meaningful manufacturing presence in the city to the fashion PR apparatus.

His brow furrowed. "Where do you want to live?" he asked.

"New York," I replied sheepishly.

"Next time, just say that," he said.

SPALY LEFT FOR Chicago to start his new job. I spent my days shuttling between the group house, where I still lived, and where we had stashed our inventory, and a yurt behind our friend Erik Allebest's house. Erik, a classmate, had been an e-commerce entrepreneur before coming to Stanford—he'd built a chess-gear website—and so I'd offered him an equity slice of Bonobos if he would help launch our website. Spaly also admired Erik, so he was just as enthusiastic about the partnership.

The rest of the summer is a blur, freeze-frames flickering by: driving into San Francisco to pick up finished batches of pants, leaving money for Hong Ning and Seymour at the factory, folding the inventory neatly and stacking it in a hallway closet, doing photo shoots of friends wearing the product, writing pants stories for the website, and pacing Erik's driveway while taking phone calls from our investors and lawyers to pull together the angel round that Peterson and Andy were leading.

As midsummer approached, I had an idea. While moving from Palo Alto to New York, I'd be stopping in Chicago for the wedding of my friend Jim. There'd be a huge crew of friends from college in town, many of them Cubs fans. I asked Spaly if I could take the lead in designing a style for my friend's wedding. He agreed, so we found a playful liner patterned with baseballs, and I matched it to our trademark pinwale fabric in royal blue. We then had the pants discreetly embroidered with the groom's last name, Clark, right above one of the back pockets. Clark is also the name of a street near Wrigley Field. This was the only time, to my recollection, that I was the model for a pair of pants, courtesy of a couple of pictures Erik snapped of me outside his house in Menlo Park.

The look was just the sort of matchy-matchy styling Spaly would poke fun at: a red shirt, white belt, red running shoes, and royal blue pants. As he said to me on a couple of occasions, "You dress the way my mom used to dress me when I was eight."

I wanted to prove that I could be helpful on the design side of the house as well—coming up with a concept that could be a hit with the local circles of friends in our target market. After all, I'd been successful selling Spaly's designs in conjunction with two other weddings.

I didn't sell a single pair.

CHAPTER 6

PANTS ON FIRE

WITH TWO SUITCASES OF PANTS SHOVED IN THE TRUNK, MY TAXI approached the apartment building I was moving into, one I had never seen before. The next morning I would wake up to join the cutthroat competitive ranks of one of New York's proudest and most exhausting industries—fashion—and I'd be pursuing a business model that, as far as I knew, was completely unprecedented, a digitally native, direct-to-consumer brand. Moreover, I would be doing so as a first-time founder, an inexperienced CEO, and a twenty-eight-year-old male— a trio of titles and attributes that would come to simultaneously serve and undermine me.

As the storefronts and bars of Murray Hill and Little India whizzed by, I stared out the cab window, neither excited nor afraid. What I remember feeling is the weight of responsibility, a profound sense of what I owed to my co-founder, our first investors, and a small but growing base of excited customers. All of our angel investors were friends or mentors. I had no idea how the company we had advertised to them would actually materialize, but I believed, with a fundamentalist's zeal, that of course it would.

My first days in New York were magical, like building a

workshop at the North Pole. I ordered a mattress for my
room and put it on the floor. My Stanford friend Jason Torres
called his handy uncle, and we bought shelves at the Home
Depot on Twenty-third Street. We slipped the guy at the exit
ten bucks and he let us take the shopping cart out of the store.
We wheeled it down Broadway, the shelves jutting out of the
cart. After my friend's uncle hung them in my bedroom, I
unloaded four hundred pairs of pants and stacked them by
size, navy khakis alongside a handful of pop colors, like the
seafoam-green pinwale corduroys we called the Mint Juleps.

The apartment was a three-bedroom off Irving Place, a
tree-lined slice of urban oasis that begins at Fourteenth Street,
heads north, and ends in the stately and dignified vale of
Gramercy Park. The street is inviting, with neighborhood in-
stitutions like Pete's Tavern and Friend of a Farmer dotting its
six short blocks. I shared the apartment with Ben and Robin,
who both worked for Bridgewater, the hedge fund giant. Ben
was another friend from Stanford, an early customer and an
angel investor. He quickly and literally became my confidant
in residence.

Ben and Robin paid nearly all of the rent, and with this
generous living arrangement I was able to maintain the pre-
tense of solvency as a New York bachelor. In reality I had no
savings, $150,000 in debt, and a cash-flow-negative startup
that wasn't yet fully funded. Contrary to popular belief, New
Yorkers don't worship money. They worship chutzpah. I'd
come to the right place.

But Spaly was right: for a guy running a fashion company,
fashion was not my strong suit. I wore weird combinations.
We had a thicker orange corduroy pant, with fatter wales,
called the F. Scotts. I paired those with a tight-fitting T-shirt

I'd bought on eBay, a replica Walter Payton Chicago Bears jersey, matching the orange pop of the Bears' stripes to the pants. As Spaly would say: "Oh boy."

New York was different from Silicon Valley. At a local coffee shop, 71 Irving Place, Ethan Hawke sat calmly in a black corduroy suit, nose behind a newspaper. I wondered if he'd soon become a customer. When a friend was in town we had breakfast with Natalie Portman. For weeks, I considered the possibility that she'd one day become my wife. Hollywood royalty and future president. Was I starting to slip?

Back then, transaction notices came directly to my inbox, each bringing a tiny hit of dopamine. I scoured each incoming order to see who was buying what, and from where. Most of our customers in those early days were New York finance guys. One day, however, the flashy CEO of a Fortune 10 company placed an order. Then an NFL quarterback ordered some pants. To this day, I'm not sure how they heard about us. There are people who just find things, and then those people tell other people.

Largely because of its strong cappuccinos, 71 Irving became my office for meetings. One day I called Bryan Wolff, who was now living in New York. After Joel and Andy, he became our third angel investor. I told him I was drowning in a startup sinkhole. He suggested I hire our first employee, a logical idea, and introduced me to a writer friend of his from college. Dane Huckelbridge and I met at 71 Irving, and as we sat in a little outdoor nook, we struck a deal on the spot. He'd become employee No. 1 at the company. A novelist by trade, and a scrappy Gristedes shopper, he accepted my offer of ten dollars per hour. He asked where he should start. We headed up to the pants apartment. I suggested he take inventory of the pants as a first step before doing pick, pack, and ship for the day. He marched into my bedroom and began laying neatly folded stacks on the bed. "Well," he declared, "it's time to count the pants."

Dane was a human Swiss Army knife and an instant godsend. He commandeered the morning coffee making and provided comic relief over lunches on Third Avenue. He couldn't care less about capitalism, which made him a very relaxing person for a stressed startup founder to be around, and his quiet artist's energy offset my entrepreneurial overdrive. He was also discreet, letting himself into the apartment and printing out invoices while I was still sleeping off the previous night's bender. As the pressure built, having a literary raconteur as a day-to-day partner became good for the soul.

One day while away at a lunch meeting, I got a call from Dane. We had received unexpected PR coverage in a fledgling publication, a men's blog called *UrbanDaddy*; somehow they'd figured out who we were and had run a piece titled "Monkey Pants." We had our biggest sales day ever: $2,000. Panicked by what felt like a tsunami of incoming orders, Dane asked me if we should turn off the site, presumably because he was the single point of failure on packing and shipping orders. The question soon became moot; our site crashed.

As I hustled to keep up with the company's growth, I felt full commitment to one mission: to build Bonobos and, in so doing, serve as inspiration for how brands would be built in the digital age. Serve as inspiration? That sounded like the Ghost talking. A grown-up boy with a grown-up gift: Here's the future of retail. I made it for you. Enjoy. I had trouble discerning megalomania from startup thinking. Aren't those sometimes the same thing? I began to believe that I could see a future no one else could see, that all brands would one day be built digitally. Grandiose, sure. Such a thought wasn't a product of mania, which is a state of certifiable insanity. It stemmed from mania's antecedent: hypomania. If you can keep it in bounds and stay on the ground, it's a wonderful place to be. As Dr. Z likes to say: might we all be hypomanic all the time.

WE BOOKED $100,000 in sales in our first six months, five hundred transactions, against a barely organized, couple-hundred-line Excel file of expenses. It hadn't been tracked thoroughly by the frenetically busy founders on the go, so there was a lot to excavate. We found an accounting firm that wasn't too expensive and quickly hired them.

We didn't check any references.

The accountants spent six weeks at the kitchen table in the Seventeenth Street apartment, where Dane and I worked, poring over the files. Melody and her partner were warm and engaging. It felt like they were part of the team. There was only one problem: they never delivered the work on time, and when they did, it was always incomplete and riddled with mistakes. Trusting that they'd eventually get it right, I kept paying them anyway, and never directly confronted them about the errors that were piling up.

Less than a year into the job, three of my biggest flaws were already on display: implicitly trusting my intuition about people and, even worse, my intuition in general; acting in-congruously with how I was feeling and not getting in touch with my negative and vulnerable feelings; and avoiding the difficult, candid conversations that are literally the bedrock of startup CEO life.

The flaws of a founder are sewn into the foundation of the firm.

We were now $7,500 in the hole with the accountants. With inventory payments flying out the door, and our first equity round still not fully raised, this felt like an enormous sum. When their next invoice came, I snapped. Our second employee, Dave Eisenberg, a recent college grad who we brought on as chief of staff, hired another accountant, this time someone vetted, and sent the new accountant, Heather, all the work Melody's team had delivered. Heather came back with lightning speed. The work Melody's team had done was compromised. Multiple people had been in the QuickBooks file, including some folks with an IP address in India. Heather hypothesized that they were farming out the work overseas, and when that work came back with errors, they weren't fixing them.

In short, they were stealing from us.

"Correction," said my housemate Ben. "They're stealing from our company. It's slightly different. We can be more rational if we think about it that way."

I squinted. I knew what he meant, but to me it was an unnecessarily nuanced point. Because he was an angel investor, I thought he'd be upset. Instead, he was concerned with how personally I was taking it.

In naïve and optimistic startup-founder fashion, I sent Melody an email laying out my grievances—three pages of feedback we could discuss in person. I felt confident in my approach and pleased that I'd chosen to deliver the message over lunch at a nearby restaurant instead of inviting them back to our apartment.

When I got to Casa Mono, a happening Spanish restaurant at the corner of Seventeenth and Irving, Melody was standing by the bar rather than sitting at the table under my reservation. She was accompanied by two men in black leather jackets. One was big, clearly the muscle, and the other one was shorter, beefier, and menacing. He shook my hand hard before launching into his speech. It soon became clear that we would not be eating lunch. He flashed a toothy, mocking grin and began:

You and Melody have a disagreement. You're right, she's right, doesn't matter who's right. Nobody's badmouthing anybody. You seem like a bright guy. Congratulations! You know who else is pretty smart? Melody. So here's what we're gonna do. Today, you're going to pay Melody, in full.

He shook my hand again, hard, gripping my knuckles and pulling me close. My heart pounded at what felt like two hundred beats per minute. Adrenaline, laced with anger and fear, surged through my body. Emotionally flooded, I was voiceless. So I stared. I could only look at Melody as she blew by me on her way out the door. The heavies walked by first. She looked right at me.

"Enough talkin', Andy. I'm tired of talkin'."

My feet carried me to the lobby of a safe place, the lobby of a hotel down the street. I called a good friend. He'd grown up in a neighborhood where you had to fight whenever challenged, and was the only person I could think of in my orbit who might know what to do.

"Give me their address," he said.

I was tempted. Though I knew what he was getting at, I asked anyway. "Why?"

"Nobody has to know," he said.

"What are you going to do?" I asked.

"They need to know they can't get away with this," he said, with an odd mix of menace and enthusiasm.

This is how shit starts, I thought.

Bypassing the retaliation route, I called Andy Rachleff.

"You're kidding me," he said. "In Silicon Valley, this would never happen. But I can see how in New York it might." I was reminded of my conversation with him about basing the company in Manhattan instead of the Bay Area. As someone who'd grown up in New York, he got it.

"Pay up," he said. "And just be glad," he added, "it isn't a hundred-thousand-dollar bill. Next time, make sure you don't tell someone you're not going to pay them before the meeting. Tell them *at* the meeting."

AT THE TIME, we were operating the company on Bonobospants .com. Our technology adviser, Erik, was an armchair URL trader. We had been hunting for Bonobos.com.

One day Erik called me, excited.

"Andy! I can get us Bonobos.com," he told me.

"No way. How much?" I asked.

"Thirteen grand," he replied.

While that was a lot of money, having the right URL for the brand, one that didn't limit our concept to just pants, was to me a no-brainer. I told Erik to go for it. It was a steal. Only after I got off the phone with Erik did I realize that I hadn't thought to ask Spaly, even though we had a pact to talk about all major expenses.

Then I did something weird. I called Spaly in Chicago to ask him if we could do it. He told me Erik had just called him to share the good news that we were getting Bonobos.com, and that he understood that I'd already given Erik the green light.

While he'd played it cool with Erik, I was now trapped in a lie. I catastrophized that if he shared this with our investors, I might be fired as our CEO. When Spaly and I met in Los Angeles for a wedding the next weekend, he eventually let me off the hook. Left unanswered was the real question:

Why had I felt compelled to lie?

THOUGH SPALY WAS working the private equity job in Chicago, he had resolved to work on Bonobos nights and weekends. I was carrying the load seven days a week, and he flew to New York on the weekends. On Saturdays, we'd head up to the new factory we were working with in Manhattan's Garment District.

Unlike the sleepy San Francisco shop, this one was buzzing. It was a sample shop for big New York labels, and its employees did great work: twenty sewing machines whirring at a time, with the two owners solemnly walking around, holding the seamstresses to a high bar and interacting with their fashion industry clientele with the bare minimum of friendliness. I saw through it, though, and felt a twinkle of admiration for these fellow entrepreneurs—and, of course, they were privately cheering us on, since we were their customers. Spaly loaded up on fabric at the famous Mood Fabrics, where many an aspiring designer has bought rolls and swatches to pursue their fashion dreams. We carried rolls of fabric over our heads to the cut-and-sew manufacturer, put in an order with a button taped to a sheet of paper, a swatch of the liner, and the contrasting stitching color to match Spaly's creative sensibilities.

Spaly kept making hit designs, dreaming up combinations like navy corduroy with a floral galaxy liner featuring bright red and orange flowers. Those we called the Last Starfighters. When we got into cotton twill, he paired a sheeny khaki with a swirl of color in the liner; these were named Serie A, after the Italian football league they invoked.

With the geographical separation, our partnership was prospering, and working together was fun.

When Spaly was in town, we'd work on Saturdays until eleven P.M., then go out. A half dozen rum and Diet Cokes later, it was three in the morning and we were still going. Partying, dancing, dating in the big city: the candle burned hot at both ends. During the week, Spaly would return to Chicago. I'd keep it rolling, going out every single night, for a late dinner, drinks, or both. During those go-go first two years, I can count on two hands the number of weeknights when I stayed in and ate dinner at home.

This wasn't what the experts call a "scalable" approach to being an entrepreneur. Nor were our word-of-mouth and in-person trunk shows a solution for generating sustained attention for our brand. We needed to find a marketing and customer acquisition channel we could grow with, and we needed that channel fast.

At the time, a burgeoning money-burning social media company called Facebook was finally launching the money-making part of its business model: advertising. One of our angel investors headed up the initiative, and we were one of the first fifty companies on the platform. Back then it was cost-effective. As we began spending money on Facebook, sales surged. The momentum was amplified by the second-best form of marketing after customer word of mouth: PR. We hired Polly Ryerson to help us build the buzz. She was a publicist with her own agency, and an absolute rainmaker. Over the next year, we were everywhere: fashion magazines, men's blogs, the *Today* show, and on a local cultural news segment that played in the back of taxicabs. In pre-Uber New York, this meant we were ubiquitous.

My first PR encounter was a desk-side meeting at a fashion magazine in Midtown. Desk sides were a strange concept: roll up next to a journalist's desk on the editorial floor, sit down with the posture of a courtroom typist and the demeanor of a porcelain gargoyle, show the writer your latest fashion item, and hope for the best. I was sweating bullets. A woman who looked like a cross between a librarian and a Brooklyn hipster, with what appeared to be a mini-sword through a bun in her hair, regarded me over her glasses and said:

"Isn't it a bit fraternity-boyish of you to name your company after a monkey that likes to have sex?"

"Actually, it's an ape" was all I could say, defensively, sparing her a condescending primer on how most monkeys have tails, but apes don't. It would only have buried me deeper.

In retrospect, she's one of the few people I met in late-2000s New York who called us on our bullshit. What I couldn't see at the time was that she had a point. We fancied ourselves as outsiders to the fashion scene. We thought the fashion establishment looked down on us. The reality was that the fashion establishment wasn't looking at all. Her comment stung. But partly because I failed to see past my own nose to consider it.

· · ·

SIX MONTHS AFTER launching, the company surged to a $1 million run rate. This meant we were selling nearly $100,000 worth of pants each month—let's say one thousand pairs a month—or thirty pairs a day. It took only fifteen orders each day, at two pairs per order, to get there, but we'd gotten there quickly. We were just a year from Spaly's trip to Los Angeles to buy fabric, when the brand was just a twinkle in his eye.

The mood was kinetic.

Living in a bedroom full of pants, I found that the boundaries between work and life had been obliterated. One night a grandiose vision came to me that the innovation emanating from this little apartment on Seventeenth Street, building brands on the internet, would revolutionize every corner of the retail industry. Holding this secret of our company's radical potential, and what it meant for the whole retail ecosystem, was almost too much to bear. In a dream I saw a burning image of a lion in the sky, a free association from the Broadway version of *The Lion King*. Being overserved with early entrepreneurial success, women, and alcohol, working around the clock, fantasizing about being an industry titan when we had four employees—it was a cocktail of frenetically ascending emotions. The beauty of hypomania is that it's an engine for creativity, optimism, and vision. On the one hand, this is what is required to change the world. On the other, the line between fantasy and reality can become threadbare.

In that way, bipolar disorder is an illness that can undergird greatness and seek to destroy it at the same time. It's a Faustian bargain: here is this power, but if you don't respect it, treat it, medicate it, and be clear-eyed about it, it will take you down.

My mood climbed upward, soaring from helpful hypomania to crackles of erratic behavior. The company had outgrown my apartment, and as we looked for our first office, I visited a potential space farther west on Seventeenth Street. As I checked under the sink, I crouched down on the ground to inspect the pipes. This was an unusual measure for prospective tenants, although not entirely surprising. What happened next, however, was: with a start, I kicked my legs back as if doing a burpee, to be able to look deeper underneath. It came on unexpectedly and out of nowhere.

The broker became alarmed.

"I've never seen anyone do that," he said. I smiled, but in the moments that followed I felt unhinged and confused, afraid and embarrassed.

Monica was in town and was with me on the office visit, but she hadn't seen me acting strangely. My heartbeat raced as we walked down the sidewalk toward Fifth Avenue. Anxiety welled up inside me. I had no language to express it, no thoughts as to what to do about it, and no plan. As the Ghost of my diagnosis stirred, tapping his fingers diabolically, I imagined him thrilling to the possibility of rising again. The demilitarized zone between hypomania and mania is treacherous territory. My blinkers of denial were on.

My sister's were not.

WHILE OUR FAMILY had not come to terms with my diagnosis, they were highly attuned to my moods. Subliminally it was understood that I was to be monitored closely. The methods our family employed were not the right ones, like therapy, medication, and open acceptance and dialogue around my diagnosis. In their place we inserted a more difficult regimen: an attempt to monitor or control the uncontrollable ourselves.

My mom was the worrier in chief, and Monica was deputized as the better-positioned diplomat as sibling. She became the unofficial sentinel of my sanity, texting me every night before bed to check in, and every morning to confirm that I'd slept. The hope was she could feel out my moods without causing me to snap "I'm fine," or dodge my family's inquiries outright. Trying to figure out how I was doing became a core family enterprise, and trying to evade surveillance became my learned, immature response.

Meanwhile, there was my Ghost, grinning, just around the corner.

MONICA SENSED THAT the grandiosity and elevated mood I was experiencing that spring were a throwback to my darkest secret. She had flown out to New York from Chicago, where she still lived. Having decided to eat dinner at my apartment, we ordered Thai food. I was irritable, and uncharacteristically slammed my plate onto the table. She suggested I get out of the bedroom full of pants for a few nights. She checked me into a hotel room on Union Square, and secured sleeping pills through one of the family doctors.

Out of the pants apartment, and with chemical help from the pills, I slept for twelve hours. By morning, I was back from the brink of an upward spiral. The embers were out. I felt numb. When hypomanic spells are broken by a long sleep, the unchecked acceleration into mania is averted. But it comes with a price: a sudden and disorienting decrescendo in mood.

We got lucky. Monica had helped me avert an episode. It was the closest I'd been to mania in eight years, ever since the episode in 2000. Just when we'd almost caught sight of my Ghost, he was gone, leaving everyone, including me, wondering if we had even seen him at all.

PART II

PANTS LABYRINTH

All of them, all except Phineas, constructed at
infinite cost to themselves these Maginot Lines
against this enemy they thought they saw across
the frontier, this enemy who never attacked that
way—if he ever attacked at all; if he was indeed
the enemy.

—John Knowles, *A Separate Peace*

The depressed person was in terrible and
unceasing emotional pain, and the impossibility of
sharing or articulating this pain was itself a
component of the pain and a contributing factor
in its essential horror.

—David Foster Wallace, "The Depressed Person"

CHAPTER 7

SHADOWBOXING

WHEN YOU'RE FIGHTING A HOLE IN YOUR OWN SOUL, THE FIRST step is to invent a real-world enemy to stand in as a proxy. The second step is to disguise that enemy as your friend.

The next year and a half of my life was like my own personal version of *Fight Club*. I was shadowboxing my Ghost by taking aim at my co-founder.

IN THE SPRING of 2008, my phone rang with a call from a Chicago area code. I thought it was Spaly, who'd just told Gary, his current (and my former) boss, that he was quitting.

"Spales! How did it go?" I said, picking up the phone.

"It's not Brian," said a voice I quickly recognized as Gary's. "Brian just quit. Is this pants thing really taking off? Or does he just want to say he runs a fashion company in New York to meet girls?"

My heart raced. My former boss still held a spell over me. Since I had introduced Spaly to him, I felt bad. But I told him my best version of the truth.

"It actually is kinda taking off."

As we eclipsed a $1 million annualized rate of sales, we

reached a level where a company with a little bit of angel money can afford the salary of not just one MBA but two.

Spaly arrived in New York in the spring of 2008, and we dove into the work. He took on the title of chief creative officer, but we functioned more like co-CEOs. He handled design, merchandising, sourcing, and all things creative. I led marketing, finance, technology, recruiting, and dealing with investors. We shared operations.

After outgrowing my bedroom shelves and kitchen table, we needed a real office. Spaly raced around the city, cellphone attached to his ear, looking at potential spaces. At one point, we talked about finding a combined work-living space, a pants loft, where we could run the company and live together, again, as roommates. I mentioned the plan to Monica and Nick Ehrmann over dinner. My closest friend from college, Nick now lived in New York, and Monica was once again in town.

"Spaly and I are talking about living together, to run the company from our apartment," I said.

Nick looked at me and laughed. Monica was just off the heels of her hotel intervention for me. They both knew something I didn't. I needed to create a geographical boundary between work and home, as a starting point, with the possibility that this separation might be mirrored in my psychic world.

"No. Fucking. Way." Nick was still smiling, but he was dead serious. Monica agreed. That was that.

While Spaly and I didn't live together, we found the next best thing: a lofted office at Sixteenth Street and Sixth Avenue. Spaly moved in some of his furniture from his condo in Chicago: a beige corduroy sofa and an Oval Office–worthy desk, with metal rivets on weathered brown leather. He said it had originally been used by the boss of a Chicago pickle company.

We did some modest rehab on the space: installing a better bathroom, dividing the room into two halves by adding a wall with windows, and putting in a dark brown wood floor. Dave, our second employee, memorably did a headstand on the toilet we bought for the space. This was fitting, because he dealt with our shit in more ways than one. As "chief of staff," Dave did a little bit of everything: recruiting, analytics, customer service, business operations, finance, and accounting. Most important, he was someone both Spaly and I trusted, which created a release valve for our partnership.

Spaly started buying me clothing. We needed a fashion-startup front man, not a neon orange liability. He went to a Ralph Lauren sample sale and came back with a light purple cashmere sweater, a half-zip cotton pullover, and a prep school black-and-red embroidered jacket. He'd suggest which pants I should wear with each item and advise me on compatible shoe purchases. I offered to pick up the tab; he declined. Our pattern of behavior drew on several themes: it reinforced the narrative, established during that conversation in Stanford, that I wasn't a fashionable CEO. It also solidified a story in my mind about his generous nature. In retrospect, it may have done one other thing I didn't recognize at the time, even though I felt it: it gave him power over me, the recipient of his magnanimity—the original gift being that he'd invited me to become the co-founder and CEO of a company that was his idea, not mine.

I WOULD LATER hear that the DNA of your first few enduring hires sets the culture. The early folks who stay on are the source code, and once that gets set, it never really changes. It just replicates.

After Dane, our all-hands-on-deck first employee, and Dave, our chief of staff, came Kevin Kelleher, a college football player we brought on to help Spaly on the fashion side of the house. We found Marshall Roy, one of our first full-time customer service ninjas, on Craigslist. (We picked the word "ninja" because "customer service rep" sounded uninspired, and we wanted to give the folks on the front lines of customer service a title that would inspire a high bar.) Adam Sidney joined to run operations; his first job was to buy a bunch of industrial shelving and set up the inventory.

Not long after, we hired Sarah Gray and Tiffany Poppa. Tiff had just returned from working for a nonprofit in Bolivia. Her slapstick sense of humor and scrappy get-shit-done mentality were a buoyant force for the team, and she'd become known for introducing hundreds of new hires over the years. Her town hall–style interviews became a rite of passage: Before, you were just an employee who had accepted a job offer. Afterward, you'd been welcomed onto the team by its unofficial gatekeeper. She was at once magically self-effacing and a revered leader.

Chris Travers left a partner track at a law firm when I offered to pay him in pants. He'd become our general counsel, sometimes head of HR, and an in-house therapist for all of us. Ten years my senior, he played the role of both wise older brother and loyal second-in-command. He was my foil, in every way: balance-beam steady to offset my mercurial tendencies. Whereas I loved attention, Travers shunned it. Whereas I liked to dream about best-case scenarios, Travers, ever the lawyer, liked to remind me of what might go wrong. He spent his days trying to protect us from all kinds of problems—some endemic to our company, and some endemic to my personality.

Tiff and Travers became the integrated spiritual center of Bonobos. John Rote manufactured the cultural glue, leading the ninjas team by day, and leading the entire team out at night. Matt Mullenax, a reformed investment banker, and another college football player, joined to help on finance and operations. He and Kevin grew attached at the hip. D. Craig Elbert, a brainiac from Iowa with a sneaky sense of humor, came on to run analytics. Kate Fulk (née Grimm) was our first hire from the fashion world, a planner from Bloomingdale's. She found a way to thrive in every iteration of the company, and became a lifer.

Dane, Dave, Kevin, Adam, Sarah, Tiff, Travers, John, Matt, Kate, Marshall, and Craig were graduates of places like Princeton, Harvard, Stanford, Duke, Dartmouth, and USC. You'd expect some sense of entitlement from them. But then consider their states of origin: Iowa, Illinois, Michigan, Tennessee, and Ohio, with a couple New Englanders thrown in. We built a New York fashion company with a mostly midwestern heart. The company's sense of grit, humor, humility, empathy, and tenacity—it all derived from this founding group of employees.

What was absent from this list was arrogance, insecurity, infighting, and posturing.

Spaly and I supplied all of that.

BY MID-2008, Spaly had been boots on the ground in New York for a few months. We were coming up on one year in business. Sales were strong. The team was energized. And yet, in a span of the one hundred days since he'd moved out here, our working dynamic had imperceptibly slid from fun, to less fun, to totally draining. We still agreed on the core premise of what we were doing—selling pants to guys in a new way, online—but we found ways to disagree about almost everything else, from the speed of hiring to decision-making and product strategy.

At the core of our business partnership was an incompatible truth: Spaly was a scrappy bootstrapper, and I was a swing-for-the-fences dreamer. He was there to sell pants. I was there to change the way brands were built. We had become founders for different reasons. It had been a great way to get into the room together, but it was a bad premise to be working from once we got there.

As we raised more money from existing investors and new angels drawn from our customer base, we started burning money at a faster clip—from thousands of dollars a month to tens of thousands of dollars a month to hundreds of thousands of dollars a month. What might have become a break-even operation became a money-losing one. Laced into these discussions about spending, from my end, was insecurity about, and resentment of, Spaly's creative authority and financial acumen.

While I was comfortable with Spaly's status as our pants model, I was resistant to his ideas for our business model. I began to blame our cash-vaporization issues on him. He was buying too much inventory, I'd tell myself, rather than looking openly at my side of the ledger. Determined to make Bonobos a technology company in addition to a pants retailer, I was hiring too many people, including two pricey software engineers from Zappos.

When I once again called Andy, and showed him our

cash-burn crisis, he pointed out that what Spaly had been saying was valid.

"You don't have an inventory problem; you have an operating expenses problem." Andy was referring to our acceler-
ating payroll. Because it wasn't what I wanted to hear and
didn't support my narrative that Spaly was the problem, I ignored it and sought out other opinions instead, ones that
would buttress my worldview rather than refute it. I wanted
the facts to fit my feelings. That's a devastating trait for any
leader, and for startup CEOs, it can be fatal.

Dr. Z and I still talk about the rising anger I initially feel
in my chest when someone disagrees with me. Competing
ideas are more threat than opportunity. (The only exception
is if they can be reappropriated as my own.) I took Spaly's
challenges and diverging views as a personal affront, and
when I couldn't match his reasoning or wit, I found myself
tongue-tied. I met his candor and cutting commentary with
stonewalling.

But why?

During my childhood, my mom was the person who
called it like she saw it. When my sister and I needed to do
better, she held us accountable. One day I didn't hold the
door open for her as we were leaving a clothing store.

"Andy, I think you forgot something," she said as we began
the car ride home. She went on: "You need to hold the door
open not just for me but for anyone like me." I didn't know
exactly who she meant, but I also kind of did.

Mom's communication style was such that when she was
upset, we knew it. When she was worried, we knew it. When
she was disappointed, we knew it. She and Dad didn't argue
a whole lot, but when they did, she seemed out of control to

me. Hot in the ears, fiery in the eyes. She was often right, but not always calibrated. Dad, on the other hand, didn't get externally upset. He never returned fire. His crossed arms, deep breaths, and unwillingness to engage in conflict: that seemed like the way to be.

When it came to the modeling of difficult bilateral conversations, I had no data. I assumed that an argument, where both people are going back and forth, was the beginning of the end. What I learned later is that it is the absence of the back-and-forth that spells the end of the beginning.

ONE AREA WHERE Spaly and I were aligned was raising money at the highest share price possible. Whereas public companies have market valuations, private companies, including startups, are valued at a price that the investors and the entrepreneurs agree to. Our initial valuation, in 2007, when the company was a PowerPoint deck and $30,000 in total pants sales, had been $3 million. That number is crucial because the higher it is, the smaller a piece of your company you are selling for an equivalent amount of dollars. At a $3 million valuation, if you raise $1 million, you're selling 25 percent of the company to your investors. At a $9 million figure, if you raise that same $1 million, you're selling only 10 percent. (The math works like this: The amount of money you're raising added to the valuation is called the post-money valuation. If you divide the amount you are raising by the post-money valuation, that equals the percentage of the company you are selling.)

Now, a year later, with surging momentum in the business, we tested the waters with our existing investors to raise more money. We discovered a market to raise another $2 million in new money at a $10 million valuation. As our commitments piled up, we decided to raise the valuation to $15 million and increase the size of the capital raise to $3 million. This was a bold gambit based on what we saw was a high level of interest. Initially, we fell well short of raising the full $3 million. Then I got a cold email from a man named Andrew, a customer in Kuala Lumpur who had bought two dozen pairs of pants. He expressed interest in investing in Bonobos. I didn't want to take money from someone I'd never met, so I asked him to fly to New York. He had never been here. Andrew, his wife, and I had dinner downtown. It went well. He ended up investing $1 million, which got us fully subscribed on this round.

But raising the valuation from $10 million to $15 million did not sit well with our original investor, Joel Peterson. Though his deputy had signed off on it while he was out of the office, when Joel returned, he was shocked that the price had increased by 50 percent. Injured by the implication that our company wasn't worth what we thought it was, I penned a condescending email to Joel, with Spaly's blessing, about how this round would separate "the wheat from the chaff" when it came to who really believed in us.

All of this was complicated by the father-figure role Joel played for me professionally. Our dynamic had echoes of my relationship with my real dad: they both had unreachable levels of integrity, civility, and decency. Joel replied with a power move, indicating that he wanted to sell his shares, even at a discount, unloading them at the price implied by the new round. The message was that he would take a haircut just to get out of business with us. It hit me like a punch in the gut.

.   .   .

MY GROWING CONFLICT with Spaly escalated, especially when sales were soft. When revenue doesn't meet projections, the cash burn rate of a startup only increases. The timeline to going broke accelerates, tightening the window to either get to profits or raise more money to keep the lights on. This is the dance of death, one most entrepreneurs don't survive: raising more money, burning it more quicky, and needing more money sooner than expected.

In advance of St. Patrick's Day, we made a pair of green corduroy pants called the Shamdaisies. An early crack in my relationship with Spaly emerged over the color of those pants. Later that year, during one of our long runs that doubled as a meeting, it became clear to both of us that I didn't know that kelly green was an intense, pure shade of green directly between blue and yellow, reminiscent of Celtic coastlines. He castigated me for it. Humiliation washed over me.

The adversity crept into every corner of our work. Fighting over the names of colors and pants sat side by side with fighting over things that mattered. We fought over inventory investment decisions. We fought about the people who worked for us and the people we were hiring. We fought over product strategy, about what to make next. We fought over whether or not I should hire an assistant. He laid into me.

Don't be such a diva.

The truth of the matter is that having an assistant at a thirteen-person startup is indeed a bit of a luxury. The other truth of the matter is that we weren't sparring over whether I needed an assistant; we were debating as to whether or not I deserved one.

I fumed, flooded with emotions: defensive about how hard I was working, and how much help I needed; anxious that Spaly was on some level right; nervous to push back openly for fear of getting wounded further; angry at his tone; scared, both of him and of my reaction. The result of that Molotov cocktail of feelings was that I didn't say anything. Stonewalling was becoming my go-to response.

As Spaly deepened his hooks into my superego, which Dr. Z describes as being like a critical parent or a tough coach, my actual ego began to shrink. I was hemorrhaging self-esteem. My insecurities battled his criticism every day.

According to relationships guru John Gottman, the Four Horsemen of the Apocalypse, the ingredients that spell doom between partners, are criticism, contempt, defensiveness, and stonewalling.

Check, check, check, and check.

While my relationship with Spaly was disintegrating on the outside, my mental health was disintegrating on the inside. The problem was that I was paying attention to only one of those two problems. Which made both of them worse.

I became obsessed with answering the obvious question:

How am I going to deal with Spaly?

But I forgot to pose two other important questions:

How is he going to deal with me?

And, to do what author Byron Katie would call the second turnaround:

How am I going to deal with me?

CHAPTER 8

SINE CURVE

ON A FLIGHT TO VEGAS FOR A MINI-REUNION WITH MY COL-lege friends, I was perfectly well rested. Before arriving at the airport, I'd slept a solid twelve hours. On the plane, I slept another four. A tendency had crept up on me in the preceding months: the more I slept, the more I craved sleep. In the mornings, I didn't want to get up. It wasn't a groggy hangover but a genuine desire not to face the day at all. My usually resilient joie de vivre was missing, first for days, then weeks at a time.

As we made our way from JFK to LAS, I noticed others nodding off. People get tired on flights. They sleep. My sleep was different, though: I slept because I didn't want to be awake. It was on that flight that a darker thought kept entering my mind. Each time I tried to push it away, it would announce itself more loudly:

I wish this plane would crash.

That impulse highlights the contours of bipolar disorder, or manic-depressive illness: there's one pole where you want to sleep forever and another where you believe you don't need sleep at all. Dr. Z says that for the patient with bipolar disorder, depression is so awful that mania is the flight away from depression. It is so grim that you'd rather sprint away from it forever than slip back in. Still others say mania is actually the most extreme form *of* depression.

Once in Vegas, I called Spaly and Dave to check on the business. They had decided to call one of our next pairs of pants the LeBrons. They were a gorgeous pair made from tweed wool, dark brown with a gold accent. I argued that we might end up in a trademark conflict with the world's most well-financed athlete. The debate escalated, voices rose, and what might have been a two-minute back-and-forth took forty-five minutes to unwind. Paymon, my oldest friend, witnessed the whole spat at the sports bar while he sipped a beer. "Jesus," he said when I got off the call. "I've never heard that intense of a conversation in my life." Paymon would go on to describe my tone as acidic.

I might have been with my best friends that weekend, but I didn't care. Or, more accurately, I couldn't care. The day would unfold like this: not wanting to exist, binge on coffee to summon baseline energy, start drinking as early as possible, and use the bounce of caffeine to alcohol to fuel hypomanic romantic pursuits by nightfall. Rinse and repeat.

When you associate yourself with vibrancy, when others associate you with contagious positive energy, you must appear to love life when you're around others. If you can't be the person you want to be when you're sober, maybe you can become that person when you're drinking. Substances become critical to this endeavor, and so mental illness and addiction become interlaced. The life of the party is almost always dying inside.

The fantasy becomes: If I can't be me, the me who has charisma and magnetism, then I'd rather not be anyone at all. So I'll either tuck myself away or be out at night, going big. *The most important thing,* I remember thinking, *is to tell no one*. I became an expert at camouflage. Hide in workaholism, hide in alcoholism, show no vulnerability, do no serious self-inquiry, and have no hard conversations. In other words: get no help.

Back in New York, I left myself no time to reflect on my underlying condition. The pace of the company—a speed dictated by a set of priorities that I myself had set—left no room for feeling low, or for rest of any sort. The tone-setting implications were awful—but I didn't contemplate those for years. Sometimes, during the week, when I needed to, I would schedule time on the calendar for "external fundraising meetings" and go home and sleep for ninety minutes, then power back to work. I was either out and about—or sleeping. Either way, I was a ghost.

You can learn a lot about people from how they keep their calendars. Here's what a depression calendar looked like for me circa 2008. When Friday evening rolled around, I'd eat cereal for dinner. The sofa would sing a siren song, and I'd say to myself, "Just a quick nap," and pass out at seven P.M. Next thing I knew, it was two A.M. Sometimes I'd rally and catch the tail end of the night. More often I'd move to the bed, and crawl in. Ten hours of sleep later, it was noon the next day. More cereal. Then back to sleep until four P.M. The last bowl of Honey Nut Cheerios. Back to sleep again. Now it was seven thirty P.M. on Saturday. I'd slept just shy of twenty-four hours.

"What did you do today?" a friend might ask over an eight P.M. drink. An after-dinner cocktail for her. Breakfast for me.

"Oh, been working like crazy, so took it easy last night and slept in big-time today," I'd say.

"Me, too," my friend would say. She meant ten in the morning. I meant seven forty-five P.M.

With my energy somewhat restored, I'd spend Saturday night riding an electric energy, racing away from the day's malaise. I'd flip from sleeping to having ten drinks. Then home. I'd go back to bed and sleep until five P.M. Over Sunday night dinners with friends, I'd pretend all was okay, tell the story of the previous night to burnish my image as a swashbuckling entrepreneur. The narrative was convenient. It blinded me to the truth. Over a forty-eight-hour weekend, I might spend ten hours awake and thirty-eight hours asleep.

"Acute depression." That's the term for what I was experiencing, even though I couldn't name it. If depression is characterized by feelings of loss, worthlessness, and fatigue, acute depression is the *knowledge* that you are lost and worthless and will never have your normal energy again. Suicide becomes a logical escape hatch.

For me, suicidal ideation wasn't rooted in a desire to kill myself. It was born of the desire to end the depression. My body would just be the collateral damage. You don't eat because you want to be full. You eat to end the feeling of hunger. No one says, "I want to be full." They say, "I'm hungry." The suicidal tendency is not a desire to be dead. It's a desire to no longer be living with the feeling of already being dead.

The Ghost had his hand over my mouth. To use the word "depressed" would be to acknowledge the possibility that the slump I was experiencing was the flip side of the mania I had experienced in 2000.

When the words describing my diagnosis did arise in my conscious mind, I felt a sickening drop, a traumatic connection, because I knew that bipolar disorder had another name, an older name: "manic-depressive illness." Not simply a condition but a title; known not as a disorder but as an illness. To admit that I was depressed was to admit that mania could return, that my future would be riddled with yet more depression and thoughts of, or perhaps even attempts at, suicide.

Since the 2000 diagnosis, I had experienced neither mania nor depression for about eight years. In retrospect, there were signs in both directions, but my experience never crystallized into something acute, up or down. This was an unhelpful fact. I'd been healthy for nearly a decade, and the psychiatrist had said that if nothing happened for five years, it was probably a one-off psychotic event. What I didn't understand then was that, as that first doctor had said, bipolar disorder can be a differential diagnosis, a diagnosis that depends on what the future holds. This can be a dangerous invitation for denial. What I didn't appreciate then was that having bipolar disorder is like having a volcano in your brain. You can forget it's there. But it's there. Dormant. Waiting.

I kept running. Perhaps if I ran fast enough, it wouldn't be able to catch me. And as the 2008 holiday season approached, I slowly clawed my way toward a slightly better headspace. In that context, I fell head over heels for a woman named Annika. She was from Sweden, was a child psychologist, and lived in the West Village. Annika had me in "rocket-ship mode," to use a term coined by a friend. In rocket-ship mode, I could take a relationship from zero to "I love you" in about four dates, usually spread out over six days. After just two dates with her, I was exiting Earth's orbit. Then she disappeared on me. She was all I could think about, but since I couldn't get ahold of her, I kept going out with another woman I had met recently, Christine, an Irish American teacher who had grown up in Queens.

On a Friday night not long after we'd met, Christine took me to a holiday party thrown by one of her friends. Afterward we went to a club. T.I. thundered that "you can have whatever you like." On a bathroom break, my phone buzzed with a sonar ping. A welcome green bubble popped up: it was Annika.

With an unhinged joy, devoid of empathy or awareness, I made my way to Christine on the dance floor. With little explanation, I said I had to go. She seemed upset, and also concerned. She sensed that something was wrong, not just with our trajectory but with me as well. We'd had a great night. Now I was abruptly departing. She gave me the look someone gives you when you are revealing your true colors. For me, I imagine those colors as blotchy, alternatingly bright and brooding, nearly impossible to decipher. Leaving the dance floor was the last time I ever saw her.

Sprinting outside, I experienced Annika's renewed interest in me as pure ecstasy. I ran down Eighth Avenue, then hung a turn on Thirteenth Street, toward her apartment. There are no words for this kind of hypomanic joy: courting someone, getting rejected by them, and then winning my way back. Her hot-and-cold approach enthralled me, and when she brought me back in that frigid December night, she cemented and solidified feelings somewhere between infatuation and puppy love.

In the midst of a tumultuous professional relationship, you would think I would have looked for something solid, something different in my personal life. Instead, I doubled down. The push and pull of the business partnership was recapitulated in my relationship with Annika. Instead of seeking what might balance it out, I sought the same, and amplified the ups and the downs of the sine curve.

. . .

IT HAD BEEN a momentous fall. On the evening of Election Day 2008, Spaly, our old friend Bryan Wolff, and a couple of other friends gathered at my new apartment, in a gated alley off Sixth Avenue called Milligan Place. It was a yellow early-twentieth-century low-rise with a fountain in the courtyard. A wall of windows in my bedroom peered over the small courtyard, flush with cherry trees, which would blossom in the spring, only slightly obscuring the view of a castle tower. The redbrick structure looked like it was fresh off a *Game of Thrones* set or out of a small town in medieval Europe. In fact, it had been part of a former women's prison and, more recently, a branch of the New York Public Library. When the apartment came on the market, my broker told me to show up with a checkbook. Right then and there, I wrote a check for the first month's rent, the last month's rent, a security deposit, and the broker's fee. It came to $11,000, which was 95 percent of what I had to my name.

Barack Obama won that night, and I celebrated with Wolff, Spaly, and the others, all of us feeling a fierce sense of camaraderie and hope for the future of our country. The morning after, I woke up at five to grab copies of *The New York Times* from a newspaper vendor on Fourteenth Street. I got to the office early, noticing a shift in my energy from just six weeks earlier. Back then, I could barely make it to the office by ten A.M. Now I was there, a piping cup of coffee by my side, at six A.M.

Weeks later it was Cyber Monday, which was not really a big thing yet. But holiday in retail has been holiday in retail for a long time. We had a good season. Pants were flying off the literal shelves in our office warehouse. Our lofted office meant that we worked in close quarters, every day. It was an era that I didn't really appreciate at the time: when a startup feels like a family. That phase is fleeting.

On a dreamy, snowy New York night, the whole team donned red corduroy, raised festive drinks, and signed a bottle of champagne that we vowed to save for an IPO that never happened. I'd been down for months, but now I was way up. Some people think bipolar disorder means you are all over the place in the same day. No. You're the same way for weeks. Or months. And then you flip.

That night, I was on the other side of the inflection point, the days after the mood curve had changed direction, from decrescendo to crescendo. I was crazy for a woman and I felt crazy good. We made toasts to the team, to our good fortune, and to our burgeoning startup. Snow piled up on the windowsills. Gazing out, I looked down from our third-floor perch to see taxis lighting the falling snow with their beams on their way up Sixth Avenue.

With a strong holiday season, we had done $2 million in sales in our first full calendar year, and it seemed to my freshly optimistic eyes that Spaly and I were in a better place. We had found some measure of equilibrium as we developed our own lives in the city and started spending our social time, election night aside, mostly apart. It was one of those few times in startup life, occurring maybe once or twice a year, when you step back and say to yourself, "I'm proud of this team. I'm proud of what we're doing. You know what, I'm even proud of what I'm doing. I'm proud of my co-founder, and, as hard as it's been, I'm glad he's back."

As my brain raced to remain in this happier place, I clung to an impossible thought: Maybe feeling low was forever behind me; maybe the crippling depression I'd battled that year was an anomaly. Maybe my Ghost, the phantom of mental illness, was just that: a phantom.

CHAPTER 9

ABSOLUTE MINIMUM

ONE MORNING AT ANNIKA'S APARTMENT, SHE STARTED ACT-ing strangely. It was a Sunday; normally we slept in. Instead, she was hustling me out. She had brunch later that morning with her girlfriends, she told me. It didn't sit right, so while she was in the shower, I did what insecure and unscrupulous boyfriends do: I checked her phone. Although my method was wrong, my instincts were not. She was getting brunch not with her girlfriends but with her ex-boyfriend.

When I confronted her, things got apocalyptic, but not in the way I'd anticipated. She couldn't believe I had checked her phone, and was just as upset with me as I was with her. She said that she hadn't told me about the brunch because she'd known I wouldn't be able to handle it, that it was in-nocuous, and that if I were more secure, she wouldn't have had to lie about it to begin with. When I told her that I could no longer trust her, she pointed out that I was the one who had invaded her privacy, and that therefore she couldn't trust me, either. Rather than apologizing, she demanded an apol-ogy from me. As I walked out, the part of me that thought I had the upper hand expected her to follow me into the hall-way to continue the discussion and find the resolution that deep down we both sought. Instead her door remained closed, and in the coming days, she ignored me.

I went full desperado. I kept assuming I'd run into her at our favorite haunts: Morandi, Jack's Coffee, Extra Virgin. I never did. Days became weeks; weeks stretched to months. She lived just a few blocks away, but it felt like we were an ocean apart. My mood started to backslide. Every time a text came in, with that sonar ping, my heart sank and leapt at once. Was it Annika? It never was. I tumbled deeper into a darkening place.

AROUND THE SAME time, at a charity auction in Chicago, my cousin, perhaps on a tipsy whim, bought access to a timeshare on St. Kitts. My sister invited me to join her there, and I thought it would be a welcome respite from the ups and downs of New York. As we sat on a veranda, palm trees all around, sun blazing, azure Caribbean water in the distance, my sister's eyes bored into me through her sunglasses. We were in paradise, but I couldn't even motivate myself to lie on the beach.

"You know what your problem is?" Monica said, her voice quivering. "As long as you've lived, you've always gotten what you wanted. Now there's this thing you want, and you can't have it. And you can't handle that. That's life for the rest of us. We don't always get everything we want.

"And you know what the funny thing is?" she continued. "You can't yet see that this isn't even the right girl for you. You just want her because she doesn't want you back."

Monica's honesty jarred me. In place of the sympathy I'd come to expect, to crave, from my sister, I was getting tough love.

She was right. It helped me feel less sorry for myself. I had much to be grateful for, and yet my entire focus was on what was going wrong. My mood didn't fully fit the scatterplot of life. But whose mood does? That night, we went to a karaoke beach bar. The guy who ran the place was all smiles: making drinks, playing songs, singing along. I marveled at his positivity. I wondered why I couldn't be like that.

Who can say how depressed you should be from a breakup versus how much might be a double dip from a mood disorder? How do you tease out what's expected from your circumstances versus what's amplified by biochemistry? What was just my life versus this illness I had been diagnosed with?

The temporary uptick in feeling from Monica's support and the island sunshine evaporated as soon as I returned to the New York City winter. Life was impossible. Monica called and texted me multiple times a day to check in. I performed evasive maneuvers, beginning a cat-and-mouse game I would continue for years when feeling down. I'd find ways to dodge calls and text back that I was busy with work. The reality was I was in such a dark place that I couldn't summon the energy to speak.

Soon my thirtieth birthday was upon me. It was not an occasion I could hide from. I had learned to act the part when called upon: a depressed person pretending he is not. Once I got out and threw back a few drinks, I could even fool myself. *Maybe I'm fine.* We rented out the back of a bar in NoHo. Surrounded by my dear friends, all fifteen Bonobos employees, I celebrated hard. For that night, Spaly had made me a prototype of a Bonobos shirt: it was green floral cotton with a contrasting collar in pink, with snap buttons. True to form, I doubled down on the green theme by wearing it with the Shamdaisies.

The night was filled with love, and the jukebox belted out

the soundtrack of New York in that era: Rihanna. In the back of my mind, I was stuck on the same tune: I miss Annika and wish she were here. In fact, Annika had undergone a change of heart, and she had coordinated with my friend Nick to deliver a surprise that night. A birthday cake, complete with lit candles, arrived. Nick explained that it was from her. As the candles melted, so did my defenses.

Annika and I got back together not long after that. Almost right away, we took a trip to Montreal with a big group of friends. She and I were on separate flights, and as I landed, I cranked Beyoncé's "Halo" on my headphones, ruminating on the verse about walls tumbling down.

One of my former bosses happened to be in town. We met for drinks. When we'd worked together, we had talked about marriage and dating all the time. This in and of itself was probably not unhealthy. What was definitely unhealthy was my tendency to care more about others' opinions than my own. Anyone I was dating was not just in a relationship with me; they were in a relationship with everyone I trusted.

While Annika was in the bathroom, my former boss gave me what I was looking for.

"Andy, she's a great catch," he told me.

I nodded, beaming from the vote of approval.

Back in New York, as Annika and I bonded again, our intimacy deepened. She met all of my friends, one by one, and then my parents. Something was bothering me, though. The Ghost. My secret. I had to tell Annika what had happened to me in college. I hadn't been in a serious long-term relationship for nine years. My last serious girlfriend had been with me when it all went down. But in 2009, I didn't ask myself a question that seems obvious now: Had I avoided close relationships because I'd have to share what had happened?

At that point there were two groups of people in my life. There were the people who knew me in college when I went full manic: my family and my college friends. Though we basically never spoke about it, we all knew we knew. Then there was everyone after that: from my professional life, from business school, and from Bonobos. I hid the whole thing from them, effectively cleaving the world into two parts, before and after, in the know and out of the know, old me and new me.

Annika was the first person from the new world I was going to tell, an unexplored frontier of vulnerability. We were house-sitting for a friend of hers in a palatial New York condo. I should have known what might unfold from the soulless, modern white décor. The setting was clinical, like a bad art museum or the office of a fashion executive everyone loathes. It was nighttime. I had just stepped out of the elevator that opened right into the apartment when I told her we needed to talk. She sat down at a therapist's distance on the sofa, the kind where you perch on the edge, lest you mess up the pillows, and looked at me somewhere between attentively and quizzically. There was nothing to do but plunge in.

"Annika," I blurted out, "I lost my mind in college. They said that it might have been drugs, or this intense prescription medication for acne, that it might have been a one-off thing. Either that or I'm bipolar, which is what they diagnosed me with."

The words felt impossible to articulate, and yet in a remarkably short period of time, they had conveyed the basic facts of an ocean of pain. At that moment it occurred to me that issues that feel impossibly difficult, that seem like they might take hours to explain because they clock years or decades of strife, can actually be brought into daylight in under a minute. Maybe that's the best way to do it. Maybe that's the only way.

"Wow," she said. "Okay."

I waited.

She didn't say anything else. Maybe she was in shock. Whatever the reason, this was not the response I'd been looking for. Within a few days, we broke up. It's twisted, but I think I wanted to get back at her for not making it abundantly clear that she'd love me anyway. Or maybe I felt contempt for her because she hadn't shown any empathy whatsoever. In retrospect, I see that I broke up with her not because of her reaction to my bombshell disclosure but, rather, because of her lack of reaction. It would be over a decade before I'd consider the possibility that this scene had triggered underlying resentment I'd had toward everyone else who had not wanted to talk about the issue.

As we sat down on a bench in SoHo for the breakup conversation, it seemed that, if anything, I exhausted her as much as she disappointed me. Later, I would construct the narrative that we broke up because I'd told her I had bipolar disorder and she couldn't handle it. Much later, I would realize that the truth is closer to this: I had told her I had bipolar disorder, and I couldn't handle it. Whereas the previous breakup had ended with a bang, this one ended with a whimper. It felt final, because it was.

IN 2009, BUSINESS started off slower than we'd anticipated. We had projected tripling our sales, extrapolating from the torrid

pace of our first year, and in year two, we were "only" doubling. For a retailer, this is outstanding growth. With Silicon
Valley angel investors, though, and for the technology companies we were indexing against, it was merely the price of
entry at this early stage. That, plus our overhead from a team
now approaching twenty, meant that we were losing more
money than expected.

To make matters worse, our sources of investment dollars
were beginning to dry up.

So far we had relied on angel investors, who invest their
own money. The typical check size is between $25,000 and
$100,000, though occasionally angels can invest more, as was
the case for the savior from Kuala Lumpur from our second
angel round. Venture capitalists, on the other hand, can write
checks for $10 million or more with the stroke of a pen. This
is because they are in the business of OPM: other people's
money. They raise that money from university endowments,
pension funds, foundations, corporations, and wealthy family
offices. Some VCs specialize in earlier rounds, with check
sizes of $2 million to $5 million. Others write $50 million
checks for later-stage companies. For the Series A round,
which is typically the first venture capital round, the average
offer from a lead investor is likely to be between $3 million
and $7 million. That was what we needed.

The only problem: we had no venture capital interest in
our business model. It was an unusual mixture of brand and
e-commerce: one part Ralph Lauren, one part Zappos. It was
a concept with just a few historical analogues, including
Lands' End, the catalog retailer I had consulted for years earlier, and the Gap, which had originally sold other people's
brands, until its pioneer, Mickey Drexler, realized they could

make their own brand, in the brick-and-mortar era. But in the internet age, there was not much precedent for what we were building: a digitally native brand.

Without a VC who could write the multimillion-dollar check we needed to bolster our growth, we were still being funded by individual angel investors, whom I pursued with hypomanic intensity. When I was feeling up, I was relentless. I would do six fundraising meetings a day, utilizing all the social slots: breakfast, midmorning coffee, lunch, afternoon coffee, dinner, and drinks. But while raising angel money can work for a year or two, the approach doesn't scale. As the amount of capital we needed grew from hundreds of thousands to millions of dollars, there was not enough time in the day to keep pitching people for $50,000 checks. Even though the check size is smaller, the angel investors tend to take just as much of your time as VCs, and you need to kiss ten frogs for each prince (or, rather, investor). We had raised almost $4 million of angel capital at this point, already a staggering number and a multiple of the typical startup's $500,000 angel round.

At some point, the music was going to stop.

Bonobos had a small board at that time: Spaly, two of the angel investors in the company, and me. One of them was an elder statesman named Bob, the other a young tech entrepreneur, Allen. Bob had real retail experience, having been a senior executive of a multibillion-dollar American department store. He encouraged us to meet other leading people from the apparel and fashion world in New York, but our attitude was that these were the last people we should be spending time with: they still thought that stores were everything, that Amazon would be irrelevant in fashion, that e-commerce was an afterthought, and that a brand like ours, with no stores of its own, or even wholesale distribution in Barneys or Bloomingdale's, must be doing poorly.

Then Bob told us he could get us a meeting with a retail luminary. Let's call him Alfred. This was a conversation we couldn't pass up. Alfred had built one of the most impressive fashion brands of all time. Spaly, Bob, and I sat down to meet him at his tastefully decorated office in Midtown. Whether or not Alfred was a billionaire, he carried himself with the arrogance of one. He invited two young female assistants into the office to put us on a list for a party that weekend at his home in the Hamptons—something one of them could have easily handled alone. While the two of them lingered in the room, he informed us that "there will be great pussy there."

"Are you sure you're not a villain from a James Bond movie?" Spaly asked Alfred, after a long and uncomfortable silence. "Because I could swear 007 was going to burst through those windows and apprehend you at any moment."

AS VC AFTER VC passed on the chance to invest, we continued burning through our money quickly. With our growth shy of our meteoric plans, and with a large payroll to fund the team size I had demanded, it looked like the angel capital we had in the bank might last just a few more months. This cash burn created tension between Spaly and me on just about everything. Getting through conversations had become onerous, resolving conflicts had become challenging or impossible, and what had been a fun project we were building together was turning into an arena for battle.

I called a mentor to get help.

"I don't like him anymore," I said.

"Tough luck. A lot of partnerships are like that. Your job is to get value out of him."

"I think he's a narcissist," I continued.

My mentor laughed.

"Tell me something I don't know. Most founders who are product visionaries are narcissists. If you weren't one, why would you think you could so something no else could do?"

"So what do I do?" I asked.

"He's made one hit product. The pants. Maybe it's time for him to make product two."

The problem was that Spaly and I had been fighting over what product two would be.

Personally I was torn between doubling down on pants and betting on a new category. My instincts said if we went anywhere new, we should go to button-down shirts, applying our expertise in eliminating "khaki diaper butt" to the comparable above-the-belt problem: "billowing muffin top." Spaly's view was different. As our creative leader, he was confident in the panache of our prints and thought we could take on the Vilebrequins of the world with energetically patterned swim trunks at half the price.

How the shit hit the fan with Spaly that springtime I can't even remember. At some point in a relationship driven by conflict, the details become secondary—they are just vehicles for the conflict itself. It was one of those things where you look back and say, "I don't even remember what we were fighting about."

That's the nature of a business partnership: it sublimates everything in your life to talking about the business. Developing a friendship out of a business partnership works more naturally: the relationship is rooted in what started professionally and becomes personal only later. The experience of dislocation in a preexisting friendship taken *into* a business partnership is far more jarring.

A friendship that expands into a business partnership becomes riddled with obligations: obligations to employees, customers, and shareholders. It is an intertwining of financial interests and personal reputations. It can be a battle over who gets to make decisions, who gets the credit, and who takes the blame. The partnership elevates the participants' accountability to each other to a level entirely untested in the friendship phase. It is, in short, a recipe for the evisceration of a friendship. It's not that you might lose your friend when you go into business; it's that by definition you do. The foundation of a friendship is the absence of traditional obligation. There are, of course, rare friendships taken into business partnerships that defy these laws of gravity, some of which even get better. Those friendships are mythical creatures, worthy of our admiration, but rarely conjured on command and never to be expected.

As my relationship with Spaly cratered, on the heels of my breakup with Annika, I felt defeated. It felt like a two-front war where I'd lost both battles, the absolute low point of my adult life. (I didn't realize then that only in retrospect can you tell whether something is an absolute minimum or just a local minimum.) It wasn't just that Spaly and I were having this apoplectic conflict. What made it worse was that I withdrew, turned inward entirely, buried every feeling, and ended up more depressed than I'd ever been. Being awake, being alive: everything was painful. Working felt impossible. Just getting to the office, a seven-block walk up Sixth Avenue, felt like a Delta Force mission. Inside, I caved. Something had switched, and I realized that I'd reached a crossroads: *If I don't get another human being involved, I'm dead.* My sister was doing her best as my confidante, but I needed an outsider's perspective. I knew that if I didn't get professional help, I wasn't going to make it.

Around the corner from depression is something diabolical, something doctors and therapists know can be the beginning of the end, if left untreated. It's called suicidal ideation, and it's an early step on the road to self-inflicted oblivion.

CHAPTER 10

IMAGINE YOUR ENEMY

GROWING UP IN THE MIDWEST IN THE 1980S AND '90S, THERAPY |was not a part of any discussion. It was something other people might do, but not us. We didn't need it. Neither the Scandinavian American side nor the Indian American side of the family ever spoke about it. The irony is that my family, on both sides, was stacked with doctors and healthcare professionals, including two in the mental health field. The further irony is that we had already seen what mental illness could do, in our own family history.

Being in New York, in a strikingly different era, I found myself in the therapist capital of planet Earth. Still, it was two years after my arrival in the city before I summoned the courage to go see one. It wasn't a gradual climb; it happened all at once. My depression became so acute after the breakup with Annika, and the conflict with Spaly so deep, that I didn't want to live anymore. I felt trapped by the obligation to be alive.

I had to get help.

Rachel had a modest office on the Upper West Side, with a buzzer in the waiting room and a handful of magazines. To get uptown for each session, I took taxis I couldn't afford. My body physically hurting, hating life, hating myself, wanting it all to end, I did everything I could just to remain awake as the cab made its way up the West Side Highway. It felt wrong to be leaving work for something as self-centered as this— which is an illustration of how confused I was at the time about the nature of mental wellness.

I would tell Rachel everything, but not at first. In our earliest sessions, I did not disclose my bipolar diagnosis to her. It took me several weeks to work up the courage to share the secret with her. Imagine going to an oncologist for four visits, and then on the fifth visit saying, "Oh, by the way, didn't mention this before, but I've got pancreatic cancer!"

It's a testament to the power of stigma that I had to build trust over several sessions with Rachel, a therapist who deals in mental health for a living, to tell her about my mental health history. It became possible because I was desperate. For the first time in my life, I wanted to have bipolar disorder, so that at least I'd know what I was dealing with.

What she said flew in the face of this feeling.

"Mescaline, psilocybin—these types of psychedelics can be precursors to these types of psychotic episodes."

"You mean the mushrooms?" I asked, having told her about my college drug use.

"Yes. Exactly." She went on: "Andy, I don't think you have bipolar disorder. The mushrooms you took in college may have caused a psychotic break. And the depression you are feeling right now: you're in a very difficult business partnership. You've just gone through a breakup. This is depression, but it doesn't mean you have bipolar disorder."

She wanted me to start seeing her two times a week.

I didn't know what to think. On one level, I felt some relief that she wasn't cementing, was even refuting, my diagnosis. But I felt even more despair at the same time. I couldn't imagine how I was going to get out of this deepening black hole.

On a practical level, there was no way I could afford going to see Rachel twice a week. The appointments were in the middle of the day and cost $250 for forty-five minutes— insurance picked up only a tiny slice. Already I'd had to lie about taking investor meetings whenever I saw her. The indulgence of going twice a week seemed impossible to imagine. The stigma of therapy was clearly still alive, even as I was in desperate straits. The cynical part of me felt a creeping suspicion: Was she just looking to get more money out of me?

It was about ten sessions in when she stumped me. "Andy, are you in touch with anger?"

Anger . . . I thought to myself.

What's that?

EARLY THAT SPRING, I disclosed my college diagnosis of bipolar disorder to another key person in my life: Spaly. We were on a long run around the Central Park loop. It was a conversation I could attempt only because of my dress rehearsal in telling Rachel. It was a Hail Mary. I wondered if the disclosure might jolt us to a better place, by giving him some missing piece of the puzzle that could help us address our problems.

I went for it early in the run. I told him I'd had an episode in college. Awkwardly, and without going into the details, I added that I'd been diagnosed with bipolar disorder. While we ran side by side, I shot furtive glances his way, searching his eyes for some reaction. He took my news, literally, in stride. I remember what I was wearing: a bright yellow running jacket.

I remember the feeling of being hot and cold at the same time, as the spring sunshine and the brisk wind vied for supremacy. What I don't remember was fielding a single follow-up question. It was like Annika: a momentous disclosure followed by barely a reaction. On the one hand, I felt accepted. After all, he hadn't done anything I'd feared: sounding the alarm that I wasn't fit to be the CEO of the company or naming it as betrayal that I hadn't told him such an important thing earlier in our partnership. On the other hand, I felt befuddled.

My "crazy cards" were on the table, but they didn't change anything. If that couldn't fix our relationship, what could? I sought outside help from what might be a logical place to find it: our board of directors.

At an Italian restaurant in lower Manhattan, the board—Spaly, and our two angel investors, Bob and Allen, and I—sat down for dinner. Wolff joined as well, as mutual friend and an angel investor in the company, too, though not a board member. My plan was to disclose, with a vague version of Spaly's blessing, that he and I weren't getting along.

"Brian and I are disagreeing a lot these days," I began, taking the sort of indirect line that was becoming a trademark for me, soft-pedaling something that deserved a firmer push.

"About what?" asked Bob.

Bob was the requisite gray-hair at the table, the one who had introduced us to the retail luminary the previous summer, and a storied career retail leader. We'd known each other for seven years, ever since a previous job where he'd been a mentor. He was thirty years older than me and someone I admired. It had been an honor when he'd accepted my offer to become our first board member.

"Lots of stuff. Strategy. Hiring. Inventory." It sounded so small when I put it this way. I couldn't tell the truth, because

I didn't have the words to say it: that I was enraged by Spaly's dance between criticism and charisma, disappointed by and afraid of the frequent displays of his superiority complex; that I was no doubt reciprocating with my own such displays, and responding with my own basket of mixed messages, led by stonewalling and passive-aggressive retaliation. What I was learning from Rachel was that unverbalized, sublimated anger can lead to depression.

"Here's what I want you to do," Bob said. My eyes didn't light up, but I lit up inside. Here it was. Finally. Help.

"Go into a room, work it out, and don't come out until you've either solved it or one of you has a black eye."

My spirits plunged. Really? That's your advice?

THE NEXT TIME I saw Rachel, I was vanishing fast. After refusing medication for nine years, I was now eager to talk about it.

My mind flashed back to a cab ride I'd taken in 2002, one that had been seared into my memory. The taxi driver had told me about his son who had committed suicide.

He was a pill away from being okay. A pill away from being safely alive. Maybe I was, too.

"Are you able to prescribe me an antidepressant?" I asked Rachel.

"I'm so sorry, Andy. I don't do that," she explained.

"What?"

"You'll have to see a psychiatrist for that. I can make you a referral."

Dr. Edwards was in Midtown. His place looked like a history professor's office, except four times as big and with lights dimmer than those in a cocktail lounge at midnight. From the black leather sofa where I sat, the doctor's furrowed brow and facial features were barely discernible. He sat behind a desk twenty feet away, with gold-rimmed glasses perched low on his nose. I felt like I was interviewing for a job in Satan's library.

Unlike Rachel, Dr. Edwards had no interest in talking about my feelings, my world, or my problems. By this point, things were dire enough that I knew I couldn't wait until the fifth meeting, as I had with Rachel. Without hesitation, but still with the typical mix of dread and shame required to talk about my mental health—as if he also didn't do this for a living—I described my current acute depression, my diagnosis from 2000, and the contours of the episode that had preceded it. I shared with him Rachel's theory, as well as my own long-term denial that this was bipolar disorder. We were five minutes into our conversation when he rushed me along to articulate his point of view.

"Normally we don't give antidepressants to people who have a history of mania or psychosis. It can catapult you up in mood, and we don't want you to go manic again," he said.

Sadness washed over me anew. There was going to be no help. Whatever I had, it was a disease with no cure.

"That said," he went on, "there is one possibility." He began describing a relatively new medication called Lamictal, which had originally been developed to treat seizures. "It has some mood-stabilizing capabilities, so it can act as an antidepressant, and clinically it has shown some promise, without inducing mania. I'll write you a prescription."

My heart leapt. I had always hated pills, but I would do anything, take any drug, to escape the blackness.

The appointment was over almost before it began. All business. I didn't care, though; I just wanted help.

"Oh, one thing," he mentioned as I got up to leave.

"Lamictal can, in some cases, cause a rash. Most of the time that rash is fine; it goes away. In very rare instances, though, it leads to something known as Stevens-Johnson syndrome. When that happens, it can accelerate quickly into reddish-purple blisters, and you can die from it. But either way, if you get a rash, you'll probably want to discontinue use."

The side effect sounded like a distant possibility.

On a fundraising trip to San Francisco a few days later, I was crashing at the house of Adnan Chaudhry, a close friend from the GSB. I had filled the prescription in New York and taken the unopened amber bottle with me to California. I spent hours building up the courage to swallow the pill. In retrospect it seems farcical that it would be that hard. But the stigma of taking medication for the mind is a powerful thing, and the memory of the way the previous round of meds had dimmed the lights for me was still haunting, even a decade later. Now I was thirty. It was time to put my pride aside. I swallowed the pill and went to bed.

In the morning, I woke up with a rash on my chest and called one of my uncles, a physician. He told me to stop taking it and not to worry, that just one dose couldn't lead to Stevens-Johnson syndrome. What we didn't talk about was why I was taking the medication to begin with, or what I might do instead.

I'd finally summoned the courage to get pharmacological help for my problems, and it hadn't worked. I never returned to see Dr. Edwards.

I felt cursed.

THE MENTOR I had previously sought help from on dynamics with Spaly called me one day.

"I hear you and Brian are fighting," he said.

My heart began to race. I was afraid of what he was going to say, but also oddly excited: maybe this private trauma was becoming less private in some small and important way.

"That's not good," he continued.

"But you told me that my job wasn't to like him. It was to work with him," I said.

"Yes, but you have to fight behind closed doors. If people at the company see you fighting, that's not good for the team." He explained that it's like being good parents: you never disagree with each other in front of the children. It can make your employees anxious.

To this day, I still don't know who tipped my mentor off. It led me to cross a line I had never crossed before. I started asking people at the company what they thought of our partnership, what they thought of me, what they thought of Spaly. In retrospect, I played the part of a hopelessly biased prosecuting attorney: vaguely curious about the truth, warming up witnesses, and mostly looking for evidence to confirm my belief that Spaly was the bad guy and I was his embattled partner, doing my best to contain him.

Spaly had won the debate over what to produce next: swim trunks. He'd convinced me that we could translate our design panache into making swimwear our next category.

"Vilebrequin is a rip-off. We can make prints at least as good and sell them for half the price," he argued. The typical affluent Bonobos customer wore Vilebrequin swim trunks, including the matching father-son prints you would see on Cape Cod or in the Hamptons. Their price approached $200.

Spaly got our swimwear line ready to go methodically. He worked with an apparel designer we had hired, and the prints were engaging: the signature style was a whimsical banana print with our original cursive logo. We worked with an agency to develop a YouTube video to power the launch from a marketing standpoint, hoping it would go viral. In the well-executed, humorous sketch, a chimpanzee wearing our banana-print swim trunks invites two women over for a play-date in a kiddie pool. It didn't go viral, but the views started to rack up. Not long after, I got a call from a primate expert named Vanessa Woods. She let me know that chimpanzee actors are beaten into submission to perform. It was a challenging moment, given that we were a small company and we'd made a significant financial investment in producing the video. I called Monica for advice.

"Take the video down," she said. It was not what I wanted to hear, but I knew she was right.

The botched video proved to be an omen. The swim trunks didn't hit. Rightly or wrongly, my takeaway from the experience was that the fit of our pants eclipsed the unique-ness of our designs as the driving factor in why customers loved our brand.

Spaly's "product two" hadn't taken off. It was a watershed moment in my thinking, albeit an unjust one. Judging Spaly based on a single product launch wasn't fair. Companies run experiments all the time. A failed experiment can be a good sign: it means you're pushing to innovate.

I held it against him anyway, as I could spin pretty much any data point into a reason why I didn't have to work with him anymore. It wasn't the main reason, though. All it did was add some fuel to the real fire that was already burning: interpersonally, I loathed working with him, and I'd started projecting that other Bonobos employees were having similar issues with him, whether true or not.

What I was seeking, I found. I told Spaly that because of

some issues I was hearing about about his leadership, we should get some feedback from the team. He wasn't defensive about it. Spaly was good like that: he wasn't afraid of difficult truths. I collected feedback from several team members, primarily the folks who worked with Spaly, and wrote up a 360-degree human resources–style review. He was admired, but difficult. He could be charismatic, but cutting. One employee mentioned that Spaly had once said something to him so condescending that he'd wanted to punch him.

One day, years later, when the dynamic between Spaly and me became a case at Stanford business school, someone asked me a telling question.

"Where was the 360-degree review of *you*?" he asked.

"There wasn't one," I replied.

"If there is a conversation happening about who should remain at the company, shouldn't both of you have been reviewed?" he continued.

When we see the shadow of the enemy, we avert our eyes.

ONCE THE GENIE was out of the bottle, it couldn't be controlled. As soon as I was able to identify the anger I felt toward Spaly, it exploded.

"I hate you," I told him one day on Sixth Avenue, not far from the faded facade of the Hollywood Diner, situated beneath our office. It was the volcanic eruption of what had been building for years: from being told I was unfashionable, to being castigated for not knowing a color, to being disappointed when he offended someone. I wanted to hurt him with those words, to somehow return fire for the accumulated tiny bullets he had sent my way.

"I know," he said, remarkably not reacting in kind. I found

in that moment a measure of grace and indifference entirely inaccessible to the tumult of emotions I felt in telling the person I'd spent the most time with over the past four years that I couldn't stand him. The rocket I'd shot from my bazooka landed like an arrow against iron. After that, the memory blacks out.

Days later, we were at an upstairs convenience store on Sixth Avenue, a place with a few tables. It could have been a scene out of a Vince Gilligan TV show, more *Better Call Saul* than *Breaking Bad*. The smell of burnt hot dogs wafted up. It was a sad setting for a sad conversation. Spaly and I talked through how broken things were. For me, it was a breakup. Afterward, back in the office, I watched him like a hawk, to see how he appeared to be doing. He'd found some inner fortification to wall out the conversation we had just had. Perhaps he was faking it, but he was back to business. Any sense that our friendship was bleeding out was imperceptible. I marveled at his ability to just get back to work on the deck of the sinking ship that was our partnership.

Some days after that, Spaly called me at five A.M. I picked up the phone.

He said something inaudible. I could tell he wasn't well. It was unusual for Spaly to call me so early. He sounded like a small boy: distant, in dire trouble.

All of my antagonistic energy instantly converted to empathy. There was no room to play the role of the victim. We talked for a few moments, and agreed to meet later that morning at the City Bakery on Eighteenth Street.

Monica, in the preceding years, had followed my ups and downs with Spaly closely, and had advised me through all of them. As things started coming to a head, she had taken to visiting New York even more frequently, flying in every month or so to check on me. That morning when Spaly called me, she was in town. She knew I wasn't well, either, and so she joined for the coffee.

I dialed Bryan Wolff and asked him if he could come, too. Monica and Spaly knew each other, but only at a distance, and Monica was clearly in my corner. She was family. Wolff, on the other hand, was a brother to both of us, and I thought he could be more of a bridge if need be. He was on both "sides," and an angel investor—with the company's best interests in mind. Ever the dutiful friend, he agreed to meet us there. Over croissants and coffees, we sat at a small round table barely big enough for the place's trademark chocolate chip cookies—let alone the issues we were about to unpack.

"Brian, how are you doing?" I asked.

"Oh, I'm fine. Totally good." Zero sign of the vulnerability I had heard during the predawn phone call. He was a different person entirely. The stoic edifice had been rebuilt. It was as if the conversation we'd had just hours earlier had never happened. I broke down.

Monica jumped in.

"Brian, do you like yourself?" she asked him.

I don't remember what Spaly said, or if he even replied, but I do remember what she said next.

"Because I don't think you do."

Wolff punctured the awkwardness of the moment. "Coffee, anyone?"

Wolff offered comic relief. Monica offered protection. Spaly offered stoicism, perhaps even defiance. I, completely tapped out, offered nothing but sadness and despair.

Somehow, improbably, the beat went on. Spaly and I even went for a bizarre walk where we found some measure of repair. As we snaked our way south from Chelsea into the West

Village, I pressed further on my conviction that he was the broken one, the one with psychological issues. That he could accept that concept without returning fire was an indomitable gesture. It revealed a magnanimity, loyalty, and ability to endure that I was incapable of demonstrating, and showed how deeply I hewed to my side of the story.

It was also a radical act of projection to focus on what might be psychologically wrong with him.

While my bipolar disorder was now known to Spaly and me, he never held me to account for the way my mental illness exerted deleterious effects on our partnership; the way it affected my decision-making, communication, and judgment. I burned Spaly at the stake, and gave myself a pass. He never burned me back.

IT WAS ON a Saturday in August when I caught Spaly in the office. He had just returned from a sourcing trip to China. While he was gone, I had written him a long and meandering email. It boiled down to this: I wanted to be the CEO and get him out of the day-to-day business by making him a largely external-facing chairman; but, I'd added, to flee the current quagmire, I'd be happy to play either role. I thought that by presenting my willingness to take either side of the trade, we might escape the tense deadlock. The last thing I wanted to do was leave the team, but my fear of depression was so profound that I would do anything to avoid experiencing it.

The email, while passive-aggressive, was only the start of it. With the table set between us in the open, I went for the jugular behind the scenes. I began emailing the 360-degree review of Spaly to our two board members and to outside angel investors who knew both of us, and I shared in one-on-one calls that, painful though it was, I thought Spaly should leave so I could run the company without him. A couple of the investors had private discussions with Spaly about him leaving. One of those discussions took a supportive tone: "I'll back you on your next venture." Another one, as I understand it, was firmer: "You've lost the support of the team. Now you need to go."

We had a design office in the middle of the long hallway in our new space on Nineteenth Street and Sixth Avenue. As I walked in to confront Spaly, I saw that he had hung up an electric new print. White was the ground color, and lines of black were sprinkled throughout, with filled-in parts to create a psychedelic chessboard, punctuated with shapes in pink, neon green, yellow, and aquamarine blue. The overall effect was reminiscent of Salvador Dalí. There was a verve and flair to the prints Spaly picked—in this he was on par with Paul Smith and Etro, storied designers of menswear unafraid of color and panache.

The stage was set for one of the most surprisingly short and momentous conversations I would ever have.

Spaly sat at his desk, one of a couple in the shared design area, looking up at me.

"Would you be willing to step aside?" I asked him.

"What do you mean?"

"Would you be willing to step aside . . . would you be willing to leave?"

Tears crept into his eyes, but he didn't reach for them; nor did one build up enough size and weight for gravity to pull it down his cheek.

"When?" He choked out the word.

"I don't know, a month? Two?"

"Yes."

Yes.

I couldn't believe it.

Spaly didn't hole up with lawyers. He left with grace. He read a poem to the whole company at a farewell dinner at Diablo Royale. When he signed the paperwork, Chris Travers let me know the deed was done. I closed the door to my office and fell to the floor.

SPALY PAID THE price for whatever issues he had by leaving. Mine were unaccounted for.

It is what we hate about ourselves that we most dislike in others. In our feelings about others there is always a kernel of how we feel about ourselves. The Franciscan friar Richard Rohr wrote in his book *Falling Upward:* "We all become a well-disguised mirror image of anything that we fight too long or too directly."

I am not who I say I am.

I am not who you say I am.

I am who I say you are.

The year of co-founder divorce had been the hardest year of my life. Now that I was alone at the top, the blame-it-on-Spaly days were over. I could never have imagined that it was going to get worse.

In the weeks after his departure, my mood ascended. With the demons of that relationship seemingly vanquished, I fantasized that my therapist, Rachel, had been right: it hadn't been an underlying mood disorder bringing me down, it had just been a problematic partnership. With the co-founder divorce behind me, I could fly again. The truth is, that's trademark bipolar behavior. After escaping, in mid-mauling, from the jaws of a bear, what do you do?

You run.

CHAPTER 11

HYPOMAGIC

IN THE FALL OF 2009, EVERY MORNING BEGAN WITH A HANG-over and a coffee. Five coffees later, it would be six P.M. and time for my first Maker's Manhattan. In my hypomanic world, I was always running. Running from sadness, running from depression, running from my Ghost.

Whether it was a meeting, an interview, or a date, there was always an excuse to be with someone. There was always a way to avoid being alone. It's only if I was still and centered that I would have to have a hard conversation with myself. So if I was never still, there were never any hard conversations to be had at all.

SPALY WAS NOT replaceable by any one individual. As I dug into his side of the house, I came to realize that his had been not one job but at least five: merchandising, production, design, planning, and creative direction. These areas were all foreign to me. Production was the most tangible: you can't run a clothing company if you don't make clothing. So I started there.

Who was the right person to run production for a startup brand, and why? The more people I met, the more opinions

I got, and the more new introductions I received. The process opened my eyes to two fundamental and empowering entrepreneurial truths. First, nobody knows what they're doing. Second, you don't have to know what you're doing to find and hire the person who does.

Production for a startup brand was a chicken-and-egg problem. We were making pants in the Garment District of New York. While I didn't know anything about production, I knew enough to understand that production in Manhattan wouldn't scale. New York's Garment District had declined from 325,000 workers, at its peak in the 1950s, to fewer than 25,000 by the late 2000s, and it was continuing to contract rapidly.

After I'd spoken to more than a hundred people, I realized that one name had kept coming up again and again: Liz Hershfield. She had helped build Old Navy, and she'd done consulting work for brands that were just getting started.

Liz and I spoke by phone, and I invited her to come visit us in the Flatiron District in Manhattan. We had breakfast near Union Square. She was inspired by our conviction that digital was the future of how brands would be built. She believed the same thing.

Within a few weeks, Liz had moved to New York from San Francisco. She came on full-time as our first executive hire from the apparel industry: a veteran who knew brick and mortar but who believed in the power of e-commerce. She came on as vice president of production, and for the first time it felt like we were growing up as a company. Liz was tenacious, ambitious, and instantaneously loyal.

The first time I heard her talking to Christina, the owner of our New York factories, negotiating for on-time delivery and for better prices, I was a few stories up from her in the stairwell. Liz was reading Christina the riot act. Our approach to suppliers had been "Thank you for taking a chance on us." Liz's was "You're welcome for our business, and now how about a ten percent price reduction, sixty days payable instead of thirty, less variance in fit, and let's work together on fabric with a better hand feel." As I descended the staircase, my internal aversion to confrontation manifested as a stomachache, and I had two thoughts: *I'm glad I'm not on the other end of the line* and *I'm glad she's on our team.*

Now we could make clothing. But what clothing to make?

At first I didn't understand what was meant by the word "merchandising." For a retailer that mostly sells other brands, like Walmart, the merchants are the people who buy the products that the retailer sells. They decide who for, who from, how much, at what cost to buy, and at what price to sell. Simple enough. But what if you *are* a brand? Then what is merchandising? It took me a while to divine the meaning. Eventually I came to understand a merchant (or merchandising executive) at a brand is the human who figures out what products people want and then leads the team in the creation of those products.

In 2009 in New York City, there was one brand known to have the best merchants in men's apparel: J. Crew. I'd figured out that if you admire a company for a particular function, you hire people in that function from that company. I found my way to Marcela, a J. Crew men's merchant, and we met for dinner.

By the end of the meal, I felt we had to hire her. As we parted ways, I headed for the subway, and asked her if she was doing the same. What she said was a harbinger of the negotiation to come:

"I never take the subway."

Another founder once gave me a memorable piece of advice about hiring: "Do five back-channel references on anyone who is going to report to you. Not the people on their list of references. The other people. The off-list ones."

Finding five people who both knew the person but who weren't on their reference list, and who were willing to talk to me required some Sherlock Holmes investigatory work. I had to figure out who the potential hire had worked with (and ideally worked for) that I could get a conversation with, and then get to that "back-channel reference" via some shared connection in my network whom the "back-channeler" trusted. Otherwise why would they talk to me? Over the course of several weeks, I worked my way through these off-list references at the same time I did the on-list references.

On-list people *have* to say glowing things. If someone's on-list reference doesn't extol the candidate, that's a problem. No need to bother with off-list references if the on-list references' evaluations aren't superlative. I loved the work of figuring out the off-list references: networking, surfing LinkedIn, and asking on-list references who might have a diverging view. It was like being a corporate detective, and I applied my hypomanic energy to having dozens of conversations every day in the pursuit of "the truth" about whomever I was looking to hire.

We didn't end up hiring Marcela. But from the anthropological exercise of getting to know everyone in the J. Crew orbit from the on- and off-list reference process, I identified the three best up-and-coming people from J. Crew: Brad Andrews, the merchant overseeing the men's casual-shirts program, which was growing rapidly; Dwight Fenton, the second-in-command in men's design, and the one who did the hard work of managing the design team; and Erin Ersenkal, who was overseeing merchandise planning for the surging e-commerce business.

I met with all three of them in the following weeks. The good news was that all three were intrigued. The bad news was that none of them was ready to make a move yet. Things at J. Crew were going gangbusters, and Bonobos was an unproven startup. In time, they all would join us.

Who would run the fashion side of the house in the meanwhile? Enter Steven La Guardia, aka SLG. SLG was a luxury fashion executive I was introduced to by a recruiter named Maxine Martens. Steven had been running a division of a fashion house at the time. He was one part merchant, one part designer, and one part creative director. When he joined our little team, I was stunned. His arrival was validation that maybe the fashion world was going to take our brand seriously.

SLG lived in my neighborhood, on the west side of Greenwich Village, and had a sometimes sweet manner, a cool affect, and a winsome unreachable quality all at once. One day I bounded into his office with what were, in retrospect, an ugly pair of Moscot sunglasses: they were a miss for an old and storied brand rooted in Lower East Side cool. SLG's reaction was halting but diplomatic. He hated them. "Hmm . . ." he said. It was a dose of honesty, as well as creative judgment from a fashion insider, something entirely new.

SLG whipped things into shape quickly. He led our first full-scale photo shoot with hired models, a dandy affair on a golf course in Florida. He blew up an image from it for the lobby of our new offices at Nineteenth Street and Sixth Avenue. He also suggested a fresh coat of paint and tidied up the place. As we stalled out on pants growth, due to the law of large numbers, and with the swimwear launch a commercial

dud, he innovated on product. We made only khakis and corduroys and wool pants. SLG knew we didn't want to do jeans,
so he suggested a compromise: a stretchy five-pocket in a fabric known as bull denim, offered in a rainbow wheel of colors
consistent with the flamboyant and energetic brand DNA.

DUSTIN, OUR NEW software engineering leader, arrived just in
time, as the original e-commerce platform we were built on
was falling apart.

Our technology backbone was reminiscent of the bridge
in *Funny Farm*.

"This ain't a bridge. It's termites holding hands."

It was a duct-taped, swivel-chair interface of six different
systems. It was not going to scale. With our technology situation in shambles, I applied the same technique of "DNA
importing" to our recruiting efforts. What up-and-coming
e-commerce company understood growing an online retailer
in the soft goods space?

Zappos was legendary for its customer service—something
we aspired to. Tony Hsieh, the CEO of Zappos, would soon
publish a book called *Delivering Happiness*, about the need
to cultivate cheer and positivity in your staff, particularly the
service team on the front lines of solving customers' problems. I admired Tony. It would make sense to me later that a
man who wrote about delivering happiness might not be
happy himself. I'm not the only founder with a ghost story.

By focusing on our potential as a venture-backed technology company with Silicon Valley roots, rather than a New
York City–based fashion company that happened to sell online, I was inviting a culture war into Bonobos, a war that

would be mirrored by the battle inside my own mind about who we were. Without Spaly to shadowbox with, I entered a different ring: one where I became the company's biggest asset and its biggest liability at the same time.

With the help of a headhunter, we found two star engineers to recruit from Zappos. The more senior, Dustin, became our VP of engineering. He was tall, bald, and each morning brewed gourmet coffee in a Chemex that he brought to the office.

AS WE GREW, housing our fulfillment operation in our Manhattan offices began making less financial and logistical sense. Our core pants business slowed, from doubling year on year to growing by 50 percent. While this was still fast by any other standard, it was not fast enough to keep up with the expectations we'd set for ourselves; we intended to grow more like a technology company than a traditional retailer. It certainly wasn't fast enough to finance the rate at which we were hiring. Before he'd left, Spaly had suggested that we slow down our pace of hiring. He might have been wrong about product two, but he was right about that.

To maintain momentum, we needed to keep innovating on product. Frantic for growth to stem the losses, I suggested that we start selling other brands on our site, something antithetical to our founding business model of selling only our own brand and our own designs. SLG called in all of his relationships to get this third-party brand business going. That would take a minute.

First, we had to prove selling other brands would work. A former intern, Ernie, was a men's accessories designer. He made a solid men's shoulder bag. We launched it via an email to our customer base. The first day, not a single bag sold. Over the next three days, we sold twenty-nine bags. At $300, this was the most expensive product we'd ever sold, except for a $300 pair of pants made from alpaca wool. (One day I got a call from a customer I had hand-delivered a pair of those pants to. He'd been walking down Park Avenue when he had gotten trapped in a rainstorm without an umbrella and been thoroughly soaked. He'd smelled, he told me, like a drenched llama.)

We were burning cash faster than expected, and we had to scramble to continue raising angel capital. VCs continued to lack interest in a company most of them didn't understand. Unlike Zappos, an e-commerce company where selling existing brands was the core strategy, à la Amazon, the Bonobos model of building our own brand was without clear precedent. Twice that year we were weeks from running out of cash and missing payroll or being unable to make inventory payments for future orders. This would have led to two business calamities: fraying relationships with vendors and a decline in future shipments, both of which would have impaired future sales and guaranteed that the cash squeeze would be worse down the road. If we even got there.

I raised an additional $4 million over six months, with a relentless, hypomanic energy fueling daily meetings over coffees, breakfasts, and rubber chicken dinners, piecing together $50,000 and $100,000 checks to keep things alive.

In the summer of 2010, I found myself sitting outside Bill O'Donnell's home on Lake Michigan, having breakfast with Bill and his financial adviser, Jeff Friedstein. They'd backed the company in a meaningful way already. As we sat down, I explained that we needed even more money and asked Bill to commit another $100,000. It was to be a part of an additional $2 million round.

"Andy, how do I know you'll be able to raise the rest of this? If we put in more, what if it's a bridge to nowhere?" Bill asked me.

Before VCs would back our company, the more time I spent with potential angels, the more I came to view it as inevitable that if I talked to enough people, and shared our story, we'd get the money. The hard part was getting the money in before existing cash ran out. Some of this depended on courting new investors. Some of it depended on getting inside investors to re-up. Sometimes founders forget that the most important target of a fundraising pitch is the investor who has already invested.

As we raised new money, the fresh capital coming in would dilute everyone's holdings. The fact that their portion was going to be diluted if they didn't participate could motivate existing investors to pony up. If they put in the bare minimum to maintain their previous ownership stake, that was called investing pro rata. I became skilled at convincing people to invest super pro rata, which is when they invest even more than they need to maintain their stake and, in so doing, increase it.

That day at breakfast with Bill on Lake Michigan, I had to show ironclad confidence.

"Bill, we're going to get the money. We always do."

"But what if you don't?" Bill asked.

"That won't happen. We've got a big angel base, many of them will re-up, and we continue to meet new people who are excited about Bonobos. I promise you," I said, unflinchingly, with direct eye contact, "we're going to get the full two million."

To raise money, I sought the confidence not of a charlatan but of a skeptical optimist: an entrepreneur dreamy enough to go for a big vision but realistic enough not to lose the money. Investors like Bill needed to believe I was definitely going to raise the money, and they needed to worry that they would miss out if they didn't commit. Toward the end of the round, this was easier to do, because I could use scarcity to drive action. But nobody wants to be the first penguin in the water. So I had to signal that there would be lots of other penguins, all getting ready to jump.

Bill's financial adviser gave him a glance that said, Let's do it. They committed $100,000 on the spot, and I convinced them to wire it before we had the rest of the money, which is unconventional. Most investors would rather wait to confirm that you can raise the full round, so they'll hold off on wiring until they know that the other wires are coming in. But Bill, a spiritual man whose career was built on his story of recovery and redemption from addiction, operated on faith. When I squared up and told him I'd make sure that his capital was backed up, he knew I meant it.

The lights were still on, but maybe not for long.

Back at the offices, our green but brilliant director of analytics and now finance as well, Craig Elbert, was running the numbers. He was a lanky, introverted, sneakily hilarious guy from Iowa, just out of business school, with short, curly blond hair.

One afternoon he came into my office. The color had drained from his face. "Andy," he said, "we've got a problem." My heart sank toward the floor. Craig was a painfully honest guy, so I knew that this was bad.

"We might struggle to make payroll soon."

"Are you fucking kidding?" I asked. "Even with the money Bill just wired? How is that possible?" Bill's $100,000 would have more than covered our biweekly payroll.

"It's the letter of credit we have with our factory. We've guaranteed them contractually that we won't go below a certain cash balance."

"How did I not know about this?" I was livid. True to form, Craig was taking one for the team. A bunch of other team member mistakes added up to this predicament, but he focused the blame on himself.

As I boarded a plane to California, capital was no longer feeling infinite. If I couldn't raise and close another $250,000 in a week, we might have to lay off much of the team. My headspace during that period was mixed: some days I felt confident that we were going to figure it out, while other days I gave in to near-total despair, with a sinking feeling that I was going to screw it all up.

On this emotional roller coaster, my feelings about the fundraising we had to do took on their own bipolarity, and the process of raising capital became a vicious cycle. On the good days, a relentless optimism fed on itself. In a deeply unknowable way, I *knew* we would get it done. We would raise the money, build a great company, and get everyone their money back, along with a return. Bursts of positive energy would enable me to meet more and more people, at an almost pathological level of extroverted activity. In the bad cycles, the depressive or lower-mood days, I felt despair. We wouldn't make it. There was no hope. I didn't want to crawl out of bed to get to a fundraising meeting, let alone spin tales of success to raise the money.

In that way, with the clock ticking, the need to fundraise

itself became a sort of antidepressant for me. There are two ways a startup fails: either the founder gives up or the company runs out of money. If I was perpetually depressed and didn't get the money, we were by default going to go out of business.

Depression is in my wiring. Losing is not. I've always hated it. The only thing I hate more than losing is letting other people down. Or maybe those are the same thing. The visceral desire to not fail our employees, customers, and existing shareholders always forced me into action.

As the plane made its way to San Francisco, I felt horrible: bone-tired even though I was doing nothing, plagued by a throbbing headache, entirely undesirous of living. But I had a job to do that affected other people's lives, and so I summoned a better mood state, not by meditation or prayer but by the tangible step of putting one foot in front of the other on the way to fundraising meetings, because I had no other choice.

After arriving at SFO, I hopped on the tram to Hertz to pick up a car. I put down our Amex Plum Card. One day we'd done a photo shoot with Amex, and I'd been featured in the company's ads. Today, however, the card was denied. We didn't even have the liquidity for me to drive into Silicon Valley to beg for money. Once I arrived, having paid for my own rental car to get to a Starbucks in Menlo Park, I sat down with Matt Wilsey, a brown-haired, aw-shucks, Patagonia vest–wearing Silicon Valley angel investor and entrepreneur, and a kind soul. After a pitch I had no idea could end that way, both in ticket size and speed of decision, he committed $300,000 of capital from his family on the spot, and agreed to close right away.

A true angel.

Matt saved our company without even knowing it. My gratitude to him, and his family, eclipsed what he could have realized. After the successful meeting, I felt a surge of energy, and immediately converted that energy into going out drinking with some San Francisco friends. With alcohol running through my veins, I'd get a restless night's sleep and wake up early. Sleeping just four hours would jolt me out of a depressive cycle, where I would sleep ten hours or more a night. Just one morning feeling good would light me up, remind me that I wasn't going to be depressed forever, and I'd then have the energy of a god. It was like flipping a light switch. If I didn't pause to investigate my underlying state, and if I stayed amped up on either coffee or cocktails, I figured I might be able to avoid falling into depression again. Alcohol, of course, is not an upper; it's a downer. In this way, alcohol, and the poor sleep it produced, became a mood stabilizer of sorts.

I don't recommend this program.

By the time all was said and done, in our first three years, we raised $8 million in total across four angel funding rounds from more than 120 investors. This was like scoring fifty points in a football game with twenty-five safeties. I wonder if I would have been able to pull this off were it not for those frenetic episodes of elevated mood that bipolar disorder made possible. Herein lies the dual nature of hypomania: It is a gift of relentless optimism and tenacity that can enable Herculean feats of magnetism, attracting capital and talent to a fledgling enterprise. It is also a harbinger of potential doom. Around the corner from hypomania, mania is always lurking. With additional firing of synapses at the upper bound of the mood spectrum, aided and abetted by a lack of sleep that becomes both cause and symptom, the dynamic person who days earlier just seemed "up and super energized" might come apart entirely.

More covertly, even without the ascent into mania, hypomania creates a whipsawing effect of impulsiveness and poor judgment, laced with a winsome charisma that can cover up the costs. These errors of judgment might be more accurately called errors of excitement, and the magnetic nature of the mood state can seduce others into being excited about them, too. Or impressively resistant, and at loggerheads—and perhaps at the risk of being fired. The result: a leader who is maddening and inspiring at once. One of the worst things a leader can be is unpredictable.

It became my bread and butter.

CHAPTER 12

LIGHTSPEED, AT LAST

IT'S NOW THE BACK HALF OF 2010. A CRISP MANHATTAN FALL, three years into our startup journey. With the psychedelic orange, red, and yellow trees in Central Park came a binge of trying to raise venture capital dollars. The angel investor thing wasn't going to scale as our capital needs went from a few million dollars, over the course of a year, to $10 million all at once.

More than one hundred meetings with venture capitalists over three years hadn't resulted in a penny. Some firms had gotten as far as due diligence, but never a term sheet. I developed a bionic spine to handle the rejection. It was working just fine when I met Jeremy Liew from Lightspeed Venture Partners. Jeremy, an Aussie, was another Stanford GSB alum; our attorney, who knew a lot of other people who'd come out of Stanford, introduced me to him. A good attorney can be a fountain of introductions when it comes to raising money, and our outside counsel, Ted Wang, was known at the time as one of the best startup attorneys in Silicon Valley.

When I walked into the meeting with Jeremy, I immediately noted that he was wearing the Pink Party Starters (the pants previously called the Pink Panthers, during our flirtation with trademark-violating idiocy). They were pinwale corduroys in a super-light pink, nearly white, with a wavy phantasmagorical print liner. His choice in attire for our meeting—surely intentional—gave me a jolt of optimism. Jeremy already believed in the product. I didn't have to convince him. It's a lesson most VCs are too busy to remember: come to the meeting with the entrepreneur excited about the product, or maybe don't come at all.

Jeremy was a pioneer in popularizing a methodology for analyzing internet and e-commerce companies where you examine the relationship between lifetime value (LTV) and customer acquisition cost (CAC). What you want to see in your analysis is that a company is economically acquiring customers and that those customers are increasing in their value over time—driven by repeat purchases.

Fundraising moments like this one forced us to look internally way more closely than we ever had. Craig did the analysis. I awaited his call with bated breath. How did the latest "cohorts" of customers look? The short answer was this: strong. We hadn't figured out our next product line after pants, but the repeat rates within the pants business were good, and improving each year. Because we were selling our own brand, the margins were higher—which made the economics even more attractive.

Once Jeremy had digested the analysis, he was ready. After a few weeks of discussions, he invited me to come out for the next step, something most people dread: the partner meeting. It was high-stakes stuff, and I loved it. I flew back to the West Coast to present to his partnership. But before I did, he said there was another slide he wanted me to include in the deck: the total addressable market (TAM) size. Funnily enough, in three years, "What's the size of the market?" was a question

I had never answered myself—which shows the instinctive nature of my approach to entrepreneurship.

We researched the answer: Menswear was a $30 billion business in the United States at the time, with maybe 10 percent penetration of e-commerce. That meant our addressable market was $3 billion, and compounding annually with double-digit growth. This was a bit on the smaller side for a Series A investable company. What I missed at the time is how much smaller the slice of the market was at our price point, $100 for a pair of pants: this was probably no more than a $300 million market. Later, living with the reality of this shortcoming in market size would force us to find a successful way to expand into other categories.

So far, we'd thrown up a huge airball with swimwear. But our second round of experiments into selling other people's brands was working well, from Gant blazers to Jack Spade bags. The opposing challenge was that selling other people's stuff was both a distraction and a lower-margin business. In retrospect, however, it was a valuable endeavor: it provided a road map for the products we might develop ourselves. Our success with Gant blazers, for example, had inspired confidence for our in-house designs of our own line of casual blazers.

Building Bonobos products in new categories like shirts and blazers was an endeavor with a longer lead time, one that would require more expensive up-front investment in the team that could design them. The experiments selling other brands lit the way and bought us time. Once we were developing our own product, it would be a higher-margin game: more investment, more reward, and deepening brand equity, to boot.

We used that confidence to expand our own assortment into categories like woven button-down shirts and tailored clothing. Before we went there, though, we tested our mettle in denim. Having dipped our toe into the water with color-dyed bull denim, we'd decided that it was time to build a proper blue jean, something we had never done. After all, Bonobos had initially been launched because all guys were wearing were jeans. At some point in our growth, though, and with our credibility for fit well established, it was time for us to take jeans on.

It would be the following year—when Brad Andrews, who finally left J. Crew to become our merchant, and Liz, our head of production, teamed up—that we would execute the extension into other product categories. Brad was a former high school quarterback. He was competitive, cerebral, and impossible to read. He was also a brilliant men's merchant and a good foil for my personality. We made a launch video for our new denim line that featured Liz and Brad talking about the heritage of our fabric source, a mill in North Carolina. The early wash and construction were done out of Los Angeles.

Denim was a success, and the business took off. We did an oxford shirt next, and discovered the best fit by leveraging a beta test. We found our product testers via social media and email. At first the shirts weren't great, chunky in fabrication and not yet slimming. As we iterated, and introduced a slim fit to complement the standard, that business began humming as well.

We had discovered a road map for how to grow: by expanding a brand built around fit in the three big categories—pants, shirts, and, later, suits—rather than smaller categories like swimwear and polos. Bonobos was no longer just a pants company. It was a menswear company.

BETTING ON THE potential for new categories ahead of the proof, Jeremy and the team at Lightspeed extended us our first-ever real term sheet: an offer to invest $7 million in the company at a $30 million valuation. Pacing on the cobblestoned driveway in front of the Rosewood hotel, situated on a beautiful oak-canopied property on Sand Hill Road in Menlo Park where I'd taken meetings with countless investors who had said no, I talked the proposal over with Jeremy.

"Can you give me a couple days to get back to you?" I asked him.

"How much time do you need?" he said.

"A week or so," I replied, tentatively. I was nervous that I'd lose the offer, but I was also careful to give the impression of a competitive process, and I wanted to suss out another potential key player in the deal. I didn't have in mind swapping someone out but rather adding someone into the mix, a specific someone who could kill three birds with one stone: get us even more money for the business, get me out of debt, and buy out Spaly.

Sometimes I wondered: What if Spaly had stayed and I had gone? Would Bonobos have been more focused and raised less capital, and built a profitable business sooner? The real world would provide me with its answer to that question within just a few years. In the meantime, things were awkward. I had lied to him when I'd said I'd stay in touch, call and ask him for advice. I never did.

I was still afraid of him—afraid of failing him, and afraid

that a major shareholder of the company might hate me. Sure, Spaly was no longer a Bonobos employee, but he was still a part owner, both of the company and my psyche.

Spaly was physically gone, but *Fight Club* lived on.

SAMEER GANDHI WAS an affable Indian American with a baby face that belied the wisdom of his years in the business. Another Stanford alum, he'd been an apprentice at Sequoia, and was now making more than a name for himself at Accel. I'd met him a few years earlier when he'd visited one of our classes at business school, and I'd been impressed: he kept his perspicacity hidden underneath a projected humility, a warm smile, and a steady-as-can-be demeanor. Meeting with him was calming; plus, he'd offered me a bit of capital earlier as a part of one of our angel rounds. It wasn't a lead offer, but it would put another strong firm on our capitalization table.

When Sameer had offered a check the first time, I'd called our outside counsel, Ted, for advice. Ted, ever wise, had suggested that we not take a small check from Accel, because if they didn't invest in a bigger way later, it would be a negative signal to all other potential investors.

At the time, Accel was in the news a lot as a major investor in Facebook. It was still a contrarian idea that Facebook would become big; its business model was nascent. As one of the first advertisers on Facebook, with early success in acquiring customers through its new advertising platform, I was a believer—in both Accel's prescience and the halo it would shine on their firm and therefore any investment in us. Sameer was also not shy about e-commerce: he led Accel's investment behind an entrepreneur named Marc Lore, who'd had the audacity to challenge Amazon by selling diapers through a business aptly named Diapers.com. While I didn't know Marc, I looked up to him—and entrepreneurs notice the entrepreneurs VCs are backing as a way of understanding which currents those VCs are surfing.

I'd wanted Accel's money that first time, but I'd heeded Ted's advice. With the term sheet from Jeremy, I had a new opportunity—not to swap Lightspeed out but to add Accel in.

THE DAY I presented to Accel, my niece was born to Monica and her husband, Rob. Monica and Rob had met as partners in pharmaceutical sales. A tall, soft-spoken, blue-eyed man with brown hair and a closet sense of dry humor, Rob cut a familiar figure to our dad, not an atypical story. He was a dedicated husband and was about to become a dedicated father. My niece's arrival felt like an omen. I'd flown home twice to try to be there for the birth, but when she finally arrived, I missed it. I had to be in Silicon Valley to present to Sameer's partners at Accel. Normally the presentation would have occupied and perhaps overtaken my thoughts, as well as my ability to sleep the night before. But that night, all I could think about was Monica and her health. Her pregnancy had been normal. Still, I was worried. As I went to sleep, she went into labor.

I woke up to a call from Monica, and the two best words I'd heard in my then thirty-one years.

"She's here."

In that moment I knew two things: My sister was okay. And I had a niece.

The rest of the morning was a blur. The presentation to Accel went well, I thought. As everyone gathered around a square table with, uncharacteristically for VCs, white furniture, surrounded by glass walls (inviting questions and intrigue about which entrepreneurs were passing through for pitches), the discussion was warm. It felt familial, and more like a conversation than the grilling I'd grown accustomed to.

That night I was aglow. Being an uncle was more on my mind than having finally climbed the entrepreneurial ladder to present to a hot firm. As I drove down El Camino Real toward a dinner engagement, the phone rang. It was Sameer. I pulled over to gather myself. We spoke briefly. Accel was going to be in as well.

Looking down at my iPhone to find the address where I'd be having dinner, I didn't even pay attention to it—Google Maps was removing, in real time, the need to even think about where you were going.

I was going to see the Wilseys—the family whose angel investment had helped save the company with a $300,000 check out of nowhere that day at the Starbucks in Menlo Park when I could barely afford the rental car required to get there. It seemed right that they'd be the first to hear that their bet had paid off, and that now we were funded by two of the best venture capital firms in the game.

As I pulled into view of their street, it occurred to me that it was just around the corner, less than a block, from the house where Bonobos had begun, and where we had stored our inventory in a closet.

As I turned onto the Wilseys' street, I finally noticed the name.

It was Isabella Avenue.

Isabella, the same name as my newborn niece.

A memory came back to me. It was my maternal grandmother's prophecy, one I'd dismissed at the time. She had said that if Monica had a daughter, she would bring with her great wealth. With Accel's commitment to the round, if Spaly decided to sell his stake so that we could make space for Accel to be included, I would also be able to sell some stock, and in so doing become a millionaire. Meanwhile, the company was getting an eight-figure infusion of fresh capital.

As I parked on the street, it all caught up to me. It was less the money, and more the idea that something more was going on in this world than meets the eye, and the epiphany that a woman educated only through the sixth grade, on a divine or celestial level, somehow saw further than the rest of us.

I HAD CALLED Spaly a few days earlier and asked him if he'd like to sell if I could line up the money. He'd need to relinquish a big chunk of his shares for the overall deal to be worth it to Accel to come in.

The phone rang. It was Spaly.

He was in. At the price offered in the financing I had arranged, he wanted to sell the lion's share of his position.

This meant a few things.

First, he'd be putting a few million dollars in his pocket— which took the pressure off me. I would no longer be the guy who'd screwed up what was originally his brainchild. Even though things had gone sour between us, I still felt intense loyalty and, more aptly, a sense of duty to do right by him. He'd given me the keys to his concept and put me in business as a CEO.

Second, it meant that another blue-chip venture capital firm would be joining our investment round. For someone who had been begging people for money for three years, this was an unthinkable development.

Third, I would be getting a big wire transfer. When the

money arrived, I called Stanford's credit union and said I'd like to retire my debt.

"How much?" asked the guy on the line. I pictured my grandfather.

"All of it," I said.

"All one hundred and sixty thousand dollars?" he asked.

"Yes, sir."

"Well, somebody had a good day," he said with a chuckle. "You win the lottery?"

"More or less, sir. More or less."

DROWNED OUT BY the momentousness of these professional events, the most important meeting that happened in 2010 went virtually unnoticed. It was a midsummer day, and the lobby of the Ace Hotel at Twenty-ninth Street and Broadway was a beehive of Apple computers and Intelligentsia cappuccinos. There, the modern-day creative class hammered away on an array of Steve Jobs's devices, all striving to meet his axiom of "Stay hungry. Stay foolish." Jobs would be dead in just over a year. The New York tech ecosystem, meanwhile, was just coming into its own.

The restaurant just off the lobby at the Ace was called the Breslin. As I walked out of breakfast with one of our employees, into the buzzing lobby, I noticed a woman standing by the stairs. She had wavy brown hair, a curvy figure on a lithe frame, and was wearing a pair of Tinker Bell–style ballet flats, bejeweled. She was glowing. I don't remember making the decision to go up to her. My feet just started walking.

"I like your shoes."

She smiled at the compliment and introduced herself as Manuela, receiving me more kindly than expected for a striking woman dallying in a hotel lobby. The details of our conversation have melted away; I retained only the contours in the years that followed. She had spent her early years in Brazil, where she was born, was educated in the United States, and had been living for the past four years in China. She was a journalist there, writing for *Newsweek*, covering food and agriculture. Later I'd find out that she'd gone to Harvard and had a master's degree from Oxford, and had traveled to more than forty countries. While I had met many brilliant and ambitious women in New York, this was about the most gobsmacked I'd ever been by a first conversation—she was open, gracious, and showed no annoyance to the stranger who had interrupted her day.

Minutes later, when I was midsentence, a man with a chiseled face and cropped hair walked in and greeted her with a peck on the cheek.

My heart, previously fluttering upward, came crashing down.

CHAPTER 13

A DIAGNOSIS DEFERRED

THE SERIES A ROUND WAS CLOSED. ALL GOOD, RIGHT?

Wrong.

We got the money, then we immediately started the next year missing on the budget, and losing more money than planned. I called Pete Harding, a friend and then venture capitalist not involved with our company. He had declined to invest as an angel, in order to keep our relationship uncomplicated. At that moment, I was grateful, because I could level with him without producing any financial anxiety or concern on his part.

"Pete, we're way off plan," I confided.

He laughed. "Everyone misses their plan after the Series A. All VCs know that the first board meeting post close is going to have bad news."

This made me feel better, but not by much. If our new shareholders, led by Jeremy and Sameer, were expecting me to accomplish anything less than I'd said I would, I couldn't tell. Having two professional VCs behind us didn't decrease my day-to-day anxiety. With fiduciaries who each had a 20 percent stake in the company now sitting on the board, I had to level up my game. Initially, at Jeremy's request, we were having board meetings every six weeks.

Stress mounted quickly that frigid January. We had nearly doubled in each of our first three years, and the budget called for 100 percent growth again. Nothing can double forever. After the frenzied launch years of 2007 and 2008, the co-founder divorce in 2009, and nearly running out of cash three times in 2010, I wondered: *How is it possible, after we finally raised real money, that this job could get harder this year?* Then I came to a classic mistaken conclusion of an immature founder: if the business isn't working, we must not be working hard enough.

If the culture of the tech world is built on the joy of innovation and possibilities for wealth creation, the fashion industry is built on hierarchy and fear. Tech is a stewardship model: the leader provides context and vision, and the team makes most of the decisions and brings the vision to life. Commensurately, the team owns a meaningful portion of the equity. Fashion, on the other hand, is a proprietorship model: the leader gives marching orders, and the team executes. Employees explicitly work for management, management works for the owners, and the owners have all or nearly all of the equity.

In post–Series A Bonobos, these two philosophies were on a collision course. I had always said we were building a company, the first of its kind, at the intersection of fashion and technology. Well, there we were, and the culture clash was becoming acute. For the tech folks, apparently there was not enough innovation to warrant working hard. Even if this was a technology-enabled pants company, it was still a pants company—and the technical problems, it seemed, were not inspiring enough for the evening or weekend work I thought was required to win. For the fashion employees, I concluded, there wasn't enough fear. That was what I set out to change.

With the encouragement of SLG, our chief creative officer, an executive from the fashion world, I developed a presentation where the basic takeaway was we could all be
working harder and giving more to the company. As I wrapped
up, the room of twenty or so folks fell silent. Their crossed
arms and sullen expressions conveyed emotions I had never
before seen on the faces of our team: hurt, resentment, anger.
Breaking the silence was a slow, loud clap: it was SLG, who
had been adamant that this was a message our millennial employee base needed to hear. No one joined him in the ap-
plause. Dustin, our VP of engineering, wheeled on his feet to
go back to his desk, stunned by this botched act of leadership.

Having come to Bonobos from Zappos, Dustin brought
with him a different mindset about how to build a winning
culture. While at the time I kept a corner office, Dustin's
previous boss, Tony Hsieh, was known for sitting at an incon-
spicuous desk with the rest of the team, offering employees a
bonus if they wanted to leave the company, in order to weed
out all but the true believers. Tony also experimented with
self-organization and *holacracy*: a management school where
there are no bosses or subordinates. Zappos had sold to Amazon for $1.2 billion just over a year earlier. Steeped in the
Zappos mindset, Dustin was dismayed, to put it lightly, by my
attempt at a fear-instilling pep talk. We met in my office the
following Monday.

"I wish you could have seen Tony at Zappos," he said cryptically. And then fell silent.

In a subsequent conversation, he shared with me a
proposition—one that felt ripped from my own playbook with
Spaly.

"You step aside from the day-to-day. Scott and I will run
the company," he said, referring to our head of marketing,

who had recently come on from Apple. My ego was unprepared for the audacious suggestion. My mind raced with scenarios of what might happen if I handed over the reins. On hypomanic days, I loved my job. On the dark days, I saw it as an impossible burden. Yet at the same time, there was no one else I could picture doing it.

I refused Dustin's offer. He resigned. A handful of the technology folks followed him out the door. Dustin had been right about one thing: how to build a winning culture. Rather than taking responsibility for the presentation that precipitated Dustin's resignation, I blamed SLG for it. While it wasn't the only reason, I fired him. Next to go was Scott.

Scott had come in to run customer experience. He was a former Apple store manager, so this made sense. Before long I promoted him to running marketing: a decision made more out of hypomanic enthusiasm for his "energy" than out of careful consideration for what he might do with more scope. When it became apparent he couldn't do a job he had no qualifications for, other than coming from a company with a great brand, I did the only thing I could do: fire him for my mistake.

With multiple executive departures in quick succession, a few other folks quit, and the company culture tanked. The turnover had shaken everyone's confidence in my leadership abilities, and made them fear for their own jobs. Everyone was beginning to recognize a pattern: a senior hire would come in, their ideas would take immediate hold as they became the new golden child, and within a year that golden child would be fired, undermined in part by the quick rise my favoritism had enabled.

Meanwhile, the numbers got worse as our business selling other people's stuff began tapering and our new growth vehicles like shirts and denim, while promising, were early days and small numbers. One of the stories I had told myself in ousting Spaly was that I was better at hiring and leading people, and therefore would be better at scaling the business. Now I was seeing clearly that at best I was mediocre at hiring and leadership, and at worst a disaster.

I needed a river guide to help me make sense of what was happening.

But who?

DEPRESSION FUNCTIONS BEST in the absence of hope. Perhaps depression *is* the absence of hope. Regardless, with my depression now severe again, and sinking to levels that matched those of two years earlier, I was catatonic on the weekends and barely muscling my way to work during the week. I began to privately acknowledge thoughts erupting from below, from an unconscious layer, the domain of my Ghost.

I still didn't want to say the word to myself. *Bipolar.* As quickly as the name of the disorder bubbled up, I pushed it back down. On the journey to coming out, first you have to be able to have the conversation in your own mind.

The words "bipolar disorder" imply instability, unsteadiness: a life at the extremes. They convey, to the untrained ear, a sense of dealing with two people, not one. Trying that diagnosis on is hard, like wearing an ugly shirt that's soaked in acid: not only is it not pretty, I felt I'd disintegrate if I put it on. But I was reaching the point of not caring. *Fine*, I thought. *If I'm going to feel this awful, give me the shirt. I'll wear it. I don't fucking care anymore.*

My aunt, a physician, was in town. I gave her a tour of my

office, and then we walked through the city. Summoning some previously unrealizable modicum of courage, I revealed a deeply held secret to her: I was sleeping all weekend. While omitting the word "depression," my admission was a cry for help.

She didn't notice.

"You have a crazy job," she said, ironic on a few levels. "Of course you need to catch up on sleep on the weekends." She offered a reassuring smile.

Although it hurt, my aunt's failure to acknowledge my symptoms did not strike me as authoritative. While I had also struck out with Rachel and Dr. Edwards, I knew I needed another opinion from a mental health professional—and perhaps someone who, while aware of the stresses of entrepreneurial life, wouldn't try to explain away the illness as a function of it.

SERENDIPITOUSLY, IT WAS around this time that an angel investor introduced me to Leonard, an executive coach who happened to be a former psychiatrist. That angel investor had no idea why the confluence of former psychiatrist and executive coach was so compelling to me; I hadn't told any of our investors I had bipolar disorder. If I couldn't even tell friends or Bonobos employees who dealt with me every day, why would I tell our shareholders? Who would trust their money, let alone the $25 million I had raised at that point, to someone who has a bipolar diagnosis?

Leonard hadn't been a practicing psychiatrist for years, since discovering a more meaningful and lucrative calling advising CEOs, entrepreneurs, and executives. His particular superpower was helping leaders navigate the intrapersonal and interpersonal struggles at the vortex of managing teams.

Leonard had warm eyes and a disarmingly attentive demeanor. He always wore a pressed suit and a silk tie to our meetings. When I asked him what his monthly retainer was, he said $10,000. That was more than my salary at the time. I told him there was no way I could afford that, but perhaps I could pay him in equity. Leonard agreed to our unusual arrangement, and we began seeing each other monthly.

One day, after we'd been working together for over a year and had built up a reservoir of trust, he and I sat down for a breakfast conversation that would alter the trajectory of my life. Unlike with my aunt, where I couldn't even use the word "depression," I broached the subject of my diagnosis head-on.

"Leonard, I was diagnosed with bipolar disorder in 2000 after a manic episode," I confided. "There have been a host of people throughout my life who have told me it was a one-off event. But with all of this depression I'm experiencing, I'm starting to wonder."

We went through the whole history, from what happened to me in college, to the asymptomatic period for nearly a decade, to the way depression had been gripping me increasingly often in recent years. I told him about my visits to the therapist who thought I'd had a single psychotic episode from taking mushrooms; the opinions of my family members, who saw the possibility that acne medication or drug use had been a catalyst for psychosis; the statement from the discharging doctor in 2000 that if I was incident-free for another five years, the issue might not have been bipolar disorder, that this was a differential diagnosis, and we would only know in time what I was dealing with.

When he finally gathered his thoughts, I felt the energy in

our conversation shift: he was moving from the asking-questions phase of the discussion to the tendering-his-opinion part. I can still remember the steadiness of his gaze and the purifying balm of his words that washed over me as he spoke.

"Andy, I've been around a lot of people with bipolar disorder," he said. "I don't experience you as one of them. There is usually a brittle nature to the illness. One's mood can break up or down pretty quickly. Like anyone, you go through different mood states, but they tend to ebb and flow like anyone's moods might, and those natural ups and downs are probably amplified by the nature of your work. You haven't taken any medication in twelve years, outside of that single pill you tried. If you did truly have bipolar disorder, you would have ended up back in the hospital at some point. You don't strike me as having bipolar disorder."

I felt a decade-long stain peeling off me. I walked up Sixth Avenue, morning sunshine painting me from the east, sun refracting through the water in my eyes. It was blustery, and I felt impervious to the wind. What he said sounded not just credible but definitive. He was not a practicing psychiatrist anymore, but he had been a decorated one once upon a time. He knew me.

My family had been right all along. I called them. The diagnosis was wrong.

Ghost begone.

IF IT WASN'T a biochemical imbalance, and having gone zero for the field in getting outside help, I didn't know where to turn other than to further probe the source of my depression. Whereas in other years I might have blamed my partnership with Spaly for the stress, and the previous year I would have chalked it up to the cash-flow problem, this year we had money and Spaly was out of the company. It was something else. It was that I had no idea how to bring the right people together to get the company past the $10 million sales threshold.

Sameer introduced me to a founder I admired greatly from afar: Marc Lore. Marc was the co-founder and CEO of Quidsi, a holding company that included Diapers.com. An Italian American from Staten Island, with a rare mixture of cunning street smarts and savant-like quantitative chops, he was a ferocious competitor cloaked in the demeanor of a gritty New Yorker. He was the only e-commerce entrepreneur in New York I knew of who had actually built something of value and transacted on that. There were plenty of companies with meaningful values on paper—at one point before it collapsed, Fab was valued at north of $1 billion. But Marc had gotten liquid when he'd sold Quidsi to Amazon for $545 million.

When I met with Marc, I quickly cut to the heart of what was bothering me.

"Marc," I asked as we sat down. "How do you hire people?"

"You're not going to believe my answer," Marc began, with a wide winning grin. "I didn't believe it when someone told me. But in, like, three years, you're gonna be like, 'Oh shit, yeah, that was right.'"

"What is it?" I asked slowly. I was already surprised and delighted that he had a specific answer, rather than one of the meandering responses most people in the startup world gave to any questions. The most helpful, I'd found, were the ones who had a strong and clearly defined point of view. Even if I later deemed it wrong, it was helpful to bump up against something I could grab onto.

"Take someone's experience," he continued, "take their résumé, and set it to the side. Yes, that's table stakes, but don't overthink it. Then put all your attention on two things. One, their passion for the mission of what you're building. And two, their fit with your culture, your core values."

I was dismayed. This was a clichéd answer, and I wasn't buying it. I pressed him further.

"C'mon, Marc, passion for the mission? How do you assess that? Everyone says the right things during a job interview."

"Yeah, I know. But you actually can test it," he continued. "You make them two offers. One offer with higher cash and lower equity, the other one with lower cash and higher equity. If they take the first one, you know they don't believe as much as they need to."

I'd heard this before from another mentor. So it resonated.

"Okay, you've got me convinced on that one. But fit with the core values? Isn't that like those inspirational posters of a marathon runner that say 'Endurance'? Isn't that what people say their company is about, but it rarely is?" I thought of the famous example of Enron's core values—respect, integrity, communication, and excellence—and how that had worked out.

"No no no, that's just the thing. It's not what you want your culture to be. It's what it actually is. You can't change it. It's set by who the first ten people are. The values they have in common: that's your culture. And you have to make sure everyone you hire from then on fits that culture, which is why you really have to get the first ten hires right."

Marc opened a portal to a new way of thinking. The executives we had spurned, the people at our company we had let go, the ones who'd departed, all felt different now, as if they were lacking some ineffable facet of our culture.

"And then," Marc went on, "and here's the hard part, you actually have to hire and fire people on those values. Like, you can have someone perfect for the job, but if they don't show those values, you can't hire them, or if you do, you can't keep them. Or someone can be performing in their role, but if they're culturally not a fit, then they have to go. It's like the DNA source code of your company—it's set from the beginning. Everyone thinks they can change the culture. But after the first couple years, you can't. It's all about who stays and goes in those early days."

There was still time for us to get it right, I thought. Inspired and energized, I went back to the office and made a list of everyone we'd ever hired. At the time, it was around thirty people. I put them into three buckets: the least compelling ten, mostly folks who had left or been fired; the ten best, the cultural carriers; and the ten in the middle. What did the cultural carriers have in common?

The values wrote themselves in sixty seconds on an extra sheet of printer paper.

Self-awareness. Empathy. Positive energy. Intellectual honesty. Judgment.

Over the next few weeks, I nerded out and created a scoring system for each of the values—both for our review process and for hiring decisions. For self-awareness, a five out of five was a Jedi: someone who could talk about why they sucked while you were sitting with them. For positive energy, a one out of five was a fun sponge: someone whose very presence zapped energy from the room.

We implemented this human values system. While it provided useful guidance on who comes in, who stays, and who goes, it wasn't enough. There was another key ingredient to consider: How did we move from a culture of fear to a culture of positivity?

I called Joel, our original investor. After he'd threatened to sell his stake, I had apologized profusely by phone, later flying to California, hat in hand, to concede what a pompous brat I'd been. I talked him out of selling his shares, even asking if he would consider joining our board to help me avoid making similar mistakes. He declined that day. I kept asking. Eventually, I wore him down. He joined the board, and became its most respected member.

"Joel," I asked, "once you've gotten the right people in the door, how do you motivate them?"

"I've always found that you catch more flies with honey," he said. "There are no diminishing returns to specific positive feedback. The quick email. The handwritten note. A few well-chosen words when you stop by. You can't do enough of it, if the feedback is specific." A lightbulb went on for me. I didn't have to play the brooding leader or learn from an unnatural playbook so I could inspire fear in others.

The combination of Marc's and Joel's advice changed everything, starting with me. I started to feel like myself at work—I could be who I was when at my best: naturally spreading positive energy.

On the surface, these conversations were about business and leadership. Underneath was something more fundamental. I had told myself a story about who I was—in this case, a leader who was good at the people stuff: talent and culture. When that story got turned on its head, I cycled into self-loathing. This is the heart of the entrepreneurial journey, the constantly changing narrative about whether you're capable or not, about who you are, or might be.

Amplified by the mood disorder, the narrative and the behavior had become indistinguishable from each other. High spirits led to exuberant decision-making, the feeling that anything was possible; strategic lurches produced new ideas, a sense that the supply of capital might be infinite. Low moods not only created pessimism about the company's prospects; they also rendered the job impossible, the future unlivable. Deprived of the life force that made all the good days worthwhile, I'd become the bare minimum of a human and retreat into my cocoon until the depression gods let up.

Marc's and Joel's answers provided me with a road map out of the darkness. Their wisdom gave me hope, as well as the energy I needed to change my company, our culture, and my story about who I was. They did so not by solving my underlying psychiatric problem but by helping me create a culture at our company that insulated us from the ups and downs of my mood cycles and, in so doing, protected me from myself, and perhaps, the team from me.

CHAPTER 14

911

WITH THIS CULTURE EQUATION UNLOCKED, 2011, 2012, 2013: those were go-go days. In September 2011, *Crain's New York Business* named us the sixteenth-best place in New York to work. We continued to recruit stars from more established players in the fashion industry, people who saw Bonobos' internet-driven approach as the future. We built a real shirts business and a real suits business, all grounded in our principle of offering more silhouettes, sizes, fits, prints, and colors as a function of our internet-driven model. The evolution from pants brand to menswear brand multiplied the size of the opportunity. What we didn't expect was that, in testing into new product categories, we would betray our roots and deepen them at the same time.

The guideshops, our next-generation retail store concept, were a classic story of innovation: notice something in the corner that's working and that is antithetical to your worldview, open your mind to it, give it some water and nutrients, and watch it flower into a centerpiece of your strategy. At the time, we were homing in on the woven shirt category, expanding from a casual oxford to a proper dress shirt. We called it the dress shirt alpha and reached out to our most engaged New York City customers to join in.

With the help of the now-departed SLG, we had built two traveling fitting rooms that we thought we could take around to events. They ended up being too heavy to move around, and so they were sitting in our offices collecting dust when we realized we could use them for the dress shirt alpha. We spruced them up and started inviting guys in for fittings.

While they had good feedback on the shirts, mostly constructive, a funny thing happened as customers started visiting: they would ask to try on our pants and to see the latest colors and prints, and then they would ask to buy them on the spot. When we explained that our model was all internet-driven, so we didn't have any inventory—something any customer visiting us already fundamentally appreciated as the means by which they had gotten to know the brand—they all said the same thing:

"No problem, you can ship them to me."

Our hypothesis that men didn't like shopping in traditional stores was being challenged—maybe they would, if we developed a new kind of store? As we wrapped our brain around the possibilities, one stood out: we could start to build clothing stores with no clothing stock. By doing fittings with just a few samples on hand, we were able to add service to the experience and subtract the complexity and the capital cost of the inventory. The "fit to ship" model was born. The only hurdle: we needed our investors, who had backed us because we were digital-only, to sign off on pursuing this new strategy.

At a subsequent board meeting we had a fierce debate about whether an e-commerce company should be opening stores. Chastened by e-commerce's difficulties and newly reborn as an open-minded person, I convinced the board that this wasn't an internet menswear brand, it was a menswear brand grounded in an internet experience—and that we'd be doing stores in a different way, without the inventory risk. It was a sleight of hand, and only partially true: there were still leases and people to deal with. But our forward-thinking VCs green-lighted the plan regardless. We had now not only helped invent how brands were built in the digital age, we had developed a leading example of how to re-imagine store experiences in the internet era.

The power of the guideshops opened our eyes to a new reality: brick and mortar wasn't dying, it was just evolving. Getting to a large national footprint of guideshops, we knew, would take years. Having glimpsed the power of selling in person in retail locations, I was too impatient to wait that long. So we cut a deal with Nordstrom. That company was the one retailer out there who, we believed, could sell to our target customer with great service.

In April 2012, we announced a $16 million Series B financing where Nordstrom became an investor in the company at a valuation close to $100 million. The luxury department store chain joined Lightspeed and Accel, who both put in more money. Faster than any of us had thought possible, we became Nordstrom's top-selling chino brand.

As we started opening stores, the team size exploded to over one hundred people, and I went back to dividing my day among breakfasts, meetings, lunches, cocktails, events, and dinners. No more days spent in bed. Most mornings I wouldn't even know in advance what I'd be doing that day. I'd wake up, look at my calendar, and just go. The PR team would hurry me out the door, we would hop into a car, and I would get a briefing on the way. One evening we were launching our suiting line at a posh new restaurant in the Meatpacking

District called Catch, with a player from the Brooklyn Nets. Midway through introducing him to a raucous crowd already on its third cocktail, I realized I had forgotten his last name.

That night I met a woman in bright yellow jeans. Layla. I was thirty-two at the time. She was twenty-two, right out of college. We started dating. Even after five dates, we'd never had a proper conversation—we were always out at loud bars and clubs. I was infatuated, and my personal and professional personas were rocketing upward. Layla and I would go out often. I'd buy bottles I couldn't afford. We would spend weekends in places like Moscow and Istanbul. I invited her to Bali, and we stayed at the Four Seasons. The bill was ten grand.

It would be years before I learned an important lesson: an elevated mood state can be even more dangerous than a depressive one.

THEY SAY THAT a startup goes downhill when the founder buys a Porsche.

In our Series A round, I had sold a little more than $1 million of stock. With that money, I bought my parents a place in my sister's building in Chicago and began to make angel investments in NYC. While I didn't tell those entrepreneurs about my own mental health battle, being able to advise them became its own form of therapy. Seeing the struggles of others lessened my own.

Within eighteen months, and a dozen companies later, I'd invested most of the money, and with a formidable tax bill I'd failed to do the math on, I had my back against the wall. They were good investments; in the long run, they'd more than pay off. But you can't eat stock in Warby Parker for breakfast.

A mentor asked me how much I was investing in private

companies. Instead of answering, I asked him about the appropriate level to be risking as an angel.

"I hope you're not investing more than ten percent," he said.

"That makes sense," I replied, as cryptically as I could. The real answer was closer to 80 percent.

I kept remembering an axiom of my grandfather's, though I couldn't summon the self-control to act on it.

Money talks. Never let it say goodbye.

In our Series C financing, nobody wanted to lead the round. I found a way to bring a rising star in venture capital, a woman redefining gender norms in the industry, onto the board. Unlike all the other VCs I had met, Kirsten Green had a background in studying and investing in retail brands. She understood the psychology of consumers. She wrote a $1 million check to lead, unheard of for such a large round, and together we raised the other $29 million.

In that round, I sold another $2 million of stock. I vowed to save most of it, but that resolution lasted about five seconds. The temptation of angel investing fired right back up—and this time the check sizes ratcheted up to $50,000 or more. This type of financial impulsivity is typical of hypomania. Perhaps anything I touched might turn to gold.

One day—bouncing off the walls from the six coffees I'd drink between nine A.M. and two P.M.—I overheard one of our designers talking about Porsches. He told me about the 993, a model of Porsche 911 built between 1994 and 1998. The cars were made by hand, with an air-cooled engine. I didn't know what that meant, but I knew that my assistant, Chloe, had a dad and brother who specialized in rebuilding Porsche 911s.

A few weeks later, I had one: black on black and black.

. . .

WE CONTINUED EXPANDING our guideshops at breakneck speed. We were approving a store-opening plan where we would be opening multiple guideshops each month—a frenetic pace unlikely to result in good deals. The early ones did well; the first store in a market by definition usually does the best. It's not a particularly good thing to extrapolate from. The next two years were a blur. The company continued to grow, but so did our losses. Rather than focusing on building the core business to profitability, I developed a new leadership pathology.

It's called shiny new object syndrome, and at a startup, it means throwing yourself into whatever is your freshest and biggest idea. Bonobos had quietly invented a better-fitting pant, a new way to build a brand—on the internet—and now a next-generation retail store. What would be next?

It was around this time that two delusional ideas came to me at the same time, and they were interrelated. One was that we were going to create multiple brands in-house in other categories, starting with a men's golf brand, Maide, and a women's apparel line, AYR. The other was that we were going to build a technology and personalization backbone to power an entire ecosystem of brands. Basically, I sought a power grab over the entire constellation of brands that Bonobos had spawned, and to prove that we could be an engine for building many such brands over time. Either idea was a leap. Together, they were pure fantasy.

Soon we had hired a women's brand team in New York and opened a technology office in Palo Alto. We were poaching engineers from Netflix and bringing on more expensive hires from the fashion industry. Our payroll skyrocketed,

while any meaningful potential revenue for these new businesses was still just a twinkle in our eye. I spent most of my
time on the new stuff, my side hobby of investing in new
startups, things on the tip of the spear of creation, and less
time on the core Bonobos business that paid the bills—
although, technically, it wasn't even paying the bills anymore,
because we had to raise money again. This time, our ever-
increasing burn rate demanded a cash infusion so large that
there might be nowhere to turn.

I brought on my longtime friend, Stanford classmate, and
early investor Bryan Wolff as our CFO to help us fix our financial problems and get profitable. One of our board members was opposed to hiring him, citing his inexperience as a
CFO. Wolff had previously been a hedge fund investor and
had worked at McKinsey, but he had never held a C-suite
role. Nevertheless, he had retail in his blood, and baseball
statistics on his mind; I'd spent years in friendly arguments
with him. I trusted him, he loved this business and had invested in it from the beginning, and I believed that he was the
right guy to speak truth to power and help us grow up. We
hired him.

With Wolff in the mix, Spaly reemerged in my life as well.
Spaly was now the CEO of Trunk Club, a Chicago-based
men's clothing service, and was building it admirably. While
things were still frosty between us, his friendship with Wolff
was still alive and well, and so Wolff provided a bridge by
which we all might hang out when Spaly came to New York.
Rogue Bar, on Sixth Avenue at Twenty-fifth Street, was across
the street from the newest Bonobos office, so Wolff and I
would sneak out of work to grab a day beer every now and
again. That day, Spaly joined; it was the three of us, and it felt
like old times.

Then Spaly said something that only Spaly could say.

"If I had told you," he said, looking at Wolff, "when we were in Colombia that I would start a company, that I'd hire Andy as the CEO, that he would steal it from me and hire you, Wolff, and that the two of you would become the Bryan and Andy who ran Bonobos, would you have told me I was crazy?"

Wolff laughed. Spaly grinned. I was left breathless by the precision of the question, then I died laughing, too. I was filled with wonder about the improbability of our journey.

One Friday afternoon in the summer of 2013, Wolff called me. I was standing in Penn Station with a distressed-leather overnight bag, in front of the big monitor where you wait like a wide-eyed baby eagle. I was heading out on a getaway weekend to D.C. It was summertime, and I was wearing a slim-fit Bonobos animal-print shirt even though I wasn't that slim, ikat-print shorts, and loafers. In short, it was a Fourth of July state of mind.

"Andy," Wolff began, "I just closed the books for June. We burned $5 million."

My stomach turned; anger rose up. Underneath anger is always fear. Always. As usual, we were losing money. But this was an enormous sum, even by our standards. Rather than tackle the issue head-on, I shot the messenger.

"Bryan," I replied, "we've talked about this. You can tell me bad news every day, and you do, but not on a Friday afternoon." I asked him to put it to me straight. "How much money are we going to need for this next round?"

"At least fifty. And then we'll probably want to refi our debt on top of that, and layer twenty-five on."

I added up the numbers. We'd raised $75 million already across seven financing rounds over seven years. The idea that

we needed another $50 million, in a single round, was crush-
ing.

The next week Wolff built a presentation on how we could
get to profitability, and we took the team off-site to talk it
through. It seemed like it landed with everyone except me.
While I knew we had to change our ways, I committed only
to the incremental changes we needed to make: increasing
our gross margins by buying inventory smarter, reducing our
photography and travel expenses, and negotiating with our
software vendors. What I wouldn't do was the one thing I
needed to: stop hiring people to fuel my delusions of grandeur. This was a pants company—not a multi-brand technology platform. We had inspired a legion of followers, but that
wasn't enough for me. I wanted us to empower the entire
ecosystem, own a dozen brands or more, and become the
backbone for the broadening direct-to-consumer movement.
(There was a little company up in Canada at the time called
Shopify that would go on to do just that. It's now worth more
than $150 billion.)

What I didn't understand at the time was that a pants
company doesn't somehow turn into a software company, or
that a cash-flow-negative brand doesn't get to start new brands.
In short, I couldn't make the leap from a co-founder with vision to a CEO with realism. We needed to do a layoff, and
instead we were still hiring.

Wolff fearlessly resisted my desire to hire at every turn.
The more he pushed, the more convinced I was that it would
just take courage to achieve this fantasy of mine. On occasion
I could cajole him into relenting, but more often we were
clashing. During one holiday party, it became a literal gong
show.

Chloe had started as my assistant, but when she'd proved

to be both a rising star and a perspicacious judge of talent, I'd promoted her to run recruiting. Whenever we hired someone new, she would ring a gong in one of our offices. Wolff's office was next door, and he had his own eccentric artifact. He would walk around the office carrying a baseball bat in his hand, one that had been a groomsmen gift at Wolff's wedding. He would tap it against one hand as he walked or play with it in his office while he was on calls. The bat, to me, signified cutting expenses. The gong sounded a note at odds.

We were dressed to the nines for the Bonobos holiday party—a ritual that had taken on a life of its own. As you'd expect of a New York City fashion company, people got dolled up and the DJ spun late into the night. When the open bar ran out, I'd usually lay down my personal credit card, and then ever-protective Tiff would come over, and tell me that I wasn't "rich enough" to be doing this. She was right, but I loved cocktails, our people, and hip-hop, and so every year I thanked her for the advice and put it on my tab anyway.

Wolff approached me at the party, wearing a light gray linen tux. For all of our conflict at work, I was genuinely excited to see him. Whereas Spaly and I had been equal partners, Wolff was an employee who reported to me. So the conflict was never as smoldering as it could be with Spaly. I had never imagined there was anything Wolff could say to me that would make me want to kick him out. And then he said it.

"Andy," he said, "whenever that gong rings, part of me dies inside. Like, what she's doing is directly opposed to what I'm trying to do. Everyone we hire puts us that much further away from ever getting this thing profitable, from ever turning us around."

A fire lit inside me. This was the most festive event of the year, and now we were talking about profitability. Meanwhile, the person whose work he was criticizing was someone I was exceptionally fond of, who was stellar at what she did, and who was only making hires we had approved in our budget—a budget process that Wolff ran. Torn between dueling loyalties, feeling violated by the setting and timing of the conversation, and with rising fear about the ongoing need to fund parties like the one we were throwing with venture capital rather than profits, I melted down inside.

In retrospect, it wasn't Chloe who was in Wolff's way; it was me, an obstinate friend dead set on conjuring an implausible vision to life. Companies have to be audacious, but within constraints. I was a dreamer, good at reacting to overreaches after they'd happened, but seduced by the next overreach right afterward. I'd learn the lesson about an endeavor that wouldn't work, but never the meta lesson about the underlying problem. Hypomania for me as an entrepreneur became like Murphy's Law: inevitably, and in cycles, I'd get distracted by something big and exciting that not only was the wrong thing for us to do but could fundamentally compromise what we were already doing.

Unwilling to acknowledge that Wolff was right, I received what he said at that holiday party not as a friend unburdening himself but as proof that Wolff and I weren't aligned on my go-big-and-change-the-world vision, that we were too codependent emotionally to make great partners, and that I couldn't rely on him to do the sort of hothouse-flower tending that my moods required.

The Series D capital raise was virtually impossible. To get a $50 million round together, we'd need a lead who could put in at least $20 million to catalyze our insiders to do the rest. With the Series C, we'd pulled off a miracle with a $1 million lead. That wasn't going to happen this time. We hired a prestigious investment bank, we built a beautiful presentation on our growth, we teased the possibilities for multi-brand and platform expansion, and we got turned down by everyone. I pitched forty-two different investors. They all said no.

And then magic struck. A retail family based in Sinaloa, Mexico, took great interest in what we were doing. From their point of view, a minority stake in our company would give them a glimpse into how to digitize their multibillion-dollar enterprise. The scion of the family, David, led a $25 million round. After we closed the round, David and his colleagues from the Coppel department-store chain flew in from Mexico for the closing dinner. We rented the upstairs of a posh restaurant on Ninth Street to celebrate, perhaps not the right message in terms of cost management going forward. Most investors would leave it to the company they had invested in to pick up the tab—in essence, using the money they'd put into the company to buy preferred stock to, in turn, buy themselves cabernet and steak—but in this case, David picked up the bill. The Coppel family: they're built differently. Scrappy retail operators who don't flaunt their wealth, they're humble, hardworking, and ambitious. In addition to David, we added another famous retailer to the board—the co-owner of a large luxury brand. We'd brought in the retail DNA the company needed, at this stage, to scale.

The night of the dinner, although both Travers and Wolff had been equally involved in the financing round, I'd brought only Travers to celebrate. He was more allied with Chloe internally, and I felt on some days like I had to pick between my top lieutenants. The truth is, there should be no picking.

What there should be is a consistent approach to leadership, untainted by recency bias and disentangled from personal proximity.

The irony is that Wolff had introduced us to David and his team. It was Wolff who was working hard to put us on the path to profitability that was the backable way forward, and it was Wolff whom I excluded from the celebration of getting it all done.

WHEN I FIRED Bryan Wolff, just after the closing, I'm sure it was noted by those on the executive team wise enough to give me a wide berth: another golden child bites the dust.

The way I fired him was itself indicative of the dream bubble I was living in. I drove the black 911 to Brooklyn with the top down, and picked him up outside his Brooklyn Heights house. I waved to his wife and we cruised back into the city to Minetta Tavern, a Parisian-style steak house with black-and-whites of Sinatra on the walls; the place's Black Label Burger is so soft you could cut it in half by looking at it. I'd order it with a side of mayo, in between a bone marrow appetizer and a rib-eye steak main course. With a Manhattan before, red wine during, and Armagnac after, it was everything to the extreme for me. I couldn't have just red meat at dinner; I needed three cuts of it. I couldn't have just one alcohol, but preferred three different kinds in three stages.

Who fires someone with such confusing fanfare?

It's one thing to let someone go and then, if you are on good terms, take them out to thank them. But this was something else. When I went to the bathroom before breaking the news, I was reminded of the scene in *The Godfather* where Michael Corleone retrieves the gun hidden behind the toilet before returning and blindsiding his dinner guests with bullets. Over the main course, I told Wolff I didn't like working with him anymore.

"If you don't like working with me anymore," he said, "then I have to go. There's not really anything to say about it. I have to go." He was gracious. I felt guilty—missing the point, of course, that that dinner was about his feelings, not mine.

Meanwhile, Spaly—who had now been at the helm of Trunk Club for not even five years—sold the company to our key wholesale partner, Nordstrom, for $350 million. I'd walked into Trunk Club to visit him one day on a trip to see family in Chicago, where Spaly was living and running his company, and the energy there had been kinetic. It was one of the most humbling moments of my life—seeing the vibrant culture there.

Not only did Spaly sell his company to Nordstrom for a meaningful sum, he did it quickly and raising only a fraction of the money we did. By capitalism's scoreboard, he had put up a big win. Bonobos' fate, on the other hand, was uncertain.

WITHOUT THE SERIES D, we'd have been sunk. If we hadn't gotten it done, it would have been a standard startup coup de grâce: a down round, in which shares are sold for a lower price than previous investors paid, followed by layoffs, talent hitting the exits, management equity becoming worthless, and investors getting their capital marked down to a discount.

That thought was unbearable. As investor after investor told us no, I buckled.

At some point that summer it dawned on me that I had thought Spaly had been impossible to partner with, but I was the one who had failed at building enduring partnerships, with both him and Wolff. When that realization finally came to me, it hit me like a punch in the gut.

For all my conflict with both of them, the unpartnerable person was me.

A periscope emerged from my mind and looked back down at me, observing myself as others might see me.

Fight Club was over.

I'd finally found the villain I'd been looking for.

It was me.

PART III
GHOST RIDER

Whatever is begun in anger ends in shame.
—Benjamin Franklin

A person is, among all else, a material thing,
easily torn, not easily mended.
—Ian McEwan, *Atonement*

CHAPTER 15

LIFE IS A DREAM

"GO!" LAYLA POINTED TO THE DOOR. IT WAS SOMETIME IN THE winter of 2013, and we had just broken up.

In the hallway, a neighbor's dog barked at me ferociously. It had snowed heavily earlier that day, but the rising temperatures had already turned the sidewalks and curbsides into foot-deep wet mush. I was wearing gray suede Gucci loafers, notable only in that they would have been worth a third of my savings just a few years earlier. I purposely trudged them through the slush as I walked home, an angry, sad, self-pitying mess. Fancy vacations, fancy cars, fancy shoes: I had become increasingly materialistic, and that night I realized none of it mattered if you don't at least have someone to be materialistic with. The old saying is true: we buy things we don't need, with money we don't have, to impress people we don't like.

With the demise of my relationship with Layla, I felt like a failure. I had finally been ready to be good to someone, desirous of redemption, a chance to be decent, and it hadn't worked.

The next morning, back at the Ace Hotel at Twenty-ninth Street and Broadway, a stone's throw from the new Bonobos office on Twenty-fifth Street, the malaise continued. It was only seven o'clock. Heartache had woken me unusually early.

I had dressed for work and wandered up Sixth Avenue in a grief-stricken haze. My parents were on the other end of the line, one of those high-stakes, all-hands-on-deck calls where Mom puts it on speaker so Dad can hear, too.

Latte in hand, an emo cliché, I tried to smother my sniffles so that the baristas and the early morning hotel guests wouldn't hear me. My parents listened, but didn't try to offer solutions. They said they understood. I knew they loved me, and I later found myself sifting through their silence for some element of parental wisdom in what had been left unsaid.

Crashing into depression after the soaring hypomania of love's first year, I began to wonder if the potential evolutionary purpose of being depressed was revealing itself: it forced the reflection, the gut-wrenching introspection, of what I needed to change about my life. I don't really believe this is true—cancer isn't evolutionarily adaptive, so depression doesn't need to be—but I clung to the idea at the time. When I was depressed, and having sought and failed to secure help, I would turn to any explanation for the hopelessness in my life.

As I muffled my sobs at the Ace, it hadn't occurred to me to consider something that had happened there years earlier. In that same hotel lobby, I'd met a Brazilian American woman named Manuela. She was in town from China after the passing of her father. In spite of the guy who showed up when we first met, I'd asked her out as a follow-up, emailing her at the address on a business card I'd snuck away with. We went out on a date, which ended dismally after my botched attempt to get us into a nightclub. I knew the doorman, as I'd promised her, but he wouldn't accommodate my red corduroy Bonobos shorts. Embarrassed, I admitted that I hadn't come up with a plan B, and we headed our separate ways.

For four years.

Manuela and I stayed in touch remotely. She and I periodically exchanged emails: Beijing to New York. She would ask me to meet someone from her world from time to time, usually an aspiring entrepreneur. I always took the meeting, hoping unconsciously, perhaps, that a kind word would be passed back to her. In the summer of 2014 she sent me a note offering another such introduction, but there was something different about it. I noticed a line about her possibly moving back to New York, and that she would soon be in town.

"I have no interest in meeting your friend," I said. "But I would like to take you out to make up for that douchey night in the Meatpacking District."

On our second date, four years after the first, I was determined to redeem myself—and I nearly messed up again. We'd both grown up, though, so my tardiness wasn't a deal breaker, and we ended up dancing the night away at the bar of a Mexican restaurant. For our next date, when I arrived at a movie theater in Greenwich Village, it began pouring. Manuela texted that she was running late this time. I made an impromptu plan to get her a gift and headed over to Three Lives bookstore, a favorite haunt. En route, I sneezed. A woman twenty feet in front of me whirled around. It was my ex, Layla, who happened to be walking down the same street at the same moment. *What are the chances?* I thought to myself. *One hundred percent*, a voice inside me answered. Layla and I had a quick, civilized chat—the universe's version of closure.

That night with Manuela, the dinner conversation pushed into substantive corners. I was blown away. She was the daughter of a Brazilian Jewish father, Jonas, a Marxist econo-

mist and international relations professor who had partici-
pated in the Communist students' movement in Brazil and
had been with Salvador Allende in Chile. Her mother, Leni,
had been one of the first feminist anthropologists in the 1960s
and an advocate of women's reproductive rights thirty years
ahead of her time.

After coming to the United States from Brazil as a little
girl, age seven, Manuela, her younger sister, Leonora, and
her parents had moved to Providence, Rhode Island, and
later East Lansing, Michigan, before settling north of Chicago. Manuela was at Evanston Township High School the
same four years I was in college at Northwestern, just a few
blocks away. She was a dancer, a journalist, and an entrepreneur who spoke four languages—including Mandarin, which
she had taught herself during her eight years in China. She
had degrees from Harvard and Oxford, was smarter than anyone I'd ever met, and yet would go on to supply 100 percent
of the humility in our relationship.

Manuela had abundant, wavy curls of dark hair and steady
hazel eyes that betrayed a profound skepticism of everyone
and everything. She was unafraid to ask hard questions, comfortable with difficult conversations, and predisposed to intellectual challenges that usually ended in her favor. As the
daughter of a Communist and a feminist, and herself an ar-
dent environmentalist, she saw issues of justice everywhere
she looked: race, class, gender, climate. I found it all enthrall-
ing: her mind, her beauty, her story, her ambition. I just
wanted to be around her.

Soon we were spending as much time together as she'd
allow, which was four nights a week. It was three fewer than I
would have liked.

The problem with falling in love when you have unmedicated bipolar disorder is that there is only one direction to go: up, up, and away.

SOME MONTHS LATER, with the ascent of my relationship with Manuela checked only by her good judgment, including her firm stance that we were not moving in together until we'd been together for at least a year, I had two vectors pointed toward the sky. Not only were chemicals surging from new love, but an escapist fantasy from my job was gaining steam: I was in the middle stages of recruiting a CEO to replace myself at the helm of Bonobos. If I couldn't blame bipolar disorder for my moods, I could blame being an entrepreneur.

It was then that I was invited to speak at an event connected to Tony Hsieh's burgeoning startup ecosystem in downtown Las Vegas. Tony was someone who I had long idolized, whose principles of how to sell soft goods online with customer-friendly policies and enthusiastic employees were embedded in the DNA of what we, at Bonobos, were doing as digital brand builders.

In our original angel investor deck, Bonobos had been pitched as "Ralph Lauren times Zappos," and Tony's book, *Delivering Happiness*, was foundational to my entrepreneurial worldview. His impact on me only deepened from my brief experiences working with Dustin, the short-lived Bonobos engineering leader from Zappos. Being invited to speak right after Tony, I felt like I'd arrived.

In the terminal at JFK before the flight to Vegas, I ran into an old friend. We had what I recall as a normal conversation. The JetBlue flight, a red-eye from JFK to LAS, was parked at the gate. I wish I could remember if I was low on sleep or what the prior week had been like. But within twenty minutes after I'd taken my seat, a thought came to me, and for some reason it stuck:

This plane is going to crash.

My fear isn't a fleeting dash of paranoia. It is empirical knowledge.

Once I start even considering that such things are possible, I'm on my way to psychotic. With the guardians of sanity gone from the gates, insane thoughts stream in freely. At that point, I'm in trouble. I am free-associating my reality. Literally anything can happen, just as anything can happen in a dream. Soon I might be taking any thought that comes to me as the gospel truth, or sharing those thoughts with others on a street corner, in a movie theater, or in a Burger King.

The plane is about to leave the gate when the flight attendants do the unthinkable and reopen the door to let in a straggler. It is a woman who is going to miss her friend's bachelorette party, supposedly, if she isn't let on. She and the bride-to-be have a teary reunion. Since the plane is going to crash, I know for a fact that this is my only chance to get out, to save myself, to see my family again.

Choosing to stay on is a spiritual decision. With the rising religiosity, and fundamentalism, of the manic mind, I show God I am willing to put my fate entirely into Her hands. Death holds no consequence to a manic person. It may even be desirable, a death wish. But that wish is usually not to die an unknown death. It's to die the death of a martyr, a hero, or a prophet.

How am I going to become one when I might have only hours to live?

This is my first full-blown episode since college, and unlike what happened during my initial one, I understand that this time I can't let anyone know what I'm thinking. It is lodged in me from being hospitalized fifteen years earlier that if you reveal who you are, you get locked up. No part of me wants to stand up in the middle of the flight and address the passengers. I decide to tweet my thoughts instead, subtly sprinkling messianic ideas like breadcrumbs in other people's feeds, so that my prophetic warnings will be discovered later, by the people who will study my life.

I look up from the screen only once during the entire flight—just as we are passing over the electric cityscape of Chicago. This is a moment meant to be so that I can say goodbye to my family from above. I imagine them looking up from below, like Santa Claus, as my date with destiny whizzes by.

As we approach Vegas, with no crash yet, I assume that the impact will happen upon landing. I have heard somewhere that the takeoff and landing are the most dangerous parts of any flight. My work is done. To eternity we go. I close my eyes, unafraid, waiting for the end—knowing that this must be it.

Then reality interferes with my prophecy.

The plane touches down. It's a smooth landing. We arrive in Vegas without incident at three in the morning. I start crying: quiet tears, no sobs. Nobody has a clue what I am thinking, or who I am. I am spared. I am so grateful to be alive. I completely surrendered myself to the certainty that I was going to perish, and getting a second chance at life feels like being reborn. On the spot, I commit myself in my heart, soul, and entire being to serving God.

The work begins now. Arriving in Vegas at six A.M. New York time, no longer discarding nonrational thoughts, and having spent the flight in an oddly calm state of paranoid delusion, I am now psychotic. And alone. In Las Vegas.

There is only one thing that might save me. Having been hospitalized the first time I felt this way, I know that I have to keep it a secret this time, or they'll take me away, and I won't be able to do God's bidding. My bidding.

Sitting in Alizé, the lounge of the hotel, which is in a glittering section of the revitalized downtown, I marvel at the blue and sparkling gold lights, at the brilliance of it all. I gaze around like a kid, all of a sudden swimming inside a coral-infused fishbowl, surrounded by the noises of the slot machines, the sports on TV, pretty people walking by, the smell of smoke. On the list of places a manic person should be, Vegas is last. My sensory experience is heightened, I have the energy of a freight train, and I am psychotic: there is no objective reality.

Anything is possible.

Should I play poker? I ask myself. I know that if I do, I'll win millions. But I also know that betting is a vice, and so I think better of it. Gambling, something I had no problem with previously, suddenly seems immoral to me. Just as it did during my college episode, a sense of asceticism is rising up.

The TVs are set to ESPN. I see a clip of a football game. The crash of helmets, normally background noise, sounds deafening to me. I picture all of those skulls crashing, the brains sloshing around, and I think of years of news stories on the dangers of the sport. I feel a surge of disdain for the Neanderthal-like violence of it all. As I'm a lifelong Chicago Bears fan who has never had a problem with the game, it comes out of nowhere, this knowledge that football is morally wrong, that one day, in the world I will remake, it will be gone.

When the broadcast cuts to the news, there is a segment titled "Like Father, Like Son" about a football family. Tears well up inside me, tied to a dizzying kaleidoscope of thoughts: in spite of my own sordid adventures in the very town where I now stand, I am "coming home" to be more like Dad after all. I've admired all these other men along the way—the lotharios I've partied with, the philanderers I've worked for—but at the end of the day, I am still my dad's son: a man of deep integrity.

I get all of that from a few minutes of TV. This is quintessential manic stuff: everything means something, everything is a sign, it's all about you, and, a familiar narrative among many: I was bad before, but I'm going to be good now, and my journey as a sinner is going to give me a heck of a lot of credibility in my new incarnation as a saint.

The next sign comes in the form of a lost charger. I have a scatterbrained approach to chargers, and I don't have one with me early that morning. My phone, after a red-eye and a commute, is fully out of juice. The guy behind the hotel desk finds me a compatible charger. He says it's on the house. I give him a hundred-dollar bill as a thank-you. He looks at me like I am crazy. He is right.

My speech is at ten A.M. There is no way I am going to be able to get any sleep beforehand. On the way to the venue, I pass a homeless woman on the street: tall, gaunt, dark. I look at her. She peers back at me from under her hoodie, and smiles a slow smile. Hairs stand up on the back of my neck as I think, *She knows who I am.* An old thought comes back: *Homeless people aren't real. They're angels. They're apparitions, sentinels to our materialism and our greed.*

When I arrive at the speaking venue, someone from the sponsor, a startup organization, gives me a T-shirt. Whereas normally I never wear conference swag, in this case I put it on right away, over what I'm wearing, in some strange show of solidarity with the audience. It is a graphic tee with a picture of a wolf howling at the moon. In spite of my insane inner monologue, I know I have to stay in disguise as a normal human and summon words that won't get me arrested. My speech is bizarre, but I somehow stay in bounds—though the bounds entrepreneurs are offered are porous. I do my usual bit about bonobos, the matriarchal chimpanzees whose societies have no violence—a herald of a better kind of humanity. It converges perfectly with my underground thought process about God being a woman, and I Her messenger. Luckily I leave out a longer bit I had just decided to discuss, about all of the world's religions and their flaws. Afterward, the friend I'd run into in the terminal at JFK approaches me with a friend of his.

"We actually thought that was awesome." The way he says it, and how readily his friend agrees, combined with the absence of other post-speech well-wishers, might indicate to me that something is off. But the part of me that might have been reading the room is closed for business.

On the way back to my hotel, I look down at the vintage Rolex on my wrist and decide that it doesn't fit with who I feel I am becoming. I take it to a pawnshop and am ready to sell it for peanuts, but there is a line of customers. At a hole-in-the-wall restaurant, I offer it to a guy who is quietly eating his lunch.

"Do you want my watch?" I ask him.

He looks at me, studies my face closely, eyes the watch, then turns his gaze back to mine.

"No," he says.

As a consolation prize, I leave the watch on the table for

anyone to grab. It's a low-key spot where the watch is likely worth more than the monthly salary of the clientele. For that exact reason, I want it gone. I head to the bathroom, looking forward to not seeing it upon my return. When I get back, it's still there. What I was going to take as one kind of sign becomes a different kind of message: working-class people, and the poor, are better than rich people. They're on my side. I'm here to liberate them.

Of course they wouldn't take the watch.

Near the hotel, I see a black bird, a raven, perched on a fence. I stop, like a small child would, or perhaps an ornithologist, and marvel at it for minutes. It is incredible to behold: jet black, muscular. I am mesmerized, and I see it less as a bird and more as a general surveying the landscape, a higher-order creature superior to all of the people walking by.

Back at the hotel, I commit to veganism. I'm hungry, though, so I order one last cheeseburger. As a function of my dual life as an entrepreneur and an angel investor, I typically get a dozen emails a week from entrepreneurs seeking advice. Normally I would triage them, then focus on one or two. In a now-manic frenzy, I start responding to all of them, offering my help.

That night, I go with some new friends to Tony Hsieh's downtown Airstream trailer park. Here is a man purportedly worth hundreds of millions living in a trailer in the desert. It's a surreal vibe, with llamas and a campfire in the middle of Las Vegas. We sit around that campfire, near Tony's trailer, and the fire, its glow and warmth, takes hold of my mind the way it might if I were both stoned and shrooming. My manic state is somewhere in the middle, though I am learning to hide my insane thoughts from others.

The ringleader of the group is a local Vegas VC who works

for Tony, a deputy who is a part of Tony's project to revitalize the city. As we sit around chatting, drinking beers, I get asked about the co-founder divorce at Bonobos. In the manic state, I decide that some show-and-tell might be useful. I search for a video on YouTube. It is a clip of Spaly and me on Fox Business, being interviewed, one of our first-ever TV segments. In my memory, which I relate to those assembled as color commentary, Spaly talks over me the entire time. I intend the clip as an illustration of how our personalities were too big to both exist at one company, and I tell them that he was the one who did the steamrolling. Then I play the video on my phone.

Minor problem. I monopolized almost the entire conversation.

As the small group takes in the contrast between my description of the event and the video, Tony's deputy jokes, a little too comfortably:

"Wow, you're really a sociopath." Everyone laughs.

I laugh, too, but nervously, as I attempt to process what is happening. To the mind that has ascended to mania, revelations can come fast and furious, entire histories rearranged based on a new data point. I know what this one means: I am in fact a sociopath. I am the narcissist I've been looking for. Thoughts race through my mind. I need to call Spaly to thank him. I don't, but I file the idea away, along with the renewed realization that I am the villain in my own life story.

Tony's deputy invites us to "Tony's house" to meet him. Inside his trailer, I greet the man himself. Brief words are exchanged. I remember something about him not being worried about climate change, because humans will innovate our way out of it. Somebody mentions a startup that will gobble up the ocean's plastic. Suddenly, and unexpectedly, Tony's dog scrambles up onto my lap. My brain, oscillating back and forth over the vanishing line between fantasy and reality, takes this as a good omen.

Tony is quiet, for the most part, sipping his drink. He seems more pensive than sad. I use the bathroom, then some of us leave. Later that night, his deputy tells me that Tony has a unique ability to see around corners in ways that others can't.

Back at the hotel, having now been awake for two days, I take a shower. As the hot water hits me, I move to the next step of the journey to insanity: euphoric sudden truths. My mind wanders to the Israeli occupation of Palestinian territories.

Any chosen people would know that everyone is chosen.

It's obvious. All humans are equal. A fierce sense of social justice wells up in me, and my anger about the Palestinians' plight surges. When I was part of a Stanford delegation to Israel in 2006, I bought a T-shirt in Jerusalem that said, FREE PALESTINE, with a picture of the Palestinian flag.

That's when it hits me: the solution. A century-long strife is being resolved, in my head, in a downtown Vegas shower.

Israel gives half of the land of Israel back to the Palestinian people. In return, the United States gives Israel a plot of land ten times the size of Israel somewhere in the western United States to create West Israel.

(Message to manic me: it's called New York City.)

In 2006, on a study trip, I'd been amazed to observe what the Israelis had created in the desert. In the United States, they will be able to quickly make magic. The most godly thing they could do would be to give half their country back to the people they have oppressed, repent and atone for the Nakba with the right of return. I picture Palestinians returning to their home, tears in their eyes, the world agog, the Jews redeemed. I realize this is something I can facilitate only once I become the American president.

As a first step, I decide I need to go shopping. In a taxi line on the way to the mall, there is a man who looks down on his luck. I invite him to get a lift with me. On the ride, he tells me about his life. He's abandoned his family. He's dying of pancreatic cancer. There is no sadness to him. I buy him a slice of pizza at the mall's food court. He takes it. It's then that I see a torn dollar bill on the ground. Another blinding insight strikes me: *Money is an illusion. So is suffering. This man is an angel, too. That's why he's not sad.*

At the mall, I go to Nordstrom and—inspired by Tony Hsieh's vision of transforming American cities in decline—buy two Shinola watches, made in Detroit. One is for my dad. The other is for me: I can't keep wearing the Rolex I tried and failed to give away. It is off-brand for a messiah. Everything I do now has meaning; everything ladders up to the broader mission of fixing America, saving the poor, healing the world.

There's no need to do my job anymore. The people at Bonobos know I've moved on to more important things. Given my focus on initiatives outside of our core business that consistently risked derailing us, there is an irony to my being "off the grid" that I can't possibly appreciate as it's happening. Manic delusions and entrepreneurial delusions, while not twins, are not unrelated. They're more like distant cousins. The capacity for one doesn't guarantee—but can indicate—the capacity for the other.

My brain spins. For no reason other than my manic intuition, I go to a casino called the Bellagio. It is the first place I'd ever been in Vegas, the spiritual home of a former roommate who loved it there. The first time I saw the fountains, years earlier, dancing to "Con te partirò," was pure magic. Seeing them now, I'm ecstatic. But the sight of people gambling is a reminder of the work ahead. It is tragic. Gambling takes people's livelihood. This is the philosophy I grew up with, what my parents taught me. In the material world, I like craps and poker. In the messianic delusion world, vice is a scourge upon humanity to be eliminated. I know that everyone will be better off once gambling is gone. How I'm going to whisk it away is TBD.

For twenty years I've had a calling card number that somehow still has credit on it. It's a phone number with a twelve-digit password, and I couldn't tell you what it is off the top of my head. But when I'm in front of a keypad, sometimes, muscle memory kicks into gear. In the floating ethereal plane I am swimming on late that afternoon, it is easy.

From a pay phone in the Bellagio, I call home to Chicago. My mom answers. We talk. I ask to speak to my niece. Bella, then five years old, gets on the phone.

"The gruffalo is coming, Mamu," Bella says to me. "Mamu" is an affectionate Hindi nickname for "uncle," and what Bella calls me.

The story of the gruffalo, from a book I had read to Bella many times, is a frightening one. In the book, a mouse wanders through a forest. The mouse keeps encountering animals that want to eat him: a fox, an owl, and a snake. The cunning mouse tells each animal that there is a huge monster, a gruffalo, that he is going to dine with. The fox, the owl, and the snake run away, fearful of the mouse's vivid description of the monster. Then, to the mouse's surprise, he meets a real gruffalo, exactly as he's described it. The mouse fears being eaten. Thinking quickly, the mouse explains to the gruffalo that he, the mouse, is the scariest animal in the forest. The gruffalo asks him to prove it. The mouse then seeks out each of the animals he told the story to, and when they see the mouse and the gruffalo together, and realize that the mouse wasn't lying, they run off. The gruffalo is convinced that the mouse *is* the scariest animal in the forest and leaves the mouse in peace.

"Who is the gruffalo coming for?" I ask Bella.

"For the one who screams," she replies.

I clench my eyes, hard, and swallow back tears. Real grief about a coming calamity sets in. I know who my niece is talking about.

She is talking about my mom. In the free association of my manic mind, my mom is screaming for a reason. She has throat cancer. An accumulated lifetime of a son's love for a perfect mother runs through me like a geyser.

The irony is that there is no gruffalo coming for my mom, though I am certain of it in that moment. There is no illness lurking inside her that I need to fear.

There is, however, a gruffalo coming for me.

CHAPTER 16

THE OPPOSITE HOUSE

AFTER THE PHONE CALL WITH MY FAMILY AT THE BELLAGIO PAY phone, I somehow find my way, like a homing pigeon, back to the hotel in downtown Vegas. Once there, I begin searching for flights home. Originally I was headed back to New York. Now I write to Ali Freedberg, my assistant, and inform her that she should cancel my flight to New York. I tell her that I am headed for Chicago but, in an unusual move, that I will be booking my own flight.

Ever reliable, Ali became like family over time. She'd visit with my family when they came to town; I'd go with Ali and her three marvelous siblings and parents on an annual ski trip. Ali could always find ways to explain my erratic comings and goings to the team. She came to know my moods better than me, figured out how to work around and through them, to make sure the company got what it needed. She provided a form of friendship that helped me stay healthy: mostly via honesty, empathy, concern, and acceptance. In this way, Ali "covering" for my sudden absence that week wouldn't necessarily raise any flags. She normally did everything for me; from consulting on dinner reservations to scheduling board meetings, advising on executive hires, and sharing insights on our people and our culture, Ali did it all.

In that way, booking my own flight is an aberration. I spend minutes staring at the options on the screen. I start searching for one-way tickets and am surprised to discover that you can fly Spirit Airlines from Las Vegas to Chicago for under $74. Even manic me doesn't really want to fly Spirit, though, so I choose a flight with an auspicious number, 2345, on American.

I leave my hotel room and sit down on a sofa in a vintage retail store in downtown Vegas for two hours. If the shop's employees wonder what I am doing there, they never say so. I buy a black-and-white backpack because I see a Mario Bros. fire flower in the pattern. Back at the hotel, I take an hour to pack, getting rid of many things, leaving them in the room as relics, consolidating almost everything into the new backpack. I make the hotel bed before I leave, something I have never done before.

In a taxi on the way to the airport, I extract from the Syrian taxi driver what I'm looking for: validation that my plan to save the Middle East and bring about world peace makes sense. Once I'm at the airport, an airline check-in agent barks at me for sitting down while in line for security. I feel scolded, like a child, at first, then afraid of her anger, before landing on pity. Pity that she has nothing but bile inside. I have not an ounce of confrontation in me. I'm not wearing contact lenses, and without them, or sanity, the airport is dizzyingly confusing. I decide to follow some businesswomen walking in heels to the tram, because women can be trusted. Their brisk, purposeful strides imply action: *Follow us.* I can't read the fine print on the arrivals and departures monitors, so I ask one of the women where flight 2345 is leaving from. While initially bewildered, she answers, and I get to the gate.

My next memory is of sitting at the kitchen table with my family. There is a plate of food in front of me that I'm unsure if I'm going to eat. After a few days of mania and no food, hunger goes away. It's physically hard to eat. Irritability is rising; I am coming undone. Food becomes a symbol of mortality. I am immortal; I don't need it. Anger rises inside me at my family for trying to bring me back to planet Earth.

"It's just us," my sister says. My stomach turns. Am I being betrayed by the people who love me most? At that moment, Bella breaks the spell by walking over, pulling the paper towel off my dinner plate, and revealing what is underneath. With grandeur, like a magician, she says:

"Carrots!"

It is hilarious. Who gets excited by cooked carrots? Her sense of humor, at just five years old, warms my heart, and I realize I can eat for her—my first meal since the cheeseburger a day and a half ago. As my mom, dad, and sister look on, I force my way through the dinner, hoping that it might convince them that I'm okay. There's pumpkin pie, my favorite food, for dessert. I make my way through it. Rob, my ever-loyal brother-in-law, returns from the pharmacy.

They have a pill for me to take, a sleeping pill. As I stare at it, I wonder for a moment if they are trying to kill me. I survey all of them: Are they for me or against me? This type of paranoid thinking is part of the tragedy of bipolar disorder. Those who are trying to help me most can become enemies in my mind, a heartbreaking dynamic for them. Violence can begin this way, though it won't this time.

No, my family won't kill me, I think. And even if they try, I'll survive it. I take the pill and sleep for twelve hours.

. . .

BELLA WOKE ME up in the morning. A long sleep had returned me to the fence between fantasy and reality.

Next to the bed, I had laid out all three of my watches. There is the vintage Rolex, alongside the Shinolas.

The part of me that still had one foot in the material world, Andy the human, wanted to keep all three watches. The ascetic in me, the wannabe Jesus, knew that material possessions hold no value. I turned this paradox over in my mind as I slid on a gradient, back and forth between sane and insane poles.

At that moment, as I was right in between, Bella said something I took as gospel:

"Mamu, one day you wear this one, one day you wear this one, and one day you wear this one!" It was as if she'd read my mind, seen through my dilemma, and resolved this conflict. In my exalted state, what I heard her say was this:

Mamu, you live in the material world. You play the game. You appear to be human. When you are with rich people, wear the Rolex. Appear to be one of them. When you are with the rest, wear the Shinola—show your "Made in America" faith and your midwestern humility. When you want to show no means, well then, just wear no watch at all. Or maybe you should get a Swatch or a Casio.

In this way, the bipolar ascetic got to have his cake and eat it, too. Unlike real ascetics, manic messiahs find ways to contort logic, spending money like it's nothing at certain moments and giving away their belongings in other moments, engaging in indulgent, pleasure-seeking behaviors one minute and decrying them or looking to save others from them the next.

It was comforting to know that Bella was in on the secret,

and that I could decipher messages from her child mind that no adult could pass on.

If my connection to the reality-based world was strengthening, there was one clear sign that the episode wasn't behind me.

Manuela and I were in a long-distance relationship at that point—she had decided to go back to Beijing to sell her company and then move back to New York permanently—and though it wasn't easy to communicate with her during the day, I convinced myself we were corresponding telepathically. No joke. In my mind, and similar to my first manic episode in 2000, part of my inner joy was due to the empirical realization that I was definitely going to marry my girlfriend. In this way, the biochemistry of falling in love interacts powerfully with the underlying mood disorder to produce bizarre behavior. Of course, discussing this with Manuela was not part of the equation, as I *knew* she also *knew*.

While it sounds bananas to believe that you can talk to people just in your mind, in the world of mania, all kinds of ridiculous possibilities about how humans relate become commonplace. Some people are undead angels: normal. Some people are actually other people: no big deal. Some people who love you become devils, out to kill you. And for me, the woman I loved became a god herself, and so the idea that I might have a cross-continental mental link with her was a no-brainer.

The fact that this could happen even after I'd had a good night's sleep shows you that when you go really high, it takes days to come back down. And sleeping pills are not enough. I needed medication: antipsychotics and mood stabilizers. With our collective denial of the illness as a family, and our attempts at self-medication through Ambien, we were flying blind into a thunderstorm with a faulty plane.

To memorialize our telepathic engagement, I sent Manuela a digital emoji of a ring and I logged on to Facebook, where I changed my status from "in a relationship" to "engaged." The Facebook news-feed algorithm loves this kind of thing, and hundreds of likes poured in. My phone blew up with dozens of text messages of congratulations.

When I finally got Manuela on the phone, she was confused.

"Andy, what is going on? People are congratulating me on being engaged," she said, sounding concerned. Her worry snapped me back to reality.

"Oh my God," I said, and I did what I had to do to not reveal my insanity. I lied. It was the same instinct for self-preservation that kept me from going completely off the rails during my speech at Tony Hsieh's Vegas conference. I lamely offered Manuela a contorted explanation: "I was updating my relationship status on Facebook to 'in a relationship' and must have selected the wrong one."

"Well, if and when the time comes, it might be nice to do it in person," she joked. She seemed to have bought my explanation—despite also having gotten the digital emoji of the ring. Had I done her the service of having told her more about my mental health issues, she might have continued to press. But since we were on a schedule where it was difficult to talk, with a twelve-hour time difference, my issues were hidden, for the time being. Later I'd tell her more about the history of my diagnosis, but I'd sell her the party line, what I'd heard from many: I likely didn't have bipolar disorder; I'd had a one-time psychotic episode in college, fueled by drug use; and the on-and-off depression I'd experienced subsequently was a function of my job. Since I'd met her, after all, I hadn't been depressed. I'd been bouncing off the walls.

You know what they say about what goes up.

ONCE BACK IN New York after a week of recovery, I had some patching up to do. Most of the team was none the wiser, perhaps even Ali herself, but in an email, I had told Chris Travers that I was doubling his equity. This was a function of the role he played as an in-house therapist and the spike of gratitude I felt toward him for always helping me through difficult times.

I let Chris know that I'd spoken too soon on the equity grant, and that I'd do my best to get him a refresh from the board. At our next board meeting, I was able to get him some more equity, but nothing close to the double I had offered over email during my manic state. To try to bridge the gap, in a highly unusual step, I said I'd like to give him some of my equity. Nobody on the board liked that idea, but they let me go through with it.

The other person I had to patch things up with was Dwight, our head of design. I'd always been insecure about not coming from a fashion background yet still running a fashion company. Though he'd never told me, I'd suspected that Dwight had little respect for my thoughts about our products or for any of my aesthetic opinions, even though over the years I'd worked hard to become more useful on merchandising and design decisions. During a phone call from Chicago, I'd lost it with him, revealing my insecurity even as I attempted to defend myself. When I saw him in the office, I gave him an awkward apology. He accepted it quickly, at least

on the surface, and we moved on—leaving an unspoken weird-
ness that we never transcended.

THE NEXT FOUR months at Bonobos were dedicated to getting
myself out of the job. I courted our new CEO candidate,
Fran Della Badia, then a senior executive at Coach. She'd
been one of the few people from the retail world who had
believed in what we were doing from early on, and had become something between a friend and a mentor over time.
After months of conversations, Fran and I decided she should
meet the board for interviews. Over several weeks, she met
everyone. Momentum and support developed for her to succeed me as CEO.

We thought it would make sense to socialize with her as a
group. I called a board dinner at Joel Peterson's house in
Woodside, California. Fran and I flew out to the West Coast
for the dinner. Ali joined for the dinner so I could get a team-
level perspective when we debriefed the next day.

The dinner was fine. Nothing revelatory, nothing that interesting. Polite conversation.

At a board vote the next day at the office, we were split
three to three on whether or not to move forward. In some
ways it was more of a referendum on my departure than on
Fran's candidacy.

One board member summarized it like this:

"We should bring her on because you don't want the job."

I cast the ceremonial tie-breaking vote. It was decided that
after she started, I would move into an executive chairman
role. Fran became the Bonobos CEO, and we sold the change
to the local tech and fashion media as a big win. Bonobos was

growing up, perhaps for an eventual IPO down the road, and an experienced retail leader was being brought in to get the company there. The co-founder and departing CEO was staying on as chairman of the board, which implied that I hadn't been fired. When I reflect on the roller coaster I put everyone through, though, sometimes I wonder if I should have been. Instead, I took preemptive action. I fired myself.

My first day in my new role as chairman, I walked to a nearby park along the Hudson River with a beach towel and a book. Appropriately, it was titled *Zealot*, had been written by Reza Aslan, a friend's husband, and was about the life of Jesus; the thesis was that he had been only one of many wandering self-proclaimed prophets at the turn of the millennium. As I lay in the sunshine, picturing the team I had built over seven years of working away in the office, I felt one emotion, and it was a harbinger for what was to come: sadness. Soon after, I flew to Seattle for a weekend to celebrate the transition with my parents, and that sadness metastasized into full-blown depression.

When a new CEO comes in and the founder moves into a chairman role, the best next step is a sabbatical to let the new CEO take over. This worked well for me, as it was, to paraphrase *Good Will Hunting*, my gotta-see-about-a-girl moment. Other than a trip to Shanghai for a week in college, I hadn't spent much time in China, and I had never been to Beijing. My plan was to fly to China and spend six weeks there. Seeing Manuela, in a place she'd lived for eight years, was supposed to be a dream trip. And it was a dream trip, except that dream was a nightmare.

Manuela and I stayed in a *hutong* district for the first two weeks—old Beijing. It should have been magical. It was awful. For the six weeks I was there, I couldn't get out of bed before two P.M. A horrific depression settled in, the likes of which I had never known. I couldn't function. I'd stay in bed for hours in the morning, desperately needing to pee, because I couldn't summon the energy to walk to the bathroom. In retrospect, it was obvious: Bonobos had not been the source of my depression; it had been the only thing that kept depression's severity at bay. Without the grueling schedule of being a startup's CEO, one where I had to pull myself out of a funk every Monday morning as best I could during depressive episodes, I had nothing tethering me to a routine. It's one of the cruelties of depression that it sometimes hits when you are supposed to be having a peak life experience, and there is nothing you can do about it. I stumbled to the shower once a day and awaited Manuela's return from work. She'd drag me out for social dinners; I'd flip on a diurnal switch and use alcohol to lift my interpersonal abilities, only to suffer its depressive topspin the next morning.

Manuela was my salvation. At first she took my malaise as a sign that I didn't want to make an effort to get to know her world in China. As the depression deepened to sleeping twenty hours a day, I disclosed to her that I was really depressed. That vulnerability changed something. She accepted me for who I was and encouraged me to get therapy when I returned to the States. The most important thing she did was what she didn't do. She didn't say she didn't want to be with me. I had always assumed that revealing my depression would make any potential romantic partner not want to be with me. Such is the power of the stigma.

While she couldn't convince me to abstain from drinking at night, every day she'd make me tell her three things I was grateful for. I remember that summer as the worst of my life, for the depression, and the best of my life, in that I fully revealed it to someone for the first time and was fully accepted despite it. I'd shown her my dark half.

The blinding-light half was yet to come.

After those first two weeks, we moved from the dusty streets of old Beijing to the Opposite House, a fancy hotel for expats and business travelers. While she was at work, I'd sleep until the late afternoon, then sit in the hotel's café. Some days I'd have four cappuccinos in a row, hoping to find some life force, and still be stuck on one page of *All the Light We Cannot See* for two hours.

I could not see that light.

I still haven't finished that book.

Hope, finally, arrived via an evening phone call, followed by a text message the next day.

The phone call was from a Bonobos executive, Erin Ersenkal. He'd made an end run around the official rules—during a sabbatical, nobody but the new CEO can contact the founder—to get my advice on a difficult personnel matter. One of our best people was being recruited; should he just let him go? He wanted to hear from me.

"Yes," I said. If that person wants to be somewhere else, we should cheer that on—and find someone for that role for whom we're their number one choice. Moreover, there were some meaningful gaps in the outgoing employee's skill set that would become apparent in the company's next phase.

"This is what I needed to hear," Erin said, relieved that he didn't have to agonize over this team member's departure. Something about the call lifted my spirits. In retrospect, it's clear: I liked Erin, I missed him, I cared about our people—

including the ones who were leaving—I wanted folks to be making good decisions, even if those decisions weren't good for us, and most important, I craved feeling needed again.

The next day, the momentum built. I texted Brad and asked him how it was going.

"To be honest, not well," he replied. "Everyone's looking forward to having you back."

My heart leapt up. I should have felt the opposite way: it had been a year of chess moves to bring Fran on so I could get out of a job that had become, on its hardest days, a ball and chain. Instead, I was happy to hear that I was missed. Flickers of hope returned, and I flew back to New York, on schedule, in just a few days.

It later occurred to me that we were staying at a hotel called the Opposite House when all of this happened. While we were there, Manuela had told me about a Chinese parable known as "The Lost Horse." In the story, every blessing becomes a curse, and every curse becomes a blessing.

It was in Beijing that it crystallized for me: Bonobos was not the source of my ups and downs. It was an avatar for the expression of them, but I would have had those ups and downs whatever I was doing. My depression in China was so acute that I came to perceive my job as, if not a mood stabilizer, certainly an antidepressant. By demanding so much of me, by insisting that I show up and keep the lights on at the company, the business gave me a purpose that transcended my malaise, that over time, in fits and starts, could pull me out of the doldrums and into the rhythm of success. Once I was out of the depths, it provided a vehicle for me to run, to live life intensely, to interweave a vibrant social life and a job leading hundreds of dynamic and mostly young people. It was an amazing job, and it took not being able to do it for me to wake to the privilege of it all.

In 2015, I escaped my job to reclaim my sanity. Eighty-six days later, I started another game of chess to get my job back. Why? Same thing: to reclaim my sanity. The bullwhip effect it had on everyone who cared about the company—primarily the board and the employees—was a perfect manifestation of the disorder itself. Whether people knew the name or not, whether they held the diagnosis in their minds, didn't matter. They suffered the consequences regardless.

Before I left China, Manuela and I had many discussions about the future. Her plans remained to sell her company and return to New York, at which point we could explore a future together in NYC. We spent our last days together in Hong Kong, surfing a trade show where she gave a pitch presentation. In the lead-up to it, she had stood on the balcony rehearsing again and again. Whereas I winged everything, apparently even corporate governance, she was practiced.

As Manuela faced outward rehearsing her speech into the wind, she couldn't see me. I stood some paces behind her, quietly, just listening, again and again, to her do something I never could bring myself to do.

Prepare.

BACK IN NEW YORK, I plowed my energy into getting back in the saddle. I felt alive again, for the first time all summer. Three of our top executives were leaving. I swung into action to re-recruit the core team and managed to persuade all three of them to sign back on.

With the top down on the Long Island Expressway, I drove

out to meet Fran in the Hamptons, where she was staying for the weekend. I knew it wouldn't be an easy conversation, but as an intuitive and savvy operator, she knew what was coming. With the support of the board, I asked her to step aside, and she did so with grace and dignity.

"I'll always be like a sister to you," she said, and because of how she handled the transition, it felt that way. She treated me with the sort of kindness and acceptance you'd grant to your mercurial kid brother when he realized he wanted his toy truck back after having given it to you in a strange moment of confusion and altruism.

Back at the office at the end of a two-week sprint resecuring our staff behind the scenes and planning the PR strategy, I announced to the team that I was back. The room started buzzing. People cheered. I quickly ducked out and took a slow walk to Madison Square Park, sat down, and just stared into the sun. There were dogs barking, kids playing, couples strolling, finance guys chatting into their cellphones, and tears of gratitude rolling down my cheeks.

I vowed to never again blame my job for my highs or lows. Sure, it provided the fuel, but it wasn't the engine. The engine was in my brain. It was an engine that could come to a halt or rev too hot, even go up in flames. There'd been, over the past fifteen years, and the eight Bonobos years in particular, a lot of halting, and a lot of revving too hot.

In Vegas, I had veered perilously close to an explosion. In China, I'd had a blackout. Neither held a candle to what was coming.

CHAPTER 17

KING ARTHUR'S TAVERN

BACK ON THE JOB, I FOUND THAT TIME WHIZZED BY. I HAD A call with one of our board members shortly after I returned. I let him know that I was afraid of the interpersonal implications of shutting initiatives down, walking back on things I had said were our future, and the cost cutting that would be required to get us profitable.

"Andy," he told me, "you've got as much goodwill as any entrepreneur in the ecosystem. Now it's time to spend it."

"What do you mean?" I asked him.

"Don't come back like Andy Dunn. Come back like someone who doesn't need everyone to like them. Because people already do. Come back like Steve Jobs." It was an inspiring pep talk.

Still, Steve Jobs I wasn't.

But I was at the helm of Bonobos again, and my energy surged back to a controlled hypomanic state. I wasn't going off the rails, but I was *on*. And I'd had some epiphanies during my sabbatical. The sad truth is that what I became convinced of were things that many board members and executives had been trying to persuade me of for years.

At the heart of it was this: We needed to be more focused on building the one thing right in front of us, a men's brand called Bonobos, and stop trying to innovate outside the core. We needed to stop pretending that we were a technology company and stop making investments we couldn't afford in projects that weren't going to work.

Why the hell did we have three brands when our first brand wasn't even profitable yet?

As I was gripped, for the first time in my life, by a desire to have our company do less, not more, I felt like a real CEO at last. Like they say, strategy isn't just about what you do; it's what you don't do that often counts more. While a spirit of innovation is important, the nature of experimentation is that some things aren't going to work. When they don't, it's important to stop doing them.

We closed one of the new brands and spun out the other. We stopped deluding ourselves that we were going to build Shopify inside Bonobos and instead focused on our core business and getting it to profitability. We crossed $100 million in revenue run rate, which meant we were doing more than $8 million in sales a month. We had some profitable months for the first time since our first two years in business.

This kind of trajectory meant the company was worth at least $250 million, if you apply a reasonable 2.5 revenue multiple to a growing business. This would have eclipsed the valuation of our previous round, meaning that even our most recent shareholders were likely "in the money." So where to go from here? There were two paths: Keep building and go for an IPO. Or sell the company.

The leadership question was also more resolved. We had tried hiring an outside CEO, and that hadn't worked. This wasn't to say we couldn't try it again, but I was more firmly in the chair now. I had also learned a valuable lesson: Bonobos wasn't the source of my ups and downs; I was. With Manuela by my side, I was a more settled leader.

Or was I?

One day, pacing on Thirteenth Street, a light drizzle in the air, I called Bryan Wolff and told him he had been right about our need for more focus. The fact that he was still my friend was remarkable. The call was more therapeutic for me than it was for him. For me, it was a chance to own up to my guilt and set the record straight. For him, although he didn't say it, it was more of a "Thanks, asshole" moment.

There was another piece of unfinished business, this one of a personal nature. As we were clicking over from 2015 to 2016, Manuela and I went to Rio de Janeiro, her native city, for two weeks. One day, I told her I wanted to go shopping for menswear alone to check out the stores. After ducking into H. Stern, the local showroom of the jewelry house built by a Jewish immigrant to Brazil, I sat down with a Russian woman to pick out an engagement ring for Manuela. A diamond didn't seem right; nor did emeralds or sapphires. Toward the end of our session, the saleswoman brought out a Paraíba tourmaline, a translucent blue stone discovered in Brazil in the early 1980s, right around when Manuela was born. I put down a deposit.

With remarkable speed, Manuela sold her company to a Brazilian concern and returned to New York from Beijing. We moved into our first shared home, a garden apartment on Ninth Street in Greenwich Village. While I had the stone ready to go, she said we couldn't get engaged until we'd lived together for six months. For her next role, she took a job at a technology company with an office in New York. I'd never officially lived with a woman in my thirty-six years. I was as happy as I'd ever been.

It's sometimes when things are going too well that bipolar disorder plays its most insidious hand.

WHEN MY MOM came to town for a few days, I took her to see *Hamilton*. I had been an instant fan. While it was still new, my friend Jason Torres, who had known Lin-Manuel Miranda's father growing up, insisted we check it out.

The first time I saw the show, it blew my mind: the reinterpretation of America's founding history as a classic hip-hop tale, recast largely with people of color. The song that gave me chills was the first one that George Washington sings.

On the ascent to mania, works of culture can take on new meanings. They can overtake you, consume you, somehow mean something about you. The song was called "Right Hand Man." One day I played it on Spotify for Ali, singing along to it. I knew every word, as I'd already listened to it dozens of times.

"All too real," she said of the rendition.

I took that as a sign that I was channeling my hero George Washington. But then I took it one step further.

Am I George Washington reincarnate?

These self-aggrandizing thoughts are an introductory step on the ascent into mania.

That evening I took one of our executives out for a drink at one of my favorite haunts. At the time, we had a search firm working on finding a new head of marketing. My co-worker told me I should take on the role myself. It wasn't an outlandish suggestion, as some CEOs play a dual role, but I interpreted it differently: as an additional sign of my greatness, and something I should definitely do, with no further consideration. Three Manhattans deep, I made him some unhinged promises about his equity ownership in the company, just as I had done with Travers during my last spiraling episode.

As the week rolled by, I went out every night, drinking more, not getting enough sleep, not getting good sleep courtesy of the alcohol, catapulting through the morning on a half dozen coffees, into the afternoon, and then out again. It all started to blur. There might have been a board meeting. Out the night before, I had several drinks with two friends and our board member who was in town from Mexico. As we threw back a few beers at my favorite R & B spot in the city, Arthur's Tavern, a singer named Sweet Georgia Brown came on. She did covers of familiar songs. As she sang Chaka Khan's "Through the Fire," I felt a profound joy; I thought of my niece, who had given me a purpose, a sense of responsibility, and a knowledge deep down that I could never take my own life. Then I thought of Manuela, and resolved right then and there that when she returned from her final overseas trip, wrapping up the sale of her company, I would pop the question.

The ungluing continued. The next night, I had a dinner uptown. As I walked up Fifth Avenue all the way from downtown—an unusual decision, but I was driven by excess energy—I passed the H. Stern in Midtown, the New York branch of the Brazilian jeweler. I broke down crying as I thought of the engagement ring in the Rio de Janeiro branch, held by my down payment.

The leather-wrapped, wood-paneled Polo Bar was crackling with energy. This wasn't ideal, but I might as well have been Freddie Mercury: there was no stopping me now. I knew only one of the other dinner attendees well, a charming socialite who introduced me to his friends. I showed poorly.

When the topic turned to climate change, I lost it and ranted about the catastrophic potential of global water-level rise. Our host signaled me with his hands to calm down. My mood oscillated up and down in a single conversation; a telltale sign of hypomania going skyward is this rising anger and irritability, alternating with tears of joy—all within the space of an hour.

The next night, a Friday, I had a birthday party to attend at my friend Justin's house in Brooklyn. The door code was 1225, which I took as a sign: Jesus's birthday. Sparks flew, and those feelings about the Second Coming began to rumble, like a long-dormant volcano. Why else would my initials be A.D.? In the living room, we played a card game similar to Mafia. I strained to follow along. Ask a manic person the date or where they were five minutes ago, and they might be stumped. When the objective of the game was explained to me—I had to figure out who was friend and foe—I nodded knowingly: this was clearly a message for me, in my journey as the Messiah. I had to be careful. Not everyone would be on my side.

On the bathroom wall was a poster featuring a dragon, with a poem next to it. This pairing was incredibly helpful: the poem enabled me to quickly resolve a conflict I had with a dragon-like employee at work. That's who it was about, I knew. The poster might even have been that person transformed into a framed piece of art.

When I emerged, this creative Brooklyn crew had hung paper on the walls, for everyone to draw on. I hadn't done any artwork in decades, let alone while going out of my mind. What would I draw? A Christmas tree emerged, for obvious reasons, and then I drew a small black piglet underneath it. At an event earlier in the week, there'd been a baby pig. Pigs are a gift to the world, I now understood, and eating them is wrong. The squealing pig had churned in me some self-loathing for all the pork I had eaten. My work of art, I realized, was symbolic of the coming veganism of the human race.

At the end of the evening, a couple offered me a ride home. To this day I don't know if anyone there could tell that I was losing it. They said they'd go get their car, and then I could meet them outside; they took my number. As I searched for them, I got lost on the street. I couldn't figure out Google Maps; it was too confusing. They had to drive around to find me, as if I were a lost child. In the back of the car, I said little, asking only a question or two about *Batman v Superman* after we saw a billboard for the upcoming movie. I was Batman, too, on some level, and I wondered if they knew that I was going to kick Superman's ass. They dropped me off at my place, an apartment on Ninth Street between Fifth and Sixth Avenues where Manuela and I had recently moved in together.

The next afternoon, Manuela would return from a trip and walk into that apartment to a boyfriend in the early stages of mania.

THE FOLLOWING MORNING Manuela and I have plans to go to church in Harlem with some friends. After a night of some sleep, I regain a semblance of sanity. I get dressed, and notice that my clothing is loose. During mania, you eat a lot less. Your face becomes more angular. You get skinnier. You might stop shaving. Or grow your hair out. In short, you start to look good. Prophet-like.

We head up to the Abyssinian Baptist Church dressed to

the nines to meet our friends Michael and Ashley Beal, who belong to the congregation. Manuela and I are drinking coffee from a plastic *Hamilton* mug on the way up, and I decide to smuggle it in. As the security people and welcoming committee check us on the way in, I am afraid, as if sneaking a nonalcoholic drink into a church is some grave violation. It is Palm Sunday, the day Jesus entered Jerusalem, and some parishioners hand us palm fronds as we enter.

The choir starts singing. The sound of gospel music in a Black church is astonishingly beautiful, even when you've got it all together. When I hear the organ drop, with my mind primed for mania, I flip to full-blown. I am Jesus 2.0 again. It becomes obvious that the music is being played for Me. I nearly faint from the beauty of it, and from the overwhelming fear, honor, and responsibility that come with saving the world. Also from the whole not-eating thing.

Then I notice that Ashley is wearing sunglasses. She reminds me of my sister, the only other person I know who might wear sunglasses indoors, and I tell myself that she *is* my sister: that she is there to help me through this. I excuse myself and make my way downstairs to the kids' area, where I steal a granola bar to get some blood sugar going. Not very Christ-like.

As we walk out of church, I attempt to conceal my conversion. At brunch afterward with Michael and Ashley, I opine about how American technology companies like Apple and Google need to repatriate their cash. I think my points are brilliant. Later, even Manuela, the daughter of a Marxist, will wonder why I was so angry.

Brunch ends. Afterward Manuela and I stop for rum cocktails at a bar. I take pictures of everything on the way to the bathroom. It all has great significance, including a photo of an eagle. Perhaps that bird is my paternal grandfather, who served in the air force, bombing the Nazis, helping to save the West, while his future bride treated soldiers on the front lines below.

We are still in Harlem, now on our way to a birthday party. In a replay from Friday night, though I've been to my best friend's house many times, I can barely find it. It is cold out, and Manuela's face betrays some surprise, some concern: I normally don't struggle with directions.

Once we get to the party, in spite of my self-professed veganism, the smell of grease awakens me, and I eat a cheeseburger. The sound of the children's cacophonous voices is dizzying in its joy. When we decide to leave, I can't find my coat. There are coats everywhere, but this normally simple task, which might take a minute or two, takes fifteen. I notice a guy in a Bulls hat. He has the profile of my friend Jason. He smiles at me. This means he is my friend Jason. My heart warms as we exchange a knowing glance.

Within a few hours of getting back to our apartment in Greenwich Village, I am blasting Tupac. Manuela asks me to turn it down. Instead I show her a picture of her engagement ring, spoiling one of the greatest surprises of her life and a secret I've guarded assiduously from everyone for months. There is a knock at the door. The super announces himself. His name is Colt. Suddenly I realize his name is a sign, and a warning: he must have a gun. I feel genuine fear, turn down the music, tell Manuela to be quiet, and wait until the threat passes. She looks at me, bewildered, but plays along.

That evening, we go to Manuela's mom's storage unit in the basement of her Midtown apartment building to pick up some artwork we want to have in our new place and a set of shelves. On the way there, I leave my phone and keys in the

Uber: absentmindedness with valuable possessions is a tell that things are heading the wrong way. While we're in the basement of Leni's building, a black cat approaches me and puts his paw on my leg. He purrs, loudly, and begins to speak:

You can't love dogs and not pigs. If you love an animal, you don't keep it in a cage and then slaughter it.

The animals are on my side. I must be on theirs.

This vision ushers in others in my frenetically free-associating mind. The stench of trucks and trucks of dogs at the border of Laos and Cambodia, memories from a long-ago backpacking trip. The dogs are piled one on top of another in cages, headed to slaughter. Fury and disdain erupt inside me, that people could do such things. The vision of animals in cages, the pain, the resignation, the sense of unfairness, the evisceration of joy—it all courses through me.

After my conversation with the cat, I load the artwork into the van we have rented. Snowflakes are falling, but the cold doesn't feel cold. I am carrying the set of metal shelves. I envision the shelves as a cage. I feel the rage of the trapped animal, the pig headed to slaughter, the lion at the zoo.

I am a hypocrite: a meat eater who ate a cheeseburger just a few hours earlier. I feel the self-loathing of a preacher who sermonizes the very sin he commits. This is typical of mania. Hatred of others, self-hatred—same thing.

Somehow we make our way to bed that night in spite of my aberrant behavior. Manuela is picking up on only the surface of my insanity. She hopes that I'll sleep and come back to Earth from whatever is ailing me. I don't sleep. I start howling at the moon. Ever since I read *Julie of the Wolves,* I've loved wolves. Now I am becoming one. Manuela is terrified by my baying. She calls her mother.

Her mom arrives within ten minutes. She begins to rub my feet.

I continue howling at the moon.

The room crowds in on me. I think Manuela and her mother are preparing me to become the American president by rubbing my feet. I realize I have to pee. I leap up for the bathroom.

WHAM.

What can be said about the instant, penetrating shock of fractally expanding sudden head trauma?

Blood is dripping down my face. My head throbs from the slap shot–style collision with the low header of the doorway. I lunged blindly toward the bathroom, oblivious of the low rise I normally duck under smoothly and unconsciously.

As pain explodes in my head, my body fills with anger, fear, shock. I teeter, swaying with a vasovagal crumpling of the legs. Too much adrenaline. Too much confusion. Too much to do. I find a logical outlet for my growing rage. I don't remember a decision. The amygdala is its own muse. I swing hard. Glass cracks. A bulge emerges in the left pane of the bedroom window as if a tiny asteroid struck it, a Chicxulub crater. My hand rips open at the knuckles. Impossibly, the pain doubles. Throbbing surges to the point of blackout.

Blood down the forehead, blood in the eyes.

I've been shot in the head by a doorway, and I've slugged a windowpane. Searing pain is now emanating from two parts of my body, and the agony is multiplied by the mania. As a three-year-old I loved the Incredible Hulk. Now I am becoming him, as I tear off my clothes. Nearby is a radiator cover, loosely attached, lazily and imperfectly affixed over the heater. Underneath that heater are rocks and rat poison. With

the temporary and hallucinatory strength of a wannabe superhero, I rip it off the wall.

I smell a rat.

Looking back toward the bedroom, I see two women, confused, terrified, watching a naked man losing his mind.

Untethered from their world other than in physical form,
I swim on an ethereal plane where the pain at hand must be
transcended for a world outside in need of help, a world that
is about to be awash with water. Billions are to die in the kar-
mic rising tide coming for us all. Bangladesh first, Florida
second; nonexistent seawalls will leave even the First World
in need of Noah.

Manuela comes toward me. She comes to help. I cannot
see this benevolence of intent at the time. Instead what I see
is primal fear in her eyes. It becomes contagious.

Fear begets fear.

What I don't see is that behind that fear is a steely resolve
on top of which we will rebuild our lives.

The way I remember the scene is different from the one I
am watching at the time. At the Retrospect Theater, in the
memory stored visually, I see concern, love, tears, and terror.
On Live TV, with a mind descending into mania, I see her
coming at me, an *Ex Machina* humanoid robot. It is then
that my memory blacks out, the curtain comes down for in-
termission, a self-protective shield against images that would
be too hard to remember if stored. So they're archived instead, unopened. When consciousness reemerges, blood
from my head and my hand is dripping on the wooden floor
of our dining room.

I remember needing to recite all of the musical *Hamilton*
from memory to save my niece. I remember being zipped

into a bag. I remember thinking, *Perhaps I am dead.* I am walking in circles. I am singing at the top of my lungs. I take note of a book on the shelf called *What the Dog Saw,* which must mean something.

I don't remember hearing a knock.

CHAPTER 18

INSIDE THE AQUARIUM

WHEN I COME TO, I'M LYING DOWN, FLOATING DOWN A HALL-way. I can't move my arms. I see that my hands are tied. Am I on a gurney? Is this a hospital? No, it is an enemy ship in *Star Wars*. Storm troopers are escorting me. Or are they holding me captive? To prove my invincibility, I trace the symbol of infinity in the ceiling with my gaze, rotating my eyes and neck in reversing circles, again and again.

When I finally arrive in a room, waves of anxiety and terror alternate with an eerie sense of calm. I struggle against the restraints. Is this man's punishment for subjugating women for so many millennia? Am I to be held like this for all of time?

Knowing that my mind can manipulate matter, that the entire world is a projection emerging from my own God brain, calms me. When breaking the restraints with my mind fails, it occurs to me that there are several people outside, and I call to them. I ask to be untied. They free me of the restraints. They must know.

But I am far from free. I am headed to a fishbowl for the insane.

Bellevue Hospital is the oldest public hospital in the United States, tracing its roots back to 1736. The hospital sees more than one hundred thousand ER visitors and hosts thirty thousand inpatients each year. Some 80 percent of the patients who come through are from New York's most medically underserved populations; Bellevue takes anyone on, regardless of their ability to pay. The hospital's mental health capabilities are formidable: it's known for treating substance users, "criminals," the homeless, and the mentally ill. Bellevue's "pavilion for the insane" opened in 1879, the ward for alcoholics in 1892, and a stand-alone psychiatric hospital was built in 1931. The halls hold a lot of stories: this is where Norman Mailer came after he stabbed his wife and where Mark David Chapman was brought after he shot John Lennon. In his song "Where Fugees At?" Wyclef Jean brags, "I send psychos to Bellevue."

CPEP, the psychiatric emergency ward at Bellevue, houses four patients to a room; they sleep in the open, all mentally unwell, all together. Compared to the regular psych ward, the psych ER is a place where patients who are in a mental health crisis—shouting, crying, talking to themselves, walking in circles—can be separated from those facing purely physical ailments. At first blush concentrating such psychiatric patients together may seem like a bad idea, but it sort of works. CPEP—the acronym stands for Comprehensive Psychiatric Emergency Program—is filled with doctors, nurses, security personnel, and police officers. The lights are dazzlingly bright. Which seems weird. Dr. Z, who was a resident at Bellevue and who went on to run CPEP, would later tell me that Bellevue has a psychiatric prison ward, and its own state supreme court judge and courtroom.

The free association of mania while I'm in the psych ER releases a torrent of cultural references in my head. Recently I saw *The Revenant*. I was mesmerized by the scene of the grizzly bear mauling Leonardo DiCaprio. Now that scene is mashed up with the episode of *Black Mirror* where a man has to have sex with a pig on television to save a woman. That image drifts into a horrific realization: I am to be raped by a bear as atonement for millennia of male rape of women.

I crawl out of my bed and, despite the three other grown men in the room, take off my gown and lie on the hospital floor, naked. With my feet against the wall, I cover myself with a blanket and wait for the rape to begin. It is a waking nightmare. I start screaming, and nurses and doctors walk in, one by one, to talk to me. I wait for someone from my family to come and save me. No one can. No one does. Eventually some of the staff members persuade me to return to the gurney.

Like at a casino without windows, the days and nights blend together at CPEP. Bellevue and the Bellagio: same thing. One night, I wander. There are patients watching TV, reading newspapers, sleeping on gurneys in open rooms and in the common hallways. I insist on walking over to the women's side. Something about the male side scares me. Maybe it's the men having episodes. At one point I use the bathroom in the women's wing and get locked in. My fate, I realize, the price I have to pay for the oppression of women, is that I am to be locked in this bathroom forever. Panic rises up, then claustrophobia. I picture being buried alive but unable to die. Then a more hopeful thought: *I can do this.* I have friends everywhere. I look at the toilet paper dispenser to find one. It is one of those big contraptions, with the compartment for refills above. That compartment becomes a proud brow, and the roll of toilet paper becomes a smile. The whole thing transmogrifies into the face of a monkey king. It is my Wilson, like Tom Hanks's inanimate companion in *Cast Away. I can do this.* Eventually someone comes to check on me and they let me out.

While still on the women's side of the ward, I see a vat full of liquid. I drink from it. It tastes awful. The nurse scolds me.

"Don't be drinkin' that!"

I comply. It also tastes like piss. Because it is.

Speaking of which, a manic episode can delay a bowel movement for days. When one finally arrives, I am so proud of it that I take two perfect turds from the toilet, put them in a brown bag, and place it by the door for someone to pick up. When a nurse finds it, he walks over to me and says:

"Is this yours?" He gestures at the bag of excrement in his hand.

"Yes," I reply in a matter-of-fact tone.

"C'mon, man!" he says to me.

There are newspapers in the corner, but it's nearly impossible for me to read when I'm manic. My brain is moving too fast to process the words. I keep trying and then notice the crayons. Manic me returns to a childlike state. I draw all over the newspaper, the way a toddler might. There is an article about Uber. I can barely quiet my mind to read it. The toxic masculine energy of the company is what registers, and in spite of being a frequent Uber passenger, I vow to short the company, or find some other way to take it down, once I am back on the outside.

While others sleep, I traipse the halls, pacing in long patterns, eventual circles. The nurses pay me no mind. One night my foot inexplicably curls up at the toes. I can't get them to uncurl. I start limping. It feels permanent. At first I'm alarmed. Then I remember that FDR couldn't even stand up. The eagle on the American insignia comes to mind, clutching something in its talons. It is another reminder that one day I'll be the leader of the free world.

They take an X-ray of me at some point. When I hear the machine click, I feel like I've been shot in the chest. They push me around in a wheelchair, not for medical reasons, in my mind, but because I am a VIP. I stand up quickly, in a salute of sorts. I nearly fall, and the patient next to me starts laughing. This roils me. I pick up an entire tray of food and launch it at a man eating on the floor. All hell breaks loose. The noise is deafening, six grown men shouting at each other. Several staff members come over to break it up.

I picture Manhattan underwater. It seems obvious that a massive flood is taking place while I am in the psych ward. But I know that Manuela is safe, my mother-in-law is safe, and my parents are safe. If my manic episode in 2000 was all about God as a woman, this one positions Her as an angry woman, furious about the destruction of Her planet, and the plunder of man, and the link between sexual and environmental dominance. Manuela's passion is environmental activism. She as my God, Me as Her Messiah: we've come full circle.

To reach the masses as the Messiah, I will need a major social media following. While I am on the inside, I tell myself that the number of my followers is skyrocketing into the millions. Lying on my gurney bed, every time I tap my toe against the wall, I get another follower. I spend hours tap-tap-tapping, so that when I get out, I'll be ready to go.

Inside CPEP, the nurses' station has eight small circular holes carved in the plexiglass, kind of like you'd find at a bank or a Western Union office. Seeing the holes, I take it as a sign that I should have eight direct reports, and I make a note of who those should be. The Knights of the Round Table come to mind, a team of equals. I wonder why I made more money or had any more equity than any of my employees. *The evils of capitalism*, I think to myself. *When I get out, I'll make it right.*

My hair is becoming unkempt. One day, sitting on the gurney, I stare at my reflection in the windowpane and picture my hair growing to the shoulders, like Aragorn's in *The Lord of the Rings*. I decide I will stop aging at fifty-four years old. While I am sad to acknowledge that my parents will die, I recognize that my sister, niece, and future wife will be able to live forever. As I fade off to sleep, I flex my hands and calves, lengthening the muscles. My body is turning into a hybrid of a flesh-and-blood person and a Terminator-style robot. I saw an African mask at my mother-in-law's apartment the night before being hospitalized. It was blue, purple, yellow—like a *lucha libre* Mexican wrestling costume. I picture that as Manuela's superheroine outfit.

Inside the hospital, I search for Manuela everywhere. I spot a woman who looks something like her, lying on a gurney in the hall. She is wearing an Iron Maiden T-shirt. It quickly dawns on me: as we transition to cyborgs, this is a perfect way to describe my wife. The patient in the Iron Maiden tee gives me a smile as I walk by. I get a knowing tingling down my spine, the kind that accompanies a sixth sense. I know it is her. Manuela is inside, with me, in disguise.

On my third night in the psych ER, I am well enough to begin healing others. After tiptoeing around the unit for a little while, I put my hand to another patient's chest to give him eternal life. He wakes up and laughs at the sight. A nurse shouts at me:

"Hey, don't do that! Don't touch him!"

I feel sheepish. I have to take my work underground.

One of the other patients in my room I identify as the enemy. He is the original Jesus, and he had to atone for his patriarchal approach to everything. Jesus 2.0 is inclusive, and knows that God is not a man but a woman.

I glare at him, thinking I can kill him with my eyes. It is the battle of the Jesuses. He looks back, then at some point says, "Hey, man, stop staring at me." I start doing yoga in the middle of the room. Downward dog, I think, will finish him off.

"Good scene," he says, after I stand back up.

Despite all of this, I am soon declared ready to be taken upstairs—from the psychiatric emergency room to the psychiatric ward.

WEDNESDAY, UPSTAIRS IN the main psych ward, the meds were kicking in and I was coming back to planet Earth. I didn't yet know the details of how I got there, but I was beginning to remember who I was. My days were split. I had a foot in each camp.

Among my medical caretakers, one stood out: Juan. Latino, tall, fit, and with a buzz cut and a lot of big smiles. "What's up, my man," Juan would say as he took my blood pressure and pulse in the morning and administered the meds. I took the pills happily, trusting him implicitly. Other than Benadryl, I don't know what I was being given.

Despite the Benadryl, it was hard to sleep at night. I'd wander out to get snacks at the snack station, fruit and granola bars, or roam the halls, when allowed. There was a picture of a couple in San Juan, Puerto Rico—I took that as a sign that Manuela and I would get married there. There was a poster of Barcelona. That was another sign: already home to my favorite soccer team, it was a place where Manuela and I would one day live.

I was beginning to think about people again. Not just as peripheral characters in my personal, solipsistic *Truman Show*–like drama, but as humans.

My roommate was a man named Escobar, who looked to be in his seventies. Rumor had it that he'd gotten into a huge fight before coming in, assaulting several people. Though he had a lot of years behind him, he was ripped, tattooed, and clearly capable of kicking my ass. When manic, I had absolute faith in my own safety; as I was coming back down, I had some worries about having a violent roommate. I didn't yet appreciate the terrible irony of how I myself had ended up at Bellevue.

Midday, I'd pace alongside Gabriel, a white-bearded patient, energetic, probably in his fifties, with a philosophical bent. We couldn't go outside or see much sunlight, so walking the halls was a way to get exercise and blow off steam. Gabriel and I talked mostly about religion. I let him know that I was Jewish. This was an interesting comment, given that I wasn't. As my relationship with Manuela, a Brazilian Jew, had deepened, I had begun exploring converting at some point down the road. But while I had been immersing myself in Jewish traditions and attending synagogue, I had not yet committed to converting nor begun the rigorous study required. Gabriel insisted that I spend some time with the New Testament. A few days earlier, I might have said that I had no reason to read about the Messiah since I was the Messiah. But as I was starting to inhabit a human form again, the messianic delusion was receding. The antipsychotic medications accumulating in my veins, day by day and night by night, were putting to bed my delusions of grandeur.

Another notable patient was Manuel, who had a pirate-eye laugh and a name like my girlfriend's. A pirate-eye laugh is when you laugh so hard that one eye closes or starts to close. Manuela does it sometimes, and not only when she is doubled over with laughter. She also does it late at night when she's too tired to open both eyes. That connection, to joy and slumber, would rise up in me whenever I saw Manuel. What is normal eye contact can, in a hypomanic or manic state, feel like some kind of secret communication. The commonality of this little quirk between Manuel and Manuela, and the similarity of their names, brought enormous comfort to me. To the manic mind, there is no such thing as a coincidence.

Then there was Danielle. She would come up to me frequently, smile, and want to chat. Women and men were on opposite sides of the ward, but during the day, for meals and supervised socializing, we mixed. For manic me, sexual interest was absent. Danielle's flirtations were more concerning than anything. One day one of the doctors pulled me aside and cautioned me about her. They had noticed her fixation and were being vigilant—preventing romance on the floor was part of the job. With that warning issued, I avoided Danielle entirely.

My family began to visit once a day, one at a time per the rules, and they brought clothing and a toiletry kit. My mom came in, and we talked. My dad came in, and we talked. I don't remember about what. When my sister, Monica, visited, I asked her to bring me a book—a ridiculous request, given that I would not have been able, in my altered state, to read.

"Yes, which one?"

"*H Is for Hawk.*"

"I can't bring you that one. Is there another one?" She got choked up. It took me a while to realize that they wouldn't let patients have hardcover books, which could be used as weapons to harm themselves or others.

Of all the people inside on the ward, just one other had visitors. It was only in retrospect that this broke my heart. I was lucky.

Finally, one day Manuela arrived, and with her came a flood of relief. She had a deck of playing cards with her. We chatted. We played honeymoon bridge. It was then, as flickers of empathy returned, that I noticed she had a slight black eye, partially covered with makeup. While I couldn't fully process it, I felt the beginnings of pain, and shame, which would build in the coming weeks to levels I'd never known.

"Did I hit you?" I asked.

"It didn't hurt." She looked right at me.

Nothing was the same after that.

I looked down at my left hand. It was covered in gauze. Underneath, though I didn't know it yet, were stitches where the glass pane I had punched had torn open the skin between my fingers. Had I hit Manuela with the same hand?

When I had a meeting with a psychiatrist the next day, she mentioned that the authorities might want to talk to me when I got out. My conscious, planning, strategic mind started to rev back up. With each additional day of sleep, each additional dose of medication, more and more of sane me was coming back. And sane me knew that if a doctor was saying that the authorities might want to speak to me, I needed to do something. There was a pay phone. Luckily I remembered that calling card number once again, the same one that I had used in Vegas in the throes of mania to call home. I called Monica.

"Call Kevin," I said, referring to a former longtime Bonobos employee, explaining that he would know how to get me a lawyer.

"Okay," said Monica, and somewhere in New York, she swung into action.

THE DOCTOR SAID I was making good progress. It was Good Friday. I'd been in five days. I thought they might let me go, but she said they'd want to keep me for observation over the weekend. On Easter Sunday, the philosophical man and I strolled the halls. He reminded me that I should read the New Testament when I got out. I resolved to. I was coming down, realizing that I wasn't Jesus or even a superhero. This is the most disappointing phase of mania: returning to Earth, becoming an ordinary person once again.

Monday came. I'd been at Bellevue for exactly a week. As I returned to sanity on a mental ward, I went from not caring that I was inside to being desperate to get out. After days of staring through the small circular window in the ward's locked door, I was finally going to be able to go to the other side. The morning of my discharge I was filled with a sense of purpose. I could practically taste being outside again, being free, being able to leave. As the hour of my release approached, I peered through the glass, searching for faces: Mom, Dad, Monica, or Manuela.

My family was downstairs. I never saw them.

When, at last, I walked out the doors that morning, I was greeted by an altogether different quartet: four cops in navy-blue uniforms emblazoned with NYPD logos. The New York

City Police Department. They beckoned me to come with them.

The police walked me through the back of the building. It was the first time I'd been outside all week, a cold, blustery, and gray March morning. The uniformed cops handed me over to two men in plain clothes. They handcuffed me, tight. They cupped my head from above like you see on TV, and guided me into the back seat of a van that was filled with weapons of all sorts—firearms of various lengths. It was a stash worthy of a SWAT team. As we pulled out of the hospital alley, I noticed two squad cars, lights on but without sirens, escorting us, front and back.

I felt like El Chapo.

As we made our way through Manhattan, my mind tried to come to terms with what was happening—a transition from one surreal place to another. Was I imagining it all?

We started in the high Twenties and landed on West Tenth Street, where we pulled up to a fancy restaurant I'd been to dozens of times: L'Artusi, one of my favorite spots in the city. It was a spirited Italian place where I'd spent many nights drinking Manhattans with perfect ice cubes and eating orecchiette. Sometimes the server would bring out a complimentary portion of sautéed mushrooms with a fried egg or fresh ricotta with crackers. Now I was on the other side of the street, the other side of society, the other side of the planet. I knew they weren't taking me out for lunch.

Having lived in the neighborhood for eight years, I had often noticed the police station across the street from the restaurant. I had walked or run by it countless times, often on the way to a jog on the West Side Highway. It looked more like an elementary school than a venue for law enforcement, with its brick facade and blue-painted shield, the affect blending in nicely with the brownstones of the West Village. It was almost inviting. It had never occurred to me that, even in a million years, I'd be pulling up in an unmarked van, in cuffs.

We turned into a driveway I had never noticed.

One of the plainclothes cops said it was probably nothing, that I'd be out of there soon. He was wrong.

He led me upstairs to an office, where I was told I was being charged on two counts: misdemeanor assault and felony assault of a senior citizen.

A *senior citizen?*

From Manuela's visit and her partially camouflaged black eye, I knew I had hit her. What I didn't know was that I had pushed her mom to the ground and kicked her while she was down.

My family, who had come to greet me at the hospital, had gotten word. They drove to the police station. I was not allowed to talk to them, but I saw them at a distance. Mom, Dad, Monica—they were all there. Manuela was with them, too. The last thing I remember seeing was Manuela wiping away a tear as they walked me, cuffed, through the station to the holding cell in the back.

CHAPTER 19

NOOSE TO THE SKY

WALKING OUT OF A PSYCHIATRIC WARD THAT, AFTER A TIME, had begun to feel like jail and being transported to an actual jail easily made for the worst day of my life.

In the back of the Sixth Precinct, Officer Diaz took my mugshots and fingerprints. As I saw my pictures show up on a computer, I envisioned *Business Insider* having a field day. Paranoia set in. I asked if this would be public.

He whirled around and said with a smile:

"Dude, you sell pants. You're not the founder of Google."

I couldn't help but laugh.

I asked if I could go to the bathroom. Another officer escorted me. He said I had to keep the stall door open, and he put a garbage bin between me and him, making any exit more difficult; then he uncuffed me so I could do my business. I've always been urinal-shy, but with a cop behind me waiting for me to finish the job, that stage fright reached Broadway-like proportions.

"What?" he said, with a Staten Island Irish accent. "Ya never peed on anybody before? Ya scay'd when somebody's watchin'?"

I laughed for the second time that day, and the stream flowed.

They took me to lower Manhattan, to 100 Centre Street, the Criminal Courts Building, which houses the NYPD's central booking office. The seventeen-story building is set in a sea of courthouses and public offices not far from City Hall. Underneath is a jail. For now, I was upstairs, handcuffed to a chair. There were signs everywhere about where "prisoners" were allowed and where they weren't allowed. I vowed never to forget how being labeled by that word felt.

They took me down to a holding cell to await the judge. Officer Diaz gave me instructions on how to handle the questions.

"They're going to ask you if you are taking any medications," he said. "You're going to say no." This seemed like a strange set of instructions, seeing as I was coming out of a mental ward, but I gathered that protesting would be ill-advised.

With humor and empathy, Officer Diaz was there with me on the worst day of my life. When a police officer is someone who sees the best in you, that's privilege. When I see videos of men of color in the throes of what appear to be manic episodes, the outcomes look different: spit hoods, beatings, bullets.

At some point, Officer Diaz passed me on to a different officer, who held the cuffs between my hands and walked me toward the holding pen.

The jail, officially called the Manhattan Detention Complex, is located below the courtrooms and is often referred to as "the Tombs," which is exactly what it feels like. The only thing missing from the dungeon-like space is torches. As I got escorted toward the staircase that led down, I heard voices I recognized. They were the voices of my family, in a waiting area around the corner, outside the courtroom. I heard my niece's voice. I was in handcuffs, and I knew she would never forget the sight. Terrified of scaring her, of scarring her, I stopped dead in my tracks.

"That's my niece," I whispered, through clenched teeth, to the officer, stopping so abruptly that he ran into me from behind. "She can't see me." He seemed to understand; he turned and took me on a different route.

Once I cleared a security check, I was escorted into a large cell with another fifteen or so "prisoners." Leaving me out of it as the token windu, there was only one white guy. He was wearing a Vineyard Vines vest. He looked glassy-eyed. Everyone else there was a person of color. I vowed never to forget how fucked-up our system is. There was one toilet right in the middle of everyone, with barely a stall around it. I said a prayer of thanks that I didn't need to use it. It was a weird feeling: going from being God to needing God.

Some guys were playing a game that involved rolling quarters between cells. The cops on duty snapped at us. At some point they passed out sandwiches. One by one people were summoned to see the judge. Technically they could hold you for seventy-two hours. With the help of Mark Bederow, the attorney Monica had called, I was lucky enough to be called that night. They put me in a second holding cell, where guys were high-fiving each other.

"See you at Rikers, buddy," one guy said to another, with a hand clap and a backslap. They were so nonchalant about it, like they were chatting about vacation destinations at a bar. I vowed never to forget that, either.

It was close to midnight when I got called out front. Seeing Manuela and my family, minus my niece, on the courtroom benches gave me a flicker of hope. My attorney said some words. The judge said some words. It was a blur. All I knew was that they were going to let me out, with the condition that I'd come back for a hearing in a week. I was not to see Manuela during that time.

As I walked out of jail, just twelve hours after walking out of a psychiatric ward, nothing was sinking in. I no longer thought I was God, or even God's messenger, but that night I clung to the proverbial life raft that this was part of God's plan. It shielded me from having to interrogate myself about what was going on. The intense religiosity of the manic experience still had hold of my psyche.

The truth is, I was lucky as hell. I didn't know if I could handle being imprisoned for a mental health episode right after experiencing a mental health episode. Yet that's what our system so often does: it conflates issues of mental health with criminality. Dr. Z refers to an all-too-common quartet as another kind of Four Horsemen of the Apocalypse: mental health problems, addiction, homelessness, and criminal justice. It's an interwoven cluster of pain. Every possible element of privilege was on my side, and I still barely made it.

ONCE I WAS back in the outside world, my mom and I rented a hotel room in the Flatiron District. My entire family had dropped everything and set up indefinite accommodations in New York. Manuela would stay at her mother's apartment. The apartment where Manuela and I lived on Ninth Street was empty. My mom picked up clothing for me from there. Sleeping in the same room as my mom was a childlike rehabilitation, comforting. When I couldn't sleep at night, she'd tell me to meditate.

After my first hospitalization in 2000, I had insisted on going to school as soon as I got out. This time, I insisted on

going to work the next morning. Similarly, there was no talking me out of wanting to resume my life, reclaim my freedom, and reassert a sense of normalcy. I just wanted to be me
again. Saving humanity was no longer the goal. Figuring out
how to either raise our next financing round or sell the company was going to be hard enough. I was a mess, filled with all
kinds of medications and unprocessed feelings and thoughts,
my hand still covered in gauze. No one knew where I had
been, but I filled in a small group of people who needed to
know: Ali; our now general counsel, Travers; our head of HR,
Sara Patterson; our CFO, Antonio; and our PR team. I told
them the whole story: the bipolar diagnosis from sixteen years
earlier and the details of the episode I had just had, including
the violence. Their minds were both blown and not blown.
While the severity of what had transpired was shocking, an
underlying mood disorder made sense, given my behavior
over the years.

They shielded the rest of the organization from the news.
It was easy enough just to say that I'd been out. What I
couldn't help, when it came to the rumor mill, was that people in the office might simply observe that I was unwell.

It just so happened that day that I would be on display in
front of a huge group of people for the most high-pressure
thing I did at the company. Called "CEO investment review,"
the all-day affair involved fifty people, the core team of those
who merchandise, design, and source our apparel, who came
together to present to me everything we were making and
how much we were buying. The entire meeting was a conversation between me and whoever was presenting. I'd ask them
questions, give feedback, and banter with them about where
might we be going bigger, what might we be buying too much
of, what was the history of what had been happening in, say,

our wrinkle-free button-down dress-shirt program, and what the implications might be for where these businesses would be going over time. In a retail company, the biggest investment you make is in inventory, and this was the meeting where tens of millions of dollars' worth of investment was being finalized.

In short, there would be no hiding in the office that day.

I put on an Oscar-worthy performance. I managed to hide everything that had happened, including some lurking but still present irrational thoughts, and, as if nothing had happened, I chattered about how many olive-green chinos we should be buying and where the opportunity was to expand into new fits in tailored clothing.

There was one group, however, where masking the truth wouldn't be an option.

For a call with our board of directors the next day, I invited my sister. Monica joined me in the room for what would be the hardest conversation I'd ever had with our board. I didn't tell anyone she was there, and she couldn't hear what was being said on the other end of the line. We both knew she was there for an unspoken reason—in case I had a breakdown or couldn't get through the call.

We sat in my tiny office, tucked away in a corner of the fourth floor of Bonobos headquarters. A regal bust of a bonobo, the great ape, sat on a matte-gold pedestal in the corner. A waist-high wooden statue of an elven musician stood near the glass door. The ape and the flute player presided over the proceedings as I dialed in for the call.

There are playbooks for almost everything in the startup world. But not for this. I sought strength from a different source. The knowledge that just two days earlier I'd been behind bars prompted a rapidly evaporating thought: *I have my freedom, I'm out of the mental hospital, I'm out of jail.* Anything going forward was therefore made more possible; anything that needed to be done could be done. And with that, not knowing where to start, I began.

My strategy was to get everything out in the first few sentences:

"I just spent the last week in the hospital. I had an episode, what they call a manic episode, during which I lost my mind. Before getting to the hospital, I struck both Manuela and her mom."

For a moment, there was silence on the other end of the line, then somebody spoke. "Yes, I was afraid it was something like this," said one of our elder-statesmen board members, softly. It was an important first comment, because it set a tone of understanding and acceptance.

It also broke a spell for me. We hold this idea in our heads that something that is stigmatized simply cannot be spoken of. It is unspeakable. Before this phone call, I couldn't imagine that even in a thousand universes I would ever divulge to the board that I had mental health problems. In a dark and twisted way, what had happened was a blessing: I had no choice but to tell them everything.

My thinking went like this: I'd been arrested. It was therefore a matter of public record. Reporters from the *New York Post* and other places routinely troll police blotters and courtrooms for exactly this kind of a scoop. Officer Diaz had been right: I wasn't the founder of Google. But in the burgeoning corner of the world that was the New York tech ecosystem, and the broader Silicon Valley multiverse, I was an outspoken and reasonably well-known founder. If the *New York Post* didn't know who I was, *Business Insider* certainly did. Its reporters would have loved to be the first to get this story. I could picture the headline:

FOUNDER OF STARTUP NAMED FOR PEACE-LOVING APES
CHARGED WITH DOMESTIC VIOLENCE

And just below that:

ENTREPRENEUR HELD FOR MISDEMEANOR AND FELONY
ASSAULT OF GIRLFRIEND AND HER MOM

Even if an underlying mental illness was the reason, that didn't mean it would be reported that way. I also knew that in the world of social media, the story is the headline. The vast majority of people would not be curious enough to find out any of the details; besides, most of those details weren't known yet—not even by me. Was I going to be able to keep my job? Was my girlfriend going to stay with me? Would I be going back to jail?

While I had no way to keep such a story from coming out, the snowball effect would have been hard to recover from. It would have been a stain on the company. There were hundreds of employees and over a hundred million dollars of capital counting on my good reputation. Even if I was moved out and made into a pariah, the enterprise would have taken a huge hit.

With that possibility, I had to tell the board what happened. And in order to do so, I had to give them the full story.

When the time does come, I would later reflect, all you have to do is say the words.

I went on:

"When I got out of the hospital, I walked straight into handcuffs. The City of New York charged me with misdemeanor assault and felony assault of a senior citizen."

"Has there been a diagnosis?" Joel Peterson asked.

"The diagnosis is bipolar disorder type I. I was originally diagnosed when I was twenty, and I've been in denial about it for sixteen years."

A brief silence.

"I know a few folks who have dealt with what you're dealing with, Andy," Joel said calmly, holding true to his role as my professional father figure, "including more than a couple of entrepreneurs. It's entirely manageable. I have full faith in you to take care of yourself, and I have full confidence in you as our CEO."

Joel's sage words at that moment lifted an anvil of anxiety off my chest and loosened the noose of shame around my neck. A tear streaked down my face. We were less than two minutes into the call. When it comes to disclosing a diagnosis, the good news is this: It took only a minute to actually say what it took me an ocean of time to be *able* to say. When I got there, after all that time, it was stunning how fast it came out.

My eyes moved from the small window overlooking Twenty-fifth Street to meet my sister's gaze. She couldn't hear what was being said on the other end of the line. She didn't know that my vulnerable disclosure was being met with calm and loving attention. Her brow was furrowed. She looked somewhere between proud and on the verge of tears.

The call went on. I shared with the board the game plan I had developed. The forty-eight hours after I got out of jail were the highest-stakes moments of my career. First, I talked to them about the attorney who was working on the case, and shared his point of view that the charges would ultimately be dismissed. Then we discussed the crisis-management PR firm we were retaining in case something did come out in the press or through a police blotter website. We talked about Dr. Z, my new psychiatrist and therapist, who had just taken me on as a patient, and who I would be seeing religiously on an ongoing basis. And, of course, I confirmed for them that I would be taking medication daily under Dr. Z's supervision.

Both Dr. Z and the crisis PR firm were referrals from my former executive coach, Leonard, who used to be a psychiatrist. He was trusted by the board, as he'd attended several board meetings over the years. He had visited me at Bellevue, and I'd asked him to join the call. For Leonard, who had once "freed" me from my diagnosis with a passing comment, there was now no doubt about my having bipolar disorder. I took his actions at that time—including finding me a doctor who would anchor my sanity and wellness from now on, Dr. Z—as an act of redemption from a man who'd been a loyal adviser for a decade.

The board took it all in. They didn't have a lot of questions about the game plan. I didn't spend mental energy on whether I was going to lose my job. I had decided to focus on doing it well while I had it, and doing it well meant protecting the company from negative PR and securing my own sanity to lead the enterprise going forward. Individually, the board members knew me well. Many of them had met my family over the years. It wasn't uncommon for me to bring my mom to a breakfast with one of our board members when she accompanied me on my travels. All of them knew of Manuela, and more than a few of them had met her.

"How is Manuela?" one of them asked.

It was the one question I didn't know how to answer. How was Manuela? I wasn't allowed to see her or communicate with her. It was the hardest part of my first few days out. I gave the best answer I could, which was that I hoped she was well, and I hoped she wouldn't leave me, but I didn't know.

When the call ended, after forty-five minutes, my sister mustered a shaky smile and said:

"That's the hardest thing I've ever seen you do."

HOW WAS MANUELA?

Manuela later relayed to me what had taken place when she was summoned to visit the protective services case manager assigned to ensuring her ongoing safety. She and her mom had given a police report the night of the episode, and protective services was following up. Manuela went to a building downtown, near Chinatown, and met Rebecca, a young woman around her age. She shared with Rebecca that she believed that what had happened was a mental health episode. Rebecca said that they would not be able to lift the restraining order keeping us apart; the law requiring the order had been put in place to protect women until the legal system can sort out what is going on. "The law is more conservative than this situation seems to require," Rebecca said. She seemed sympathetic, but she wasn't able to change anything. Manuela and I still couldn't see each other. And I still wasn't sure, when we did, if we would be breaking up or moving forward.

Mark, the defense attorney Monica had tracked down after I'd called her from Bellevue, was fierce, friendly, and measured all at once. With my court appearance scheduled for a week later, he and I sat together multiple times to strategize. My mom joined us for a few of those meetings. Mark assured us that the case would ultimately be dismissed, but he added that, judging from the way the city handles such cases, which prioritizes protecting victims, it might take a while.

At the same time, we were all waiting for a PR hammer to drop—one that we knew could destroy so much. Pure agony. Agony wondering if I would be vilified in the news, agony wondering what might happen legally, and, most of all, agony over not being able to see Manuela.

We returned to see the judge. Anxiety threatened the functioning of my legs as I walked to meet Mark at the front of the courtroom. My parents were sitting in the back. The self-loathing I felt as my name was called knew no depths. I was an accused criminal in the eyes of the law. Mark addressed the judge, explained to her that from the vantage point of the medical establishment this was a mental health episode, and advocated for the immediate dismissal of the case.

The judge said no. She said that even if this was a mental health episode rather than a domestic abuse case, the best she could do would be to "ACD it." ACD, I learned, stood for "adjournment in contemplation of dismissal"; this meant that I would be under observation for six months before the case could be fully dismissed and the records sealed. (Later, I would often think about what happens to people without a pricey lawyer, a loving nuclear family, and a compassionate and tolerant mother-in-law and girlfriend.)

It was good news overall, and I processed it as such. On the one hand, this meant six months of waiting for this to officially be over, six months while the incident was still a matter of public record. But on the other, I was now allowed to see Manuela. Since I'd left Bellevue, we had not even been allowed to communicate. The only sign of life I'd had from her was a heart on an Instagram post of mine. I've never been so happy to see a notification. The day of the hearing, she passed a card to me through my mom, asking her to give it to me after I walked out of the courtroom.

I love you as much as Kanye loves himself.

Mom took care of me every day. She artfully parried my desire to go to a business conference in Utah hosted by Joel. She had a way of not directly challenging me but instead finding a quiet opposition that enabled me to work out the right answer. Now that I had the green light to finally see Manuela, I'd walked down from our hotel in the Flatiron District to Eighth Street, around the corner from our unoccupied apartment. I met Manuela at a foot-massage spot there. A public place was appropriate for the meeting, and we had side-by-side foot massages. I have no idea what we talked about, but the fact that she still wanted to see me felt like salvation.

The next night, I asked my mom if I could stay with Manuela. She said no. But she offered a solution that is hilarious in retrospect: Manuela could stay with us at the hotel. Manuela and I slept in one bed, my mom in the other. My doctor would later remark that it doesn't get any more Freudian than that. Manuela and I slowly started seeing each other again.

Later that week, I saw Manuela's mom, Leni, for lunch. I couldn't imagine that she would endorse her daughter's decision to stay with me, given that the last time she had seen me I had been naked and insane, and had pushed her to the ground and kicked her.

But she was as warm as ever for our greeting. It felt miraculous. "Andy," she said, her hand on my hand, "it's just like diabetes. It's no different than that. You have to take care of yourself. As long as you take your medication and see your doctor frequently, we're good."

I couldn't hold back the tears. Being accepted by your own family in the face of a mental illness, while not a given, is an expected level of grace for the fortunate among us—it's called unconditional love, after all. But being accepted by another family, one that didn't have to stick with me, was the stuff of redemption. She forgave me. Manuela's sister, Leonora, a few years younger, was equally loving and accepting. The love I felt from Leni and Leonora was a balm, a salve for a stained soul. They provided a case study for how a family might approach mental illness: clear-eyed, lovingly, without stigma, and with profound empathy.

It was difficult to take stock of what had happened. I'd nearly lost everything I loved. The freedom to walk out of the mental ward, and then out of jail, was a gift. The knowledge that I wouldn't likely have to return was a gift. Manuela's decision to stay with me, to see how it went, was a gift. Leni's forgiveness was a gift. The ironclad support of my mom, dad, and sister was a gift. The understanding of our board was a gift. The acceptance of the key members of the Bonobos team was a gift. The ability to keep my job was a gift. My intact reputation, the absence of negative PR, was a gift. The defense attorney who got my case adjourned was a gift. The mercy of the judge was a gift. The medication working was a gift. The most unexpected gift of all came in the form of someone I had only just met, but whom you've known for a while now.

Dr. Z.

I HAD WALKED up to the precipice and peered over. But, thanks to others, I had been yanked back.

After glimpsing the devastating consequences, the absolute loss of control, the harm I'd done to others, the possible destruction of the best relationship I'd ever been in, what could have happened professionally, the challenges I might have brought upon our company—all I wanted to do was stay mentally healthy. I was maniacal about never becoming manic again. I knew I needed, and everyone knew I needed, a good doctor. Getting discharged after being hospitalized for a manic episode isn't the end of your treatment. It's the beginning.

After the referral from Leonard, my mom had called Dr. Z to schedule an appointment, and Dr. Z had returned her call right away. This impressed her. We took the subway down to the Financial District. He and I instantly clicked. Dr. Z was a therapist and a psychiatrist at once: he could be both the healthcare professional I talked to and the one who monitored me and prescribed my medications. Normally psychiatrists and therapists are two different people. And there may be good historical reasons for that. For me, having someone who was both, meaning a psychiatrist who also could do therapy, so that I didn't have to shuttle back and forth, changed my life. I began to see Dr. Z two times a week, and together we sought to rebuild my psyche, one brick at a time.

The horror I felt at having hit my girlfriend and her mother, regardless of the mental health "excuse," blotted out any feelings of self-worth I had. A crime of insanity becomes its own form of punishment. I plunged into a depression unknowable.

Intellectually, I understood my luck at having gotten through it all—with girlfriend, family, job, and sanity intact—but emotionally I felt so much shame, so weighed down by the stigma, that I couldn't function. Even though only a small cohort of people close to me knew the humiliations of my mania—the delusions of grandeur, the violence, the insanity—the fact that they knew, that the people I loved and respected the most had seen me this way, was excruciating. It was those feelings that Dr. Z and I would talk about.

Dr. Z's office—blue walls, plants and books everywhere—was inviting and mentally calming. He had a way of nodding as I spoke that affirmed everything that came out of my mouth. He listened with infinite patience, and when he did speak, it was either an intelligent question or an incisive comment.

In my attempts at therapy previously, the idea that I had bipolar disorder had itself been a matter of debate. No such time was wasted with Dr. Z. With the recurrence of mania, even with a sixteen-year gap, it was now without question that my original diagnosis of bipolar type I was 100 percent spot-on. With that medical reality and diagnosis as table stakes, the real work of how to confront that illness, and my past, could begin. It wasn't linear, but we began to excavate my whole life, from birth to the present moment.

We talked about my family, and our history of being in denial about the illness. We talked about Manuela. Dr. Z was clear that he could help me process what I was dealing with, but that we needed a professional for both of us, independent of him, to help us navigate our relationship's challenges together. He referred us to a relationship therapist, Eliona.

Whenever Manuela and I got stuck, we scheduled time with Eliona, who would begin our session by asking us to sit a bit farther apart on the sofa. Then she would prompt us to get into it: Manuela's concerns about my failure to be an equal partner at home; our differing approaches to conflict (Manuela: engage; me: avoid); our sometimes converging and sometimes diverging dreams about the future; Manuela's own experiences with depression; and, of course, the episode, and my bipolar disorder. Eliona helped us work through it all, not by resolving issues in her office but by creating a space where we both felt more heard, and could relax, and could then return to our own one-on-one dynamic with deeper empathy. She would get us unstuck. We saw her a dozen times over the course of two years of building, and rebuilding, our lives.

Meanwhile, at the insistence of our head of HR, Sara, who was fully in the know about my episode and diagnosis, and who had her own family history with mental illness, we hired a new executive coach for me. With all the twists and turns with Leonard, we decided that it was time to find someone new and brought on Vivian. During one of the most acute moments of my post-episode depression, Vivian led a two-day offsite retreat. It was among the hardest two days I've ever had at work. My stomach was filled with dread, just at being alive, and I was called to role-model giving feedback in real time to all of the members of the executive team. For ten years, this had been my core leadership challenge: being direct with people—embodying my mom's willingness to get it out there, messy though it might be. I went around the circle, and in a centered and calm way, I was 100 percent honest with everyone on the executive team about my feelings—including the negative and vulnerable ones—for the first time. Vivian was flabbergasted. I didn't have the self-worth to feel proud until later.

A new version of me as a leader came to life. I felt called to operate at a higher level. I had lost my mind, and almost lost it all. Having regained so much, things that felt hard before suddenly became easier. Day-to-day work became an opportunity to apply the fortitude I had cultivated from more difficult trials. How hard is it to run a meeting on next year's

budget compared to a board call about having been in a psychiatric hospital? Forget being the Messiah. I was happy just
to be selling some pants.

AS DR. Z and I went deeper and deeper, I came to feel like an
open-heart patient, laid out on the table, but it was my psyche
that was being opened up. In these sessions with Dr. Z, the
foundation was laid for a house I didn't even know I was
building: the confidence to tell this story.

When it comes to bipolar disorder, though, therapy alone
doesn't cut it. We tinkered in a cabinet of medications to find
some alchemy that would give me both mood stability and
buoyancy.

Dr. Z likes to say that Lamictal is so good, it should be in
the municipal water supply. It started off as a drug to treat
epilepsy, and at some point folks figured out that it could be
used for bipolar disorder. The beauty of the drug is that it is
both anti-manic and anti-depressive, so it can limit one's
mood from taking off toward mania *and* provide insulation
from depression. It narrows the band of moods, and it reduces
the amplitude of the peaks and valleys in the sine curve.
Hence the designation "mood stabilizer."

He started me at 25 milligrams a day to make sure the rash
I had gotten the previous time didn't show up again. He ti-
trated that up to 200 milligrams a day within five weeks, and
made our way up, over a period of experimentation, to 300
milligrams.

What Lamictal does for me is pure sorcery.

Those of us with bipolar disorder don't go off our meds
because we're idiots. We go off our meds because many of the
prescribed medications—like Depakote for me—might elim-

inate the possibility of mania but do so by vanquishing almost all feelings of positivity and inspiration. It's a spiritually Faustian bargain. What if I might never be manic again but, in return, I won't ever feel fully myself again either? Would I rather be numb forever and never hospitalized again, or roll the dice, even if I had to risk it all? What if any possibilities of joie de vivre are what I have to trade for my sanity? And how might my answer change if what I am known for, by myself and others, *is* my joie de vivre?

The goal becomes finding a medical balance that takes the possibility of mania to near zero, insulates me from depression, but still allows for a range of human moods. One mood state to allow for is the peak experience: those rare days where I feel off-the-charts good. With bipolar disorder, any mood described as "off the charts" puts fear into the hearts of families and healthcare professionals, but the truth is that even people with a history of mania need to have the occasional magical day without it being a clinical emergency. Just as important, another goal is being able to access a hypomanic state, the energized and elevated mood state where thoughts and ideas come quickly, without it becoming a harbinger of mania.

For me, controlled hypomania is when I am at my entrepreneurial best: able to work long days, with high levels of endurance; generating kinetic positive energy for recruiting, fundraising, and motivating the team; and having frequent sparks of ideas, perhaps even moments of vision. Everything is clicking, everything is making sense, life has purpose. Colors seem brighter; gratitude flows. This is the zone where creativity and productivity flourish. We all have days like this. With untreated bipolar disorder, I had eight years of it, on and off, and I don't think I could have built a company without that gear. But it comes with a price: manic potential if unchecked, and interspersed, long phases of clinical depression. The possibility of ascending into mania is an unacceptably high level of risk on the upside, and the possibility of sliding into depression is an unacceptably high level of suffering on the downside. And so the psychiatrist's job is to find the right balance of allowing for the fullness of human experience while shaving off probabilities at the extremes.

Lamictal makes hypomania acceptable and peak experiences possible. And for that I'll always thank God. Maybe Lamictal *is* God.

I'm kidding. No, really.

Even Lamictal, though, isn't perfect alone. It couldn't protect me from deeper black holes of depression, the deepest of which consumed me in the six months after leaving Bellevue. What most people do to solve depression—at least the ones vigilant and lucky enough to be in treatment—is take an antidepressant. The problem is, because I have bipolar disorder type I—meaning I've been manic in the past—I couldn't take antidepressants, as Dr. Z rightfully feared that antidepressants might catapult me upward and right back into mania.

I began to better understand the cycles of my moods. Depression is the long night. It robs me of everything good, including the capacity to socialize, to enjoy the company of others, to read, to work, to hope, to dream, to go to a baseball game—anything, everything. When I start to rise from it, whether it has been weeks or six months or years, I want so badly to never return to it that I start running. Like someone running from a grizzly bear who makes it to their car only moments before the grizzly pounds the door. I start driving, only the bear has now grabbed onto the back of the car, so I keep driving, faster and faster, swerving, without looking back.

This is how I flip from a long and horrific low to a fast high. I cling to a kernel of a good mood, and once it's there, I do anything I can to keep it going. I rocket upward, go from feeling that the bleakness will never end to enjoying a hypomania that I hope will never go away.

With acute depression, though, I can't get out. I can't generate the kinetic energy. The car won't start. The bear eats me. Daily.

THREE MONTHS AFTER the manic episode, in the middle of that depressive phase, and prior to my case being dismissed, Manuela and I went camping near Beacon, in upstate New York, with my friend Nick and his oldest sons, who were six and four. The dark green woods punctuated with leafy trees was a good place to talk to a friend about the future. We'd stayed up late one night, while Nick grilled meat for the boys, veggies for us. After the boys went to sleep, he broke out a flask of premade bourbon Manhattans. Later, a cacophonous thunderstorm woke all of us.

Manuela and I were still in therapy. Having someone stick with you after a manic episode isn't the end of a story; it is the beginning of one. But bipolar disorder wasn't the only thing we had talked about. We had also talked about kids, and Manuela had said she didn't want any. Now, seeing her play with Nick's boys warmed me inside. It gave me hope. One day I finally told her, with a smile, "I'd rather be with you than have kids. We can miss out on the best thing in life together."

The next day, as we walked down a winding hill toward a big tree with a rope jump, Nick and I had a sidebar.

"Marry her," he said, "and give her everything. Everything

of you. Everything you have. And let her decide . . . everything." That last thing he said didn't make sense. But it sort of did.

I agreed. But would she? Who, after all that, would have wanted to marry me?

On the train back from Beacon, I couldn't feel any joy. The depression was so black at that time. After watching me battle through it for three months, Dr. Z finally relented. "Relented" is the wrong word, but you get the idea. He allowed a cautious experiment with Wellbutrin, a common antidepressant.

After six weeks, God bless that medication, Welly B lifted me out. I've never been so grateful to any physical entity in my life as those little pills, that beautiful blue-labeled bottle. Wellbutrin became one of a phalanx of other medications—Abilify, Rozerem, Klonopin, and Ambien—that are in the rotation when needed. Lamictal, of course, is my daily ride or die.

With a new lease on life, I summoned the confidence to ask Manuela to marry me. It had been eighteen months since I'd sent her a digital ring and telepathically gotten engaged to her. It had been six months since I'd snuck away one day in Rio to put a deposit down on a tourmaline stone, and three months since I'd shown Manuela a photo of it during a manic episode, spoiling any possibility of surprise in the midst of a different kind of major . . . surprise.

Up to that very evening, I feared she would say no. At a restaurant called Blue Hill in Greenwich Village, she said yes. Tears streamed down her face.

I felt disbelief and a love I had never known, all at once.

CHAPTER 20

BLAME GAME

AS WE HIT SIX MONTHS FROM MY MEGA-EPISODE, IN LATE September, my case was dismissed, and the records were sealed. I made my last visit to the courtroom. Somewhere deep inside myself, I could breathe again for the first time. I no longer felt criminalized. I no longer waited for some career-and-company-destroying event. I no longer felt like the other shoe was about to drop.

It did anyway. That night Manuela and I were talking around the island in our kitchen, and she decided to say something she knew I hadn't been strong enough to hear until then.

"Do you know that in these six months, you've never once asked me what it felt like, that night, for me?"

Even while recovering from a manic episode during which I'd struck Manuela, I'd been thinking mostly of myself. I had such profound shame about what had happened that I hadn't been able to form the words.

Now, however, her revealing, painful question uncorked more conversations. Some of those we had one-to-one. Some we needed Eliona's help with. Manuela was disappointed in me, and hurt, and turned off by my self-absorbed focus. Rather than burying those feelings, she was surfacing them—

and she did so not by casting aspersions, but by asking a question. She was, in short, role-modeling how a healthy partnership works.

THE FIRST TIME I went to a Cubs game at Wrigley Field with Dad, seeing the bright green of the park and the roar of the crowd was like magic. It wasn't like a religious experience. It *was* a religious experience.

Wrigley Field was our mecca, a place where we gathered to worship.

What exactly were we worshipping?

Possibility. Hope.

I was nine years old, and Monica was eleven. That afternoon in 1987, it had been nearly eighty years since the Cubs had won the World Series, in 1908, and more than forty years since they had even been to the series, in 1945. My dad, who was born in 1946, would famously quip that in his entire lifetime, the lovable losers hadn't come close.

And it was true.

Cubs culture was built on a relentless sense of optimism, on faith in a better future, even when there was no evidence that such hope had any merit. For me, the Cubs filled a void I wasn't yet even aware of: a desire to view the world as benevolent, a need to have something to believe in.

When the Cubs finally made it to the World Series, a few months after Manuela and I got engaged, I went to every home game. Dad and I saw them lose Game 3 to go down 2–1, Manuela and I saw them lose Game 4 to go down 3–1, and I was there with Mom, Dad, and Manuela to see them win Game 5 to narrow the series, now at 3–2. After they tied the series by winning Game 6 in Cleveland, I was due to fly, on a whim, to Cleveland for Game 7.

The day of the game, I was in a pitch meeting with a private equity fund. At the time, the board was considering three strategic options at Bonobos: raise $15 million more from insiders to get to profitability, then keep going; do a private equity deal where a major new shareholder would come on, take in a similar amount of fresh capital, and take in another $100 million to buy out many of the existing investors; or sell the company. After nine years, there were enough shareholders who wanted liquidity, including many of the angel investors and VCs, that I felt we had to either do the private equity deal or sell.

That afternoon's presentation was not the kind of thing from which a CEO can play hooky—even if it had been 108 years since the Cubs last won a World Series. So I left the Citigroup building in Tribeca only after the meeting ended, which was sixty-five minutes before my flight was due to leave JFK.

Now, anyone who knows the New York area knows I had no business making that flight. I didn't even say anything to my Uber driver about the occasion. He just asked my flight time, then drove ninety miles per hour the whole way there, including on the shoulders at times—something I've never seen before or since. Somehow he knew. When I got to the airport, I skipped to the front of every line by letting people know I was a Cubs fan and was headed to Game 7. Everyone smiled and waved me through; I've also never seen anything like that. When they pulled my bag at security for an extra screening, I simply left it there, computer and all, to sprint to make the plane. Nick, also a lifelong Cubs fan, had begged the flight attendants to hold the door. They held it until the last possible second, which was when I got on.

The Cubs became champions that night for the first time since 1908.

A psychotic break. An engagement. A Cubs World Series. Sometimes, the seemingly impossible is possible.

A WEEK LATER, Donald Trump was elected. The night of the election, I was out to dinner with Micky Onvural; within two years I'd promote her to CEO of Bonobos. Micky was the head of marketing we'd long been seeking, and her self-deprecating British sense of humor, big heart, and courage to take our brand to new places earned her the promotion; as I moved on to a new role she would become my replacement.

What would my new role be?

Trump's victory, his direct-to-voter innovation, reminded me of the direct-to-consumer movement we'd helped launch at Bonobos: go around the gatekeeper. The innovation felt familiar: Trump had used social media and earned TV coverage to bypass the people who normally got to "decide" who the nominee would be. I wondered if such a move might be possible in local New York politics, and began looking into running for mayor.

Grandiosity, impulsiveness, overconfidence: these are all ingredients in high-grade hypomania. Quickly, I built an exploratory committee led by my cousin Suneil Ahuja, a local political operative. We spent $40,000 in two months on a phalanx of advisers. I called a Bonobos board meeting and asked for their blessing. At this point, they were used to it.

"Let's hire a new CEO! I'm tired," I had said to the board in 2015.

"Okay," said the board.

"Never mind, I'm coming back!" I said, eighty-six days later.

"Okay," said the board.

"I had a manic breakdown that could bring down the house," I said to the board in 2016.

"We support you," said the board.

"I'm better, I'm all in!" I said some months after.

Phew, thought the board.

"Can I have an equity refresh grant?" I asked the board in mid-2016.

"Sure," said the board.

"Wait, never mind, I'm leaving during our sale process to run for mayor. Here are some people you can promote," I said to the board now.

Somehow they still had my back. I even told a few private equity funds who were looking at buying Bonobos that I'd likely be exiting if we did a transaction—so if they had a "more professional" CEO they wanted to bring in, it could be a good fit. This strategy backfired: most firms dropped out. My hypomania was sabotaging our deal process. I convinced everyone who mattered that the mayoral run was a good idea: Manuela, Nick, even Dr. Z got on board. Only Mom showed fierce opposition.

"You haven't finished the job at Bonobos yet," Mom said. "You owe it to your employees and your investors to see it through."

"What about eight million New Yorkers who deserve a better leader than Bill de Blasio, Mom?" I asked her.

"You're about to get married. You don't even have a family yet. Why don't you prove you can be the mayor of your own house before you try to be a mayor for eight million people." Truth serum. She wasn't done.

"Charity begins at home, Andy," she said. Mom's push-back snapped me back into my senses. The exploratory committee's conclusion was I was going to get my ass kicked. I jumped back into the deal process wholeheartedly, having put the board, the senior leadership team, and my closest friends and family through yet another ride on the roller coaster.

ONCE I WAS firmly back in the saddle, the offers came in. Two were private equity, and the other was a strategic buyer, and an unexpected suitor: Walmart. The mentor who had helped guide me on how to create a winning company culture five years earlier, Marc Lore, the man from Staten Island who once built a diaper empire, had sold his most recent venture, Jet, to Walmart, and was now charged with running Walmart's U.S. e-commerce business. Marc and I struck up a conversation, and we mind-melded on the importance of digital brands to the future of retail. He said I had to meet his boss and the CEO of Walmart, Doug McMillon.

On the night I met Doug, heavy snow was falling. Given the weather conditions, I prepared to leave an hour early for what would normally be a ten-minute commute. By the time I got to the Bonobos guideshop on Crosby Street, it was almost six P.M. I was on time, but to my mortification, I walked in and Doug was already there, and had been for some forty-five minutes. The deal process was a secret, and we had told the team as little as possible. To this day I wonder if our store manager was aware that he was fielding questions from the Fortune number one CEO before I arrived.

At dinner with Marc and Doug, I realized how fortunate I

would be to be a part of the digital transformation of the world's largest company. In the coming weeks, I went from wondering if Walmart was the right owner for the company to praying that such a deal might come to pass.

After receiving a letter of intent at $310 million, the board gave the green light. But we were far from done. The transaction process was a dance. If we made a single misstep, it seemed, the whole thing might fall through. We'd gone all in and had not kept the other potential buyers warm. We couldn't—we were under exclusivity. Every time I got a call from the Walmart corporate development person, I lost another deal point. She was stellar at negotiating, and I wasn't.

As we got deeper into due diligence, I increasingly felt that I needed to go to Bentonville, to Walmart's headquarters, if a visit would be allowed. They said yes. I didn't know what to expect. Northwest Arkansas was a far cry culturally from Chicago, New York, or the Bay Area. As I jogged through Bentonville, I marveled at the flowering of churches, at the myriad of denominations present. Religion was on my mind.

MANUELA AND I started going to synagogue regularly. She is not particularly religious, but she embraces Judaism as a culture in every way. She never pressured me to convert. We met Rabbi Joe Schwartz, and I spent a year studying under him for a conversion. I was drawn to it. After a life of spiritual wandering, getting grounded in one system was appealing.

As we discussed Exodus after the day's Torah portion was read, I asked a question from the back of the synagogue: "Wouldn't the modern-day analogy here be that Netanyahu is the pharaoh, and the Palestinians are the Hebrews?" The conservative congregation, mostly people in their seventies and eighties, gasped. My recent work to become more candid—from therapy with Dr. Z to leadership coaching with Vivian, and in relationship therapy with Eliona and Manuela—had left me a little too comfortable with asking provocative questions. Rabbi Joe handled it deftly. Even Manuela was nervous for me. They let me in anyway. Or maybe they let me in *because* of the question. The Jewish tradition I experienced encourages the hard questions and the difficult conversations.

The morning of the conversion, I went to play tennis at the courts along the West Side Highway. It was sunny, with a slight breeze: a perfect day. Faith had me seeing things in new ways: things that used to surprise me were no longer surprising; things that previously seemed coincidental no longer felt random. These were neither hypomanic flashes of insight nor manic revelations, but a newly formed spiritual bedrock of a more centered and integrated worldview. Where before there was nothing, now there was a pattern. Or maybe there always had been? Was the Ghost a curse or, like the Chinese proverb, a blessing in disguise? From my conversion studies, the words of Rabbi Rami Shapiro spoke to me: "Think in terms of an electric light socket. Plug a lamp into it and you get light; stick your finger into it and you're dead. Electricity doesn't choose your fate, you do."

THE WALMART DEAL process stretched into the spring of 2017. In April, my parents came to New York—and while I was in theory healthy, there was an important lesson ahead of us: namely, that no matter how good your daily medical regime is, the absence of sleep can bring it all crashing down.

Manuela's bridal shower was on a Saturday. We stood in the kitchen of our garden apartment on Ninth Street. There was a beautiful spread laid out, nuts and cheese and bread and olive oil. My remarks to the group were brief: I expressed my gratitude to the matriarchal lineage present. It built to honoring Manuela, thanking her, and noting what an occasion it was to see her validated by a community of women—her friends, her family, and her soon-to-be family. We shuffled into the garden and collected the outdoor furniture, bringing chairs together to create a large rectangle of seating, with Manuela sitting in the center, garden foliage all around her, like a monarch holding court.

As I filmed the proceedings, the joy I felt inside me spiraled into a sudden—but by now familiar—conviction. Maybe Manuela *was* some kind of supernatural being. Some men say they worship their wives. I fought off an irrational thought that she was actually a deity. It sounds like a nice thing, but for me, it was actually a problematic one, dating back to the original "God is a woman" episode in 2000. That afternoon in the garden, I dismissed it, but I was in trouble. The manic-thought barbarians were at the gates.

That evening Manuela had to leave town to return to China for one of her last trips. Dad joined me at a temple in the East Village for a Holocaust remembrance service. It was a whipsaw of emotions, from gratitude muddled with grandiosity at the bridal shower, to anger and anguish during the service at the synagogue. Dad donned a kippah, out of respect. I'd never experienced a Holocaust remembrance as a converted Jew myself. The stories from the survivors and their descendants cut me in two.

I stay up all night, watching *Star Wars*, convincing myself that I can sleep by watching the movie with one part of my brain and sleeping with the other part, the way a whale sleeps by resting half of its brain at a time. The gates are now open, and manic thoughts are let in freely. In the morning, I go to my parents' hotel on Thirteenth Street. My mom gives me an envelope of money that my grandmother had left for me prior to her passing the previous year. I explode inside with sadness and thankfulness, spiked by a lack of sleep, and now heightened by this gift from beyond the grave from the original matriarch of my upbringing, the woman with the always-lotioned hands, the softly spoken prayers, the best roti and matar paneer in the game, and a prophecy about a baby girl bringing great fortune that came true.

"Andy, you seem tired," my mom says. "How much sleep did you get?"

"A solid seven hours," I lie.

My parents and I go to a shoe store with my soon-to-be mother-in-law, Leni. As the hours of sleeplessness rack up north of thirty, it's still the same day of Manuela's shower and the Holocaust remembrance for me. In the shoe shop, something cracks further in my brain. I'm in this world, but no longer of it. It's now a full psychic break. Inside my mind I am trying to become the Statue of Liberty. As we exit the store and part ways with Leni, we head southbound. I am carrying a bag of shoes.

Suddenly it is mission critical to my upcoming marriage that we get to Washington Square Park. I link arms with Mom and Dad and start dragging them down Fifth Avenue. I feel faint, my hands are clammy to the touch, and I ask my mom, unconventionally, if she can carry the shopping bag for me. As we lurch down a few blocks, I am no longer paying attention to the stoplights. We walk by two churches in my neighborhood. One has a black wrought-iron fence with sharp, pointy finials.

As Mom and Dad try to guide me west on Thirteenth Street, to take me toward their hotel, to get me indoors and under control, I'm trying to drag them, arm in arm, south to the park, saying, "I love Manuela. I love Manuela. I love Manuela."

As our bodies pull in conflicting directions, I fling my mom off me, my arms swinging wildly. She's five feet tall. She goes flying. The shopping bag falls. Mom hits the fence, one of her shoes comes off, and I end up on the concrete sidewalk. Dad is holding me down now, anything to keep me from running into the street.

A concerned man stops to ask what is going on. My mom tells him to call 911, crying frantically, "Somebody has to help us! It's a mental health emergency! Somebody has to help us!" Dad is holding me immobile, succeeding, for now, in subduing me. Mom is clutching her forehead, terror in her eyes, somehow contained. She is holding it together for the cascade of complexity about to unfold: an ambulance pulling up, the police soon to arrive, the trauma of history repeating itself.

The police cuff me and the medical team puts me in the back of an ambulance. The EMT assures my mom that they understand it was a psychiatric emergency. My mom gets into her own ambulance. In our separate vehicles, we head to the hospital.

It felt, Mom would later write, *like the world was ending.*

WHEN I CAME TO, I was surrounded by a half dozen cops at Mount Sinai Hospital, and somehow had snapped back to sanity—exhausted, but with the worst of this bizarre micro-episode behind me. During the psychiatric assessment, I gathered myself enough to answer questions: remembering the current date, repeating words given to me in reverse order. I explained to the team at Sinai that I'd stayed up all night, that I had bipolar disorder type I, that I needed sleep, and that I already had a scheduled appointment early that evening with my psychiatrist as a part of my regular regimen. Every brain cell in me was focused on not being hospitalized. They discharged me into the care of Dr. Z. When my mom appeared, I saw that she had some light gauze on her head. Underneath were four stitches camouflaged by her right eyebrow.

Leaving Sinai, we went straight to Dr. Z's office in lower Manhattan. He prescribed multiple days of antipsychotic medication—Abilify—and instructed my parents to stay with me at home. Dr. Z and I call Abilify "the hammer." Its job is to vanquish any developing mania. Dr. Z also increased my Lamictal dosage by another 100 milligrams going forward, to 400 milligrams daily, indefinitely, and in the aftermath we agreed to start seeing each other three times a week instead of just two, to narrow the possibility that we would "miss" something.

My parents and I went home to the apartment on Ninth Street. With Manuela gone for the week, Mom and Dad slept foot to foot on the sofa in our den. Ever dutiful, they would do so for days, keeping watch for my mental health to stabilize. There was no denial now. They were on it. We all were. I crashed hard, for twelve hours. The next morning, I began to talk—sharing with my parents, for the first time, how angry I was at them for being complicit, after my first break during college, in our collective burial of the Ghost.

"Mom," I said, "you obsessed over every physical medical issue I had. But the one issue we had staring us in the face, the mental illness that I was *diagnosed* as having, that one we decided to ignore."

Mom was crying. Dad was consoling both of us, struggling with the raw emotions and the confrontation, but for the first time ever, we were all going there, together. Mom seemed scorched by a fire of maternal guilt, and through tears, she took responsibility. Dad did, too. For my part, I saw in a new light how much they had carried. Mom reminded me this hadn't been easy for her, either. She had suffered, too— a decade and a half of worry.

Mom painted an accurate picture: an almost-impossible-to-deal-with son, pushing back on advice at every turn, bristling at any questions about mood, going off his meds at the first chance, and walking away from a psychiatrist in 2000. She mentioned my solo backpacking trip in Southeast Asia, and the half year I spent living in El Salvador, and all the days of agony she experienced when I was alone overseas, and wouldn't be in touch, wondering if I was not only off the grid, but off the rails, up or down. Gone.

"What would we do," she asked me, "if we never heard from you again? How would we know you were okay? How would we know you were alive?" Her eyes were glowing and watering at once. I was spellbound as I looked at her. Any animosity in my heart had vanished. A conversation seventeen years in the making had expunged it. Verbalizing my anger caused it to disappear.

Who is to blame for the havoc that bipolar disorder wreaks on families?

Not any of us, I decided that day.

The reverberations of mania, the smaller episodes that follow the big one, are like the aftershocks of an earthquake that has already brought the house down. The only chance the house stands is if it's been rebuilt more robustly, fortified and strengthened, in between calamities.

A FEW WEEKS LATER, just a few days before the wedding, a note from Doug at Walmart arrived; he said that he looked forward to meeting Manuela. I called Mom right away.

"Mom, what are you up to?" I asked.

"I'm at Walmart," she replied. Mom was buying paper towels.

"That's funny, because I was calling to tell you I got a note from Doug; I think the deal is going to happen."

"That's really great, Andy," she said, choking up. "You did a great job."

"I didn't do a great job, Mom. We all did. We did this together."

Mom and I celebrated together on the phone: not because we had sold the company, but because we had survived it. Ten years of unfathomable stress, ten years of hard work, ten years of burning the candle at both ends—all of it exploded into more relief than I thought was possible. At the end of the journey, what mattered most to me was finding a safe and enduring home for our team inside the largest company in the Fortune 500, a brand we get to keep building for decades to come for our customers, and a good return for all the investors who had believed in us, angels among them.

During Walmart's due diligence process, I had disclosed that I had bipolar disorder type I, and I'd described the nature of my hospitalization the previous year, the arrest, my day in jail, and that the case was expunged. Walmart's people were going to run background checks, and I wanted them to hear it from me before they found something about my arrest. The woman who ran HR for Marc Lore's group looked like a ghost as I told her about my Ghost. She said, "I understand—these things happen. I'll talk about it with Doug and the team. Thanks for letting me know."

Walmart asked for a copy of my medical records. I said, "Of course." Dad pulled my records from 2000, Ali helped me get together the records from 2016, and Dr. Z sent everything he had. I feared that these documents were being sent to a random doctor in Arkansas who would say there was no way Walmart could do a high-profile transaction with someone like me. Then I heard from Dr. Z that the psychiatrist who was looking at my records used to run psychiatry for the FBI.

These people don't mess around, I thought.

Word came back a few weeks later. The psychiatrist who'd reviewed my records basically said, "Yep, Andy's got a mental illness, he's in treatment, he's taking care of himself, he has a clean bill of health."

THE DAY OF the wedding I experienced a sense of peace unlike any feeling I had ever known.

Resolved was a fear embedded inside a more vulnerable question: With this illness I was carrying, would anyone ever want to marry me?

The circus of four hundred people who would be showing up that evening led me to make a contrarian call: I spent nearly the entire day alone, except for some time with Dad getting into our tuxedos. Dad had never worn one, so he needed a little help. Mood-stabilizing medication coursed through my veins, the dosage increased just six weeks prior.

Could I have one of life's core peak experiences without losing it?

My confidence in my own sanity was impregnable. I was ready to surf the waves of a magical day, and underneath the surface the ocean was deep, quiet, and calm.

As I rounded the corner in Central Park and saw Manuela for the first time, she didn't seem real. But here's the good news: I knew she *was* real. A real human. I grinned like a fool as I covered the distance. After the professional wedding photos, we squeezed yellow mustard packets onto a food-cart pretzel across from the Guggenheim Museum, and I prayed to no particular higher power that I wouldn't get any mustard, as much as she likes the condiment, on her wedding dress.

The night of the wedding was a dance party that raged until five A.M. In the middle of the festivities I rolled a surprise wedding video for Manuela, set to "Something Just Like This" by the Chainsmokers and Coldplay. It's a song about the heroism of love between ordinary people, the release from wanting to be, or needing to be, superheroes.

Not long after, with a band behind me, I serenaded her with an unexpected song.

"Dead and Gone" was a strange choice. The track is a collaboration between T.I. and Justin Timberlake. It's a song about a gangster becoming a new man. It's about weakness, immaturity, and insecurity. It's about loss, risk, violence, grief, and priorities. Ultimately, it's a song about family, triumph, redemption, and rebirth.

As the song hits the bridge, Timberlake's voice soars in a contrast to T.I.'s staccato rap. As I attempted to sing the Timberlake part, I walked across the stage to kiss my bride, who was draped gracefully over the foot of the steps.

I'd been singing that verse for a decade, mostly in my head, in the shower. It finally occurred to me why I had.

Swallow that pill that they call pride
The old me is dead and gone,
But the new me will be alright . . .

HERE'S TO THE "CRAZY" ONES

AT SOME STAGE WE CONSIDERED CALLING THIS BOOK *HERE'S to the Crazy Ones,* a nod to the Apple commercial Steve Jobs oversaw in 1997 as a part of the "Think Different" campaign. It never sat well with me. There was something visceral that I couldn't stomach. It's that word: "crazy."

One day I was talking with a friend about the book. He asked me what it was about.

"It's about the intersection of mental illness and entrepreneurship," I replied.

Without missing a beat, he said, "Aren't those the same thing?"

We both laughed.

Here's the thing: they are and they aren't.

Could I have built Bonobos if I didn't have bipolar disorder? I don't know.

Why?

Because I *do have* bipolar disorder. And I have no way to conceive of myself without having been through what I've been through. What if I'd been medicated the whole time? Could I have built a startup under those conditions? No idea. I was unmedicated and untreated. For sixteen years. I'm not worried about whether or not I could have built a startup. I'm just glad I'm fucking alive.

Are all entrepreneurs mentally ill? Hell no. Are some? Definitely. Are a lot of entrepreneurs mentally unwell?

Of course. So are a lot of people.

Here's to the Crazy Ones?

No thank you.

Let's not celebrate "crazy," and let's not stigmatize it, either. Let's just deal with mental illness—openly, transparently, medically, chemically, in the mirror and in living rooms and conference rooms, boardrooms and family rooms and bedrooms and, yes, rooms with trained therapists and psychiatrists—and let's, for everyone's sake, stop pretending that it's not here.

That we're not here.

THREE YEARS AFTER the wedding, in the summer of 2020, I was working on this book. Manuela was pregnant. We took refuge in a quiet house on a wooded property on Long Island.

Dad had gotten cancer a few years earlier, and it was back. He was responding to hormone therapy, but it was metastatic. The underlying medical reality lent a new urgency to asking him the questions I knew one day I might regret not having asked. The main question was this: What do you remember from the manic episodes that I don't?

Dad and I had come full circle now, from two decades earlier, me sitting across from him upstairs in our family home, in the midst of my senior-year-of-college break. This time, however, I was lucid, too, and trying to assemble and absorb the revelations he was sharing with me—fragments that inform the very story you are reading now.

It is not a conversation I could have had without all the new scaffolding holding me up, constructed and steeled by four years of therapy, solidified by years of tinkering to get to the right dosage of medications for the peaks and valleys of the mood disorder. The sleep report that I send to my wife, my mom, my sister, and my doctor every day—an innovation Mom came up with after my sidewalk breakdown, so that we all know if I haven't slept. It was all a part of a mental hygiene regimen that secured me to reality that afternoon.

Manuela told me in 2016 that the passion and commitment I poured into maintaining my mental health in the face of this terrible disease was the only reason she stayed with me. If I hadn't been willing to do the work to take care of myself, to provide her with the safety she deserved, we wouldn't be together.

As Dad and I were talking, Mom walked into the room to check on us. She asked how it was going. I said "good," and guided her to sit on a bench between the two of us. As we talked about the episodes—2000 (college), 2015 (Vegas), 2016 (Bellevue), and 2017 (the sidewalk)—and all the cycles of hypomania and depression, mostly from 2008 to 2016, Mom was fighting back tears of guilt. She told me she still has nightmares from that day on the sidewalk. That they won't stop.

Mom has carried an impossible burden alongside mine. My burden was bipolar disorder. Hers was being the mother of a son with bipolar disorder, which came for her in two phases. Phase one was the denial, arguably the harder phase: all of the symptoms and none of the treatment. Then phase two, after March 2016, was the knowing. It was knowing that I had bipolar disorder, with all the guilt and self-recrimination from getting phase one "wrong," and now the continued minute-to-minute wondering of how I was doing, whether I was taking my medication, whether I was taking care of myself, whether I was sleeping.

The discussion was heavy. The synthesis was profound. Within an hour of my conversation with Mom and Dad that summer day in 2020, I was on the phone with Dr. Z. He suggested a mixture of Abilify and Klonopin that night: Abilify to dampen any upswing in mood, and Klonopin to knock out any anxiety. This was on top of the usual dosage of mood-stabilizing Lamictal, and of course the sleep report the next day would be important. The Fitbit showed eight hours, eight minutes, including more than seventy-five minutes of REM. The REM is key. The iceberg was behind us for now. The seas were calm.

ON OCTOBER 5, 2020, Manuela and I were cooped up inside. I was tracking Manuela's contractions and packing enough fruit pouches into a cooler to feed every mom giving birth at NYU for the next month. While Manuela was in labor, our doula arrived, which calmed our nerves.

I was more than aware that major life events, particularly the positive ones, can be triggers for mania. The ice I'd felt in my veins on our wedding day flowed through me once more. I prayed that our son wouldn't inherit this illness, but I didn't dwell on the thought. What I did know was that no matter what he would encounter in life, he deserved a father who, while not the master of his illness, was on top of it.

On a hospital gurney, Manuela breathed quickly—not hyperventilating, but close. I leaned in and suggested that she could try to breathe more deeply, matching her breath with mine.

"Can you back up, can you move back?" she said, stuttering, her voice shaking, her teeth chattering, on another plane. "You are too close to me. Don't tell me to breathe. It is not helping me."

I backed up. The quarters were tight in the New York City operating room. Cords were everywhere. An anesthesiologist hovered just to my left. A half dozen doctors and nurses were on the other side of the curtain.

When they pulled Isaiah out into the world, he cried.

Loyalty to my wife expanded inside me, into caverns I didn't even know existed, and an abiding desire to honor always the sacrifices I'd seen her make in the previous year.

Gratitude for my parents and sister arose anew. I saw my own life from this moment, looking backward. I pictured their love for me like the love I had for that tiny child, and understood the way their love had been tested by an illness with no conscience.

One of the doctors handed Isaiah to me. My son, now calm, looked around the room, intent, his eyes and head rotating with a preternaturally calm curiosity. I processed it as a state of wonder, but that may have been my own.

Isaiah heard his mother say hello to him, and his head turned instinctively toward a voice he had been hearing for nine months, from a body that was now his ancestral home. Mother and child locked eyes, before she passed out as the drugs were dialed up. An hour later, in the postoperative room, she did something she rarely does. She cried, and said something simple.

"We did it."

. . .

WHILE MANUELA SLEPT most of the day, I watched her and Isaiah like a hawk. Or maybe it was a lion.

During the kindling of my manic episode in March of 2016, I had wandered down a few stairs into a kitschy antiques store in Midtown. The owner detected that I was off, and a spendy kind of off. As I reviewed his wares, he gave me a beer and a cigarette to grease the skids. He was Punjabi, my mom's ethnicity. I felt a kinship with him, while I think he just smelled a whale. Taking a shine to it, I sat in a throne-like chair; it would be one of four items I would buy, for $17,000, on a whim, in the span of fifteen minutes. A Kazakh rug, a huge stone wolf howling at the moon, a throne that the shopkeeper said was for a Persian king, and a painting.

When it all arrived at our home, Manuela started crying. When I was discharged from Bellevue, and allowed back to the apartment a week later, my mom accompanied me to that antiques dealer, and she convinced him to take everything back. The only thing Manuela let me keep was the painting. She didn't like it. But everyone who sees it does. So now she can't help but like it.

The grand painting features bright colors on canvas, an ornate frame that would be at home among bookshelves in a library paneled in dark wood, or in a cozy Chicago den. The scene depicted is of an adult lion standing guard next to a seated lioness, with three cubs in the foreground.

I've never felt more protective—of anything or anyone—than I did on the day my son was born. I felt a primal urge to see Isaiah grow old and prosper, to teach him everything I knew, whatever that might be, and to shield him from all potential harm.

It wasn't external threats that were on my mind.

It was the Ghost.

I never want my son to experience me as a liability. I never want him to see his dad manic. I never want him to see his dad in bed for weeks or months at a time.

Am I afraid of my Ghost anymore? Has writing this book expunged my fears?

Of course I'm afraid of the Ghost. Of course it hasn't expunged my fears. The day I'm not afraid of this illness is not a good day for me or anyone I love.

Bipolar disorder is a cruel illness. It's an illness without a cure. I can never let up on the constellation of efforts required to hold it at bay. But here's the good news: it is eminently treatable. Pills every day. A doctor's eyes on me at least once a week. Therapy forever. Sleep reports. Transparency with everyone I love. Honesty with myself.

I. Can. Never. Let. Up.

I looked back at Isaiah, sleeping soundly, and I knew something.

I knew that I never would.

ACKNOWLEDGMENTS

THANK YOU, KIRSTEN NEUHAUS, MY AGENT EXTRAORDINAIRE at Ultra Literary, for believing in this book. And me. I'll never forget you saying that, in a land of entrepreneurs with ghost writers, you thought I could write this myself. That gave me the confidence I needed to focus on the Ghost at hand. Thank you, Bradley Tusk, for the introduction to Kirsten.

Thank you, Paul Whitlatch, my editor at Currency. From the moment you told Kirsten and me that you had no interest in a self-congratulatory tale of an entrepreneur's success, but instead an unvarnished tale of mental illness told through the lens of an entrepreneur, I felt like you understood what the mission was here. Your listening ability, editorial wisdom, work ethic, and collaborative spirit made this fun.

Thank you, Katie Berry. You make Paul look good. You helped me avoid some major pitfalls in the manuscript, and your keen and tireless eye was critical to what we did here. Thank you, Kirby Blem. A book is a lonely journey. Having you as a sounding board and editorial strategist, and the first reader of most of this material, was epic. Thank you, Davi Sherman. Your last-minute read was solid gold. As in Halle Gold. Thank you, Halle, for the introduction, and the read yourself.

Thank you, Nick Ehrmann. Not only are you the best friend a guy could ask for, in a parallel universe you do books for a living. Your friendship and love span two decades, and the all-nighters you forced me to pull with your comments on the manuscript almost induced additional manic episodes. (Kidding, Mom.)

Thank you, Ali Freedberg and Chris Travers. You were my day-to-day work family for a decade. And you know this. Without you I'd be in jail in Havana right now. Upon release, we'd probably go straight to the beach.

Thank you, Bryan Wolff and Brian Spaly. If I had told you when we were in Bogotá that I'd be writing a book about a mental illness that I'd hidden from both of you, but that would meaningfully affect all of our lives, professionally and personally, would you have believed me?

Thank you, Dr. Z—the best psychiatrist imaginable. You're the most expensive friend I've ever had. (I know you're not my friend.) It turns out a sound mind is priceless. You are perspicacious. You are incisive. You are warm and inviting. You are Freud reincarnate, with equally good suits. Go figure. Everything is overdetermined.

Thank you, Leni Silverstein and Leonora Zoninsein. The acceptance you offered me into a new family helped me expunge my shame. Mamãe Leni, you've seen me at my worst, and you still gave me your blessing to marry your daughter. That's the nicest thing anyone I'm not related to or married to has ever done for me.

Thank you, Isabella Royer. You came along during days when I felt like I didn't want to go on. Knowing that I was your uncle and godfather saved my life. Because I was never going to leave you. I didn't know if you would ever need me. But I wasn't going to let you down.

Thank you, Charles Willard Dunn III—thank you, Dad. Thank you for being Darth Vader when I needed you to be. If I can be half as selfless as a father as you are, I'll be lucky.

Thank you, Monica Dunn Royer. You once told me through tears that you felt that part of your job, why you were put on Earth, was to keep me alive, and healthy. I don't know if that was a fair ask, but so far so good. You're the best *didi* a boy could ask for. Thank you, Rob Royer, for helping Monica help me, the whole way, and for your love and unquestioning support.

Thank you, Usha Ahuja Dunn—thank you, Mom. When we were talking about this book, I asked you, What would it take for you to forgive yourself? There is nothing to be forgiven for. You're the mother of my dreams. Your love is everything. Always has been. Always will be.

Thank you, Manuela Zoninsein. Your love has been my redemption. You saw the worst of me, high and low, and you took me in anyway. Your resolve, steadiness, and strength formed the backbone to my reintegration as a human. I hope I can meet you there and offer some measure of the same.

Thank you, Isaiah Zoninsein Dunn. Isaiah: You showed up in the middle of this book and the middle of a pandemic. Since you've gotten here, you've been nothing but positive about everything. One day we'll talk all about this, we'll watch *Ghostbusters* together, and we'll have a good laugh.

I ain't afraid of no ghost.

ABOUT THE AUTHOR

ANDY DUNN co-founded the e-commerce-driven menswear brand Bonobos in 2007 and served as CEO through its 2017 acquisition by Walmart. As an angel investor and through his venture capital firm, Red Swan, Dunn has backed more than two hundred startups, including Warby Parker, Dia & Co, and Coinbase. Dunn serves on the boards of Monica + Andy, an organic baby apparel company founded by his sister, and the tech nonprofit RaisedBy.Us. Named to *Fortune's* 40 Under 40 list in 2018, he is a graduate of Northwestern University and the Stanford Graduate School of Business. He lives in Chicago with his wife and their son.

ABOUT THE TYPE

This book was set in Electra, a typeface designed for Linotype by W. A. Dwiggins, the renowned type designer (1880–1956). Electra is a fluid typeface, avoiding the contrasts of thick and thin strokes that are prevalent in most modern typefaces.